Trade, Planning and Rural Development

Essays in Honour of Nurul Islam

Edited by

Azizur Rahman Khan

Professor of Economics
University of California, Riverside

and

Rehman Sobhan

Professorial Fellow
Bangladesh Institute of Development Studies, Dhaka

St. Martin's Press   New York

First published in the United States of America in 1990

Printed in Printed in Great Britain

ISBN 0–312–04512–3

Library of Congress Cataloging-in-Publication Data
Trade, planning and rural development: essays in honour of Nurul
Islam / edited by Azizur Rahman Khan and Rehman Sobhan.
   p. cm.
ISBN 0–312–04512–3
1. Economic assistance.   2. Economic development.   3. Commercial
policy.   4. Rural development—Bangladesh.   5. Islam, Nurul, 1929–
I. Khan, Azizur Rahman.   II. Sobhan, Rehman.
HC60.T65 1990
338.95492—dc20   90–32086
                                                                        CIP

Contents

Notes on the Contributors

Abu A. Abdullah is a Research Director of the Bangladesh Institute of Development Studies.

Jagdish N. Bhagwati is Arthur Lehman Professor of Economics, and Professor of Political Science, Columbia University.

Just Faaland, now at the Christian Michelsen Institute, Norway, where until 1988 he had been Director for over twenty years, is a former President of the OECD Development Centre. He was a member of the International Advisory Board of the Pakistan Institute of Development Economics when it was headed by Nurul Islam.

Dharam Ghai is Director of the United Nations Research Institute for Social Development.

Wahidul Haque, Professor of Economics and Mathematics, Toronto University, is currently Minister of Finance, Government of Bangladesh.

Mahabub Hossain is Director General of the Bangladesh Institute of Development Studies.

Azizur Rahman Khan is Professor of Economics, University of California, Riverside. He was a former Research Director of the Pakistan Institute of Development Economics and Bangladesh Institute of Development Studies.

Mark W. Leiserson immediately preceded Nurul Islam as the Director of the Pakistan Institute of Development Economics. Later he administered the Ford Foundation programme of assistance to the Institute for a number of years while he was Professor of Economics at Yale University.

John W. Mellor is Director of the International Food Policy Research Institute, Washington, DC.

Saburo Okita was Japan's Minister for Foreign Affairs. He is now Chairman, Institute of Domestic and International Policy Studies, Tokyo.

Jack Parkinson was until recently Professor and Chairman of the Department of Economics, Nottingham University.

Gustav Ranis, Frank Altschul Professor of International Economics, Yale University, was the first Director of the Pakistan Institute of Development Economics and a member of its International Advisory Board in later years.

Sir Austin Robinson, Professor Emeritus, Cambridge University, and a former President of the International Economic Association, played an important part in the setting-up of the Pakistan Institute of Development Economics. He was a member of its International Advisory Board.

Rehman Sobhan, Professorial Fellow and former Director General of the Bangladesh Institute of Development Studies, was a member of the Bangladesh Planning Commission when it was headed by Nurul Islam, and a colleague of his during his years with the Department of Economics, Dhaka University.

Paul Streeten, Professor of Economics, Boston University, was a member of the International Advisory Board of the Pakistan Institute of Development Economics.

Jan Tinbergen, a first recipient of the Nobel Memorial Prize in Economic Science in 1969, was a member of the International Advisory Board of the Pakistan Institute of Development Economics.

Introduction

This volume is a collection of essays contributed by the friends, colleagues and students of Nurul Islam to commemorate the sixtieth anniversary of his birth. The essays cover the three major themes that characterise the evolution of Nurul Islam's professional work and interest. The purpose of this introduction is not to provide a biographical note on Nurul Islam. Nor does it present a comprehensive discussion of his work or writings. Its objective is the more modest one of conveying some sense of the variety and richness of his work by simply enumerating some of his major contributions since he began his professional career as an economist in the mid 1950s.

The first decade of Nurul Islam's work was dedicated to the teaching of economics at the University of Dhaka. During this period he started the tradition of modern economics in Bangladesh (then East Pakistan) both in teaching and in research. An entire generation of economists was trained and inspired by him during this period. It was under his leadership that the university adopted a modern curriculum in economics. It was again his pioneering work that started the tradition of modern economic research in Bangladesh by emphasising the use of quantitative methods. He was also involved in the design and implementation of some of the earliest surveys in Bangladesh, e.g. those on the marketing of jute, the use of rural credit, and unemployment.

The next phase of his career started in 1964 when he became the first native Director of the Pakistan Institute of Development Economics. He continued in this position until the break-up of Pakistan and the creation of Bangladesh at the end of 1971. During this period Nurul Islam transformed the Institute from an embryonic organisation dependent on foreign advisers to a major centre of applied economic research in the developing world, predominantly staffed by nationals. During this phase Nurul Islam was also instrumental in setting up the organisation that later became the Bangladesh Institute of Development Studies.

Early in his career Nurul Islam became interested in social and political issues. During the 1960s he became particularly involved in the question of the autonomy of Bangladesh (then East Pakistan, the region that had been subjected to systematic discrimination by the rulers of Pakistan). As a member of Pakistan's National Finance

1

Commission, the National Price Commission and the Panels of Economists for the Five Year Plans, he consistently exposed the inequities in the allocation of public resources to East Pakistan and argued the case for self-governance for the region in all available fora.

At the end of the 1960s, the movement for the autonomy of East Pakistan took a militant form. Nurul Islam played an important part in shaping the economic content of the movement which achieved a great electoral victory in 1970. The refusal of Pakistan's military rulers to accept the result of the election was successively followed by a country-wide movement of non-cooperation, the armed attack launched by the Pakistani army on the movement and the Bengalis in general, and the transformation of the movement into an armed struggle for independence. Throughout this period, Nurul Islam remained an effective spokesman of the movement and one of its principal economic advisers.

The third phase of Nurul Islam's career began in early 1972 when he was appointed the executive head of the Planning Commission of the newly independent Bangladesh. He remained in this position for more than three years. This period witnessed the rehabilitation of the war-damaged economy which was soon ravaged by the famine of 1974. Nurul Islam found himself, an academic and a researcher, transformed into an administrator of day-to-day economic management during this turbulent period. Amid all these difficulties the Planning Commission, under his leadership, carried out the serious and purposeful work of the preparation of the First Five Year Plan.

Nurul Islam left the Bangladesh Planning Commission in early 1975, a few months before the country experienced the first of a series of bloody political changes. After an interregnum devoted to reflections on his experience at the Bangladesh Planning Commission, Nurul Islam embarked on what became the fourth phase of his career. In the late summer of 1977 he was appointed Assistant Director General of the United Nations Food and Agricultural Organisation (FAO) in charge of economic and social affairs. He served in this position for a decade. Early in this capacity, he organised the World Conference on Agrarian Reform and Rural Development (WCARRD) in 1979. In the years following the WCARRD, his has been a major voice in international discussions and debates on agriculture and rural development concerned with the issues of food systems and food security. In September 1987 he took early retirement from the FAO and started on a career of research on

similar issues at the International Food Policy Research Institute in
Washington, DC.

Nurul Islam's writings have covered too wide a range of topics to
be amenable to a quick summary. Yet it is convenient to focus on the
three themes into which the essays of the present volume are divided
– trade, planning and rural development – as the main subjects that
characterise the evolution of his work and interest.

During the first two phases of his career, respectively at the
University of Dhaka and the Pakistan Institute of Development
Economics, Nurul Islam was predominantly interested in the issues
related to international trade and development. His early work in this
area was concerned with an analysis of the relationship between
foreign capital and economic development, based on a comparative
analysis of the experience of Japan, Canada and India. This early
work was followed by almost a decade of serious research on the
structure, efficiency and mechanism of Pakistan's foreign trade.
While his research always emphasised empirical methods, his objective was to understand how trade policies affected the efficiency and
equity of development programmes. In this sense his empirical research on Pakistan was of significance for a wider set of developing
countries. His research on the structure and efficiency of the foreign
trade regime in Pakistan focused on such issues as: structures of
import and export trade; efficiency of export incentives and export
policies; interregional trade between East and West Pakistan; terms
of trade; commercial policy and economic growth; and foreign trade
and economic controls. Other trade-related issues that he worked on
include: regional and international trade cooperation among the
developing countries; the problem of external debt of the developing
countries; the reordering of the North-South relationship; and foreign
aid.

With the beginning of the third phase of his career, as the head of
the Bangladesh Planning Commission, planning became the major
subject of Nurul Islam's preoccupations. The First Five Year Plan,
prepared under his personal supervision, was a basic document
dealing with the complex problem of development that the nation
faced during a period of transition. His later writings on development
planning and development strategy in Bangladesh, looking back on
his experience, remain a valuable source of insight for practical
planners. His experience during this phase also formed the basis of
some of his writings on foreign aid. These writings strongly emphasise the political economic aspects of both the domestic issues of

development and the international economic issues concerning the relation between the donor nations and agencies on the one hand and the developing country on the other.

During the fourth phase of his career, at the FAO, Nurul Islam's primary interest shifted to the problems of rural development. His writings during this period have been concerned with food and agricultural policies of the countries of the world with an emphasis on the issue of food security for the developing world.

While the three topics on which this volume focuses represent the three main chronological themes of Nurul Islam's work, together they amount to an incomplete account of his total professional contribution. He is the author of the first comprehensive empirical study of consumer demand in Pakistan. He authored the first econometric model for short-term policy-making in Pakistan. He has written extensively on issues of unemployment, underemployment and surplus labour. He has made important contributions in the area of resource mobilisation and taxation policies in the developing countries.

Similarly, his work has included many more agencies than the four mentioned above. At various times of his career he has been a visiting fellow at the London School of Economics, the University of Cambridge, the Netherlands Economic Institute, the Economic Growth Centre of Yale University, the Economic Development Institute of the World Bank, and Queen Elizabeth House and St Anthony's College, Oxford. He provided public service as a member of many international and national bodies. These have included his work as treasurer of the International Economic Association, member of the United Nations Committee for Development Planning, member of the Council of the Society for International Development, member of the executive committee of the Third World Forum, member of the Commonwealth Expert Group on New International Economic Order, and member of the Boards of Trustees of the International Rice Research Institute and the International Food Policy Research Institute.

But as much as anything else, his contribution consists of less tangible things. He has been a great source of inspiration for his students and younger colleagues. His relationship with his professional colleagues has been marked by great generosity. As an economic administrator and international civil servant he displayed an unusual combination of common sense and technical skill. Above all, his professional work has always been shaped by a profound but unobtrusive concern for fellow human beings.

A large number of his associates, ranging from the very famous in the international arena to young Bangladeshi scholars, eagerly offered to participate in this commemorative volume. Constraints of time and space have unfortunately made it impossible for us to include all those who *volunteered* to write. Even so, the volume is hopefully a fitting tribute to Nurul Islam in recognition of his rich and varied achievements.

I Trade and Aid

1 Parabolic Welfare Functions and Development Assistance

Jan Tinbergen

INTRODUCTION

In this article in honour of Nurul Islam I make an attempt to contribute to a subject that both of us – and many other economists – have worked on for many years: development co-operation. My contribution deals with a lacuna I try to fill up, at least partly. The lacuna is that we don't know what is the *optimal* amount of development assistance. For years we have used, in many discussions, the criterion of 0.7 per cent of donor countries' GNP. It was proposed for the (First) Development Decade by H.W. Singer and his collaborators, for the Second Development Decade (1971–1980) by the Pearson Commission and recommended by the Brandt Commission. But it was hardly based on some optimality criterion. It was closer to a satisficing than to a maximising criterion; satisficing, to be sure, the donor countries. Moreover, most of the donor countries did not live up to what their own experts had recommended.

A first part of my contribution is the proposition that theoretically the most appealing criterion is *maximising world welfare*, if a sufficiently concrete form can be given to it. That depends, of course, on whether welfare can be *measured* or a '*money metric*' can be given to it. I think there is an increasing number of economists who adhere to the measurability of welfare. Elsewhere (Tinbergen, 1985, 1987) I stated that some economists in the USA, some in the UK, some in France and some in the Netherlands have been working on the subject and most of them also have done empirical work. In the next section I shall mention some details on the work of the Dutch group of which I profited for my own work, also in the present contribution. In the third section as a preparation for my concrete contribution I will discuss the phenomenon of *satiation*, which plays a central role in this contribution, of which the hard core is given in the fourth

9

section. The fifth section is devoted to some concrete elaborations of the welfare function I propose and some particular problems it faces us with. In the final section, a comparison is made with an alternative choice that has been made elsewhere.

MEASURING WELFARE: THE DUTCH GROUP

The Dutch group is the largest group of economists who contributed to welfare measurement and has been inspired and led by Bernard M.S. van Praag, now teaching at Erasmus University, Rotterdam. Their work started with inquiries about the satisfaction derived from income by a large number of interviewees in Western Europe, initially Holland and Belgium. A measurement scale from 0 to 1, subdivided into equal intervals, was characterised by the words used in primary and secondary school scores and interviewees were asked to indicate the incomes which would make them feel, respectively, very badly off, badly off, and so on, till well off, very well off and feeling excellent. In essence this means that the same words, when used in political debates are given a quantitative meaning, if the interviewees, who have been selected at random, may be quoted as representing public opinion.

Van Praag and his collaborators found a clear pattern in the answers, and were able to explain a large part of the pattern's features. Eliminating some of the parameters characterising the interviewees' age, family size, etc. they found a clear relation between the scores and the incomes. In their further research they approximated that relation by a cumulated log normal function of income.

In a 1981 publication two of the group (van Herwaarden and Kapteyn) had tried out a number of alternative functions to fit the observations and found that the *logarithm* of income gives a slightly, but significant, better fit. In addition, the logarithm's first derivative $d \ln y/dy = 1/y$ is diminishing with rising y and for that theoretical reason makes it more attractive as a welfare function. In another respect, however, it is less attractive: it does not have the property of *satiation* which is another aspect of reality and here van Praag's cumulated lognormal function is more satisfactory.

SATIATION

Satiation and, in addition, oversatiation are very real phenomena in daily life. Overeating and overdrinking in many forms are well known and may even threaten an individual's health. In today's world, taken as a whole, we are definitely oversatiated with armaments. Inhabitants of underdeveloped countries will certainly feel that many citizens of developed countries consume much more than is necessary and can, often in their own interests, live more modestly and so make available to the underdeveloped countries more development assistance.

The phenomenon becomes less clear when *total* consumption instead of single commodities' consumption is considered. The number of goods and services seems unlimited, as a consequence of technological development. Advertising encourages their consumption and so does the tendency to 'impress the Joneses' instead of keeping up with them only. Many economists have maintained that human needs, or at least desires, are unlimited and our logarithmic welfare constitutes one aspect of such behaviour. In the last decades, however, the '*limits to growth*' are a phenomenon that have increasingly occupied scientists and politicians. These limits occur, first of all, in the supply of goods, as a consequence of the existence of *finite* quantities of all sorts of raw materials. The limits to growth also occur as a consequence of *pollution* of the environment in a variety of forms: pollution of the atmosphere, of water and of the soil. As a natural reaction to this new situation some politicians and their advisers now advocate consumers' self-restraint, in their own interests as well as the general – especially the interest of the poor, and in their own country as well as in underdeveloped countries. So there are good reasons to introduce into development research the phenomena of satiation and oversatiation.

THE PARABOLIC WELFARE FUNCTION

In order to introduce these phenomena into research on development cooperation I propose to introduce a welfare function which I shall call a *parabolic* welfare function. For a single determinant of welfare such as consumption y_1 that welfare function may be written:

Jan Tinbergen

$$\omega_1 = \omega_0 - \frac{\omega_0}{y_{01}^2} (y_1 - y_{01})^2 \qquad (1.1)$$

where ω_0 is the maximum level of welfare, attained for $y_1 = y_{01}$, the level of consumption expenditure where satiation has been attained. The first and second derivatives with regard to y_1 are:

$$\frac{\partial \omega_1}{\partial y_1} = - \frac{2\omega_0}{y_{01}^2} (y_1 - y_{01}) = \frac{2\omega_0}{y_{01}^2} (y_{01} - y_1) \qquad (1.2)$$

and

$$|\partial|^2 \omega_1 /\partial|y_1^2 = - 2 \, \omega_0/y_{01}^2 \qquad (1.3)$$

We see that, for $0 \leqslant y_1 \leqslant y_{01}$ the first derivative is positive: welfare increases. It becomes zero for $y_1 = y_{01}$ and this is a maximum of ω_0, since the second derivative is negative for all y_1.

We shall consider two types of y_{01}: its value may be *given* (type I) by the attitude of the citizens of the group of countries indicated by the index 1 and meant to represent the First World, i.e. the developed market economies. Alternatively (type II) it may be chosen – as a goal – so as to maximise world welfare, or the total welfare of the non-communist world.

For $y_1 > y_{01}$ the phenomenon of *over-satiation* occurs. Welfare diminishes and for $y_1 = 2y_{01}$ it becomes equal to welfare for $y_1 = 0$, that is zero. As far as I can see, this type of welfare function was not studied by van Herwaarden and Kapteyn. It would be interesting to know whether it fits the facts better than the other functions considered by them, or less well. My own experience is limited: I can only state that in a number of models in which I used the parabolic welfare function it led to results not very different from models in which the logarithmic welfare function was used.

We may use this welfare function in a model to find the optimum value of all variables. An example will be given later.

In that model the use of type I parabolic welfare functions means that all satiation values of the variables used are considered given, as noted.

When using type II parabolic welfare functions we have to find their values by solving a second problem, namely to maximise world welfare, which we specify as the total welfare of the First and the Third World (W1 and W3).

That total welfare equals – apart from some constant terms:

$$\omega_1 + \omega_3 = -(y_{01} - y_1)^2/y_{01}^2 - 2.85 (y_{03} - y_3)^2/y_{03}^2 \qquad (1.4)$$

where 2.85 is the population of W3 in terms of W1 population.

It has to be maximised under the restriction that total consumption equals total production $x_1 + x_3$, the latter being given and for 1970 equal to 5879 billion dollars with buying power in 1975 in the USA (cf. Kravis et al., 1982):

$$y_1 + y_3 = x_1 + x_3 = 5879 \qquad (1.5)$$

The maximum of $\omega_1 + \omega_3$ requires that

$$y_1 = y_{01} \text{ and } y_3 = y_{03} \qquad (1.6), (1.7)$$

The unknowns of our present problem are four: y_1, y_{01}, y_3 and y_{03}, but we have three equations only: (1.5), (1.6) and (1.7). So we have one *degree of freedom*. This is a new situation. We can use the degree of freedom to attain one additional target. Two examples will be given.

One is that a complete *equity* is attained at once. Neglecting differences in capability (obtained from schooling, job experience, etc.) equity could be defined as equal per capita consumption in W1 and W3, hence

$$y_3 = 2.85 y_1 \qquad (1.8)$$

The solution then is

$$y_1 = y_{01} = 1527 \text{ and } y_3 = y_{03} = 4352 \qquad (1.9)$$

from which we can derive the amount of development assistance v_{13}:

$$v_{13} = x_1 - y_1 = y_3 - x_3 = 2353 \text{ or } 60.6 \text{ per cent of } x_1 \quad (1.10)$$

With today's power distribution this is, of course, completely illusory. But it is a clear way of illustrating the North–South problem's seriousness.

Another example, which seems reasonable, is that relative total consumption y_3/y_1, which in 1970 was very close to relative total incomes x_3/x_1, increase so as to be *double in twenty years*. Such doubling requires an annual increase by 3.5 per cent, or

$$y_3/y_1 = 1.035 \times 0.5207 = 0.539$$

where 0.5207 is the ratio of consumption in 1970, used as the base year. This means that in the first year $v_{13} = x_1 - y_1 = 60$ billion 1975 dollars or 1.5 per cent of x_1. This figure, although still twice as large as the 0.7, seems a realistic negotiation base.

The aim to double relative consumption y_3/y_1 in twenty years means that the majority of the Third World population (which twenty years from the base year will still be alive) is given a perspective of a substantial improvement in living conditions. Moreover, this aim is more concrete than the somewhat abstract concept of welfare, whose measurability is, among economists, still a matter for debate.

SOME EXAMPLES OF A TYPE II PARABOLIC WELFARE FUNCTION

No degree of freedom exists if a parabolic welfare function is used, of which the satiation values are known from polls. As one arbitrary example we assume $y_{01} = 6000$, $y_{03} = 17\,100$, which means that per capita they are the same in the First and the Third World. Maximum welfare for the non-communist world will be attained – if military expenditures remain the same as in 1975 – by the set of values:

$y_1 = 1458$, $y_3 = 4156$ and $v_{13} = 2255$ or 58 per cent of x_1.

Some alternative examples yield similar results. If, for instance, we assume that military expenditures are reduced to zero (complete disarmament), we obtain:

$y_1 = 1527$, $y_3 = 4352$ and $v_{13} = 2553$ or 61 per cent of x_1.

If we assume that y_{03} is significantly lower than 17 100, namely 10 000, we find in the case of no change in 1975 armament expenditures:

$y_1 = 740$, $y_3 = 4153$ and $v_{13} = 2973$ or 77 per cent of x_1; and, in the case of complete disarmament:

$y_1 = 874$, $y_3 = 5005$ and $v_{13} = 3006$, that is also 77 per cent of x_1.

The common feature of all these results is an optimum amount of development assistance much higher than is politically feasible. It constitutes, however, the *long-run aim* of development policy.

Finally, the use of *logarithmic* welfare functions produces results of the same character, as is illustrated by Table 1.1.

By coincidence the first example of type I parabolic welfare functions, where 17 100 = 2.85 × 6000, yields the same results as type II parabolic welfare functions, as can be easily shown.

A MORE REALISTIC ALTERNATIVE CRITERION OF OPTIMALITY

As we noted, the criterion of maximal world welfare yields very high amounts of development assistance. The reason is that the models used are static models. They indicate the optimal situation, but not the time path to attain such an optimum. It is clear that in the short run that situation cannot be attained. But, as said before, the models are an indication of the seriousness of the problem of underdevelopment. An important element of the huge amounts involved is the size of n_3, the population of the Third World in comparison to the First World. So an appropriate population policy remains one of the most powerful instruments that can help to accelerate the improvement of Third World welfare.

In this last section I intend to describe briefly a second more realistic criterion of optimality, or, formulated otherwise, a more realistic intermediate aim to strive for. As such an aim, we could formulate to start with, that the income *inequality of W3 and W1 together be reduced to the income inequality now existing within W1*. Estimates which will be published elsewhere show that this intermediate target requires an amount of development assistance of 29 per cent of W1 income, still an aim that cannot be reached in a period of a few years, but probably a good half-way station to the maximum of world welfare.

Summarising, we found that the nearest target appears to be doubling relative income x_3/x_1 in twenty years; as a second target to reduce inequality of W1 + W3 to that of W1 and as the final target maximising world welfare.

Table 1.1 Values of variables (billions of 1975 dollars) which maximise total welfare of W1 and W3 for parabolic welfare functions with different satiation values for non-military expenditures and for logarithmic welfare functions

Welfare functions span the six right-hand columns (Parabolic type I, Parabolic type II, Logarithmic).

			Parabolic type I		Parabolic type II		Logarithmic	
Data								
x_1 Production of W1	3 880	3 880	3 880	3 880	3 880	3 880	3 880	3 880
x_3 Production of W3	1 999	1 999	1 999	1 999	1 999	1 999	1 999	1 999
a_1 Military expenditure of W1	167	0	167	0	167	0	167	0
a_3 Military expenditure of W3	98	0	98	0	98	0	98	0
y_{01} Satiation value of y_1	6 000	6 000	6 000	6 000	1 458	1 527	·	·
y_{03} Satiation value of y_3	17 100	17 100	17 100	10 000	4 156	4 352	·	·
Variables								
y_1 Non-military expenditure of W1	1 458	1 527	740	874	1 458	1 527	1 458	1 527
y_3 Non-military expenditure of W3	4 156	4 352	4 153	5 005	4 156	4 352	4 156	4 352
v_{13} Development assistance	2 255	2 353	2 973	3 006	2 255	2 353	2 255	2 353
v_{13} as a percentage of x_3	58	61	77	77	58	61	58	61

Note: Columns 1, 3, 5 and 7 assume that real military expenditures of 1975 persist; columns 2, 4, 6 and 8 assume complete disarmament.

References

Kravis, I.B., A. Heston and R.S. Summers (1982) *World Product and Income*, published for the World Bank by the Johns Hopkins University Press, Baltimore and London.

Tinbergen, J. (1985) 'Measurability of Utility (or Welfare)', *De Economist*, 133, pp. 411–14.

Tinbergen, J. (1987) 'Measuring Welfare of Productive Consumers', *De Economist*, 135, pp. 231–6.

Van Herwaarden, F.G. and A. Kapteyn (1981) 'Empirical Comparison of the Shape of Welfare Functions', *European Economic Review*, 15, pp. 261–86.

2 Cost of Directly Unproductive Profit-Seeking and Rent-Seeking Activities: Some Conceptual Issues

Jagdish N. Bhagwati[1]

The concept of directly unproductive profit-seeking (DUP) activities, among them the subset of rent-seeking activities, has now become an important component of theoretical analysis. It has also entered the realm of policy analysis, including that of measurement, as several analysts of policy regimes in developing countries have increasingly attempted to include estimates of rent-seeking costs in assessing the costs of inefficient policies.[2]

It is important therefore to analyse clearly the underlying concepts and the measurement problems that attend the DUP-theoretic approach. Towards this end, I raise here some broad issues, arguing that wholly different conceptual problems arise concerning the cost of DUP activities, depending on their nature, and that an important distinction must be made among them.[3] I also plan to raise a somewhat novel point about the relationship between deadweight and DUP-theoretic rent-seeking costs: while they are treated generally as simply additive, I suggest that one may substitute for the other in practice.

DUP ACTIVITIES

I should perhaps stress once again that, by DUP activities, I plan to refer to all (directly) unproductive activities aimed at making profit or income without directly or indirectly producing (socially-valued) output. These are therefore profit-seeking activities, just as normal, productive activities are: the only difference is that they use resources, and should carry normal profits in equilibrium, but produce zero output (Bhagwati, 1982, 1987). I call them *directly* unproductive profit-seeking activities, rather than simply unproductive, only but importantly to stress that indirectly and ultimately such DUP activities may increase welfare. Therefore, contrary to the practice in Buchanan (1980) and several other public-choice theorists who define unproductive activities as socially wasteful, it is necessary to define unproductive activities as those directly or immediately producing 'waste' but which nonetheless may result in social good (for second-best reasons).

RENT-SEEKING, AMONG DUP ACTIVITIES

Not all unproductive (DUP) activities are necessarily rent-seeking. The latter, defined (as in Krueger's seminal article, 1974) as activities aimed at connecting rents to quantitative policy interventions such as industrial and import licences and quotas, are one of many forms of DUP activities. It has been muddling and unproductive to speak of such rent-seeking activities as if they were the entire universe of DUP activities. Elsewhere (Bhagwati, 1983), I have examined this confusion of concepts at some length.

Here, however, let me stress again the difference, because, as I argue below, the question of putting a cost on the rent-seeking type of DUP is in principle a very different matter from that of putting a cost on specific other types of DUP activities. This all too important implication is also lost in the confusing practice of lumping together all kinds of DUP activities under one umbrella, loosely described as rent-seeking in some of the existing literature.

To see the typical taxonomy of DUP activities, and how rent-seeking fits into them, consider Figure 2.1, in which I have considered only policy-intervention-related DUP activities. These may seek to make money by changing or influencing policies (I). For example, by seeking a tariff, a lobby expects to improve its earned income if the tariff protects the lobbyist's industry. On the other hand, with a quota in place, a lobby may arise simply to seek the quota and the rent (scarcity or windfall profit/premium) it carries, thus resulting in 'rent-seeking' (II A). Like heat-seeking missiles, which seek existing heat, lobbies then seek existing rents which are attached to the QRs. Finally, policy-evasion (IIB) is also a DUP activity where the policy is evaded in order to make money.

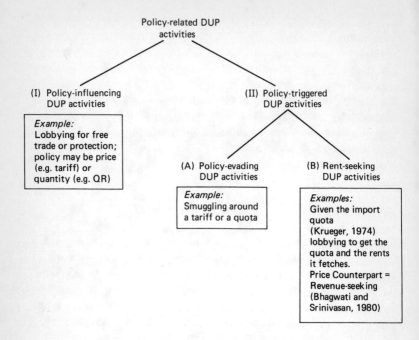

FIGURE 2.1   Policy-related DUP activities

IMPLICATIONS OF ALTERNATIVE DUP ACTIVITIES FOR SOCIAL COST MEASUREMENT

Type II DUP Activities Including Rent-Seeking

DUP activities of Type II are difficult to handle in actual measurement of their costs (or benefits) but conceptually they are easy to grasp and incorporate into conventional economic analysis.

Thus, the IIB variety of DUP activities are essentially the ones we analyse when we wish to account for the 'second' or 'parallel' economy. A considerable theoretical and empirical literature has evolved on these questions for the market and now also for Soviet-style economies, e.g. Desai, (1986, 1987), Wellisz and Findlay (1986) and Panagariya (1989).

Rent-seeking DUP activities, however, are more central to my interest here. Conceptually, I believe, they raise no problem. For example, if import quotas arise and are to be assigned, it is conceptually clear that we must take into our consideration of the cost of import protection, not merely the conventional deadweight cost of the quotas, but also the cost that would be imposed by the induced rent-seeking DUP activity. The latter would arise to secure the import quotas that carry the scarcity premia as rents. If we know what resources will be used up in such activity – this is a problem which raises acute difficulty in practice – then conventional methods can certainly be used to compute the rent-seeking costs that may be added to the deadweight costs, as nicely shown in a recent paper by Hal Varian (1989).

As is now well known, however, the early assumptions, as in the articles of Krueger (1974) and Tullock (1967), that (i) a dollar-worth of rents would lead to a dollar-worth of resources used in rent-seeking, and (ii) a primary or direct loss of resources in rent-seeking would necessarily lead to a further loss of welfare to be added to the deadweight loss, have been shown to be fragile. The former assumption is not valid except when we have risk-neutral competitive entry into rent-seeking (Tullock, 1984; Hillman and Riley, 1988). The latter is not valid for 'highly distorted' economies where resources may have negative shadow prices (Bhagwati and Srinivasan, 1980).

But I wish to add yet one more thought to this question. Gordon Tullock has rightly remarked that direct rent-seeking costs can be minimised by allocating licences to your brother-in-law: corruption is an alternative, albeit an uncomfortable one, to the economic costs of rent-seeking. Though qualifying even this line of argument is the phenomenon of 'vertical' shifts in rent-seeking: the rent-seeking may shift simply to becoming a brother-in-law (a phenomenon perhaps of more ancient vintage than modern rent-seeking lobbying).

There is a related, less discomforting view that (direct) rent-seeking costs may be less than rents because individuals are simply unlikely to be identical in the attributes that give one advantage in securing a rent. There is thus no sense in investing resources in seeking a rent if one knows that a brother-in-law is likely to be in the queue. This therefore should also cut down on the resources used in seeking rents.

But let me make an altogether different kind of point which suggests that, in certain cases, the possibility of rent-seeking in QR allocations may itself lead to methods of allocation that reduce rent-seeking and hence its costs, but then increase simultaneously and in consequence the deadweight losses. Let me state how such a *substitution relationship* may exist between rent-seeking and dead-weight losses.

A bureaucracy saddled with the task of allocating import licences and eager to protect itself from the faintly corrupting task of meeting rent-seeking lobbyist's pressures, may decide to operate by rules rather than discretion. But such allocative rules typically have little economic rationale. Thus, imported raw materials are often allocated according to installed capacity: that seems fair *and* it precludes the discretion that rent-seekers will prey upon. But when scarce imports, and QRs permitting them, are so allocated, deadweight inefficiency follows: for non-transferable pro rata allocations are suboptimal. Thus, the analysis of deadweight and rent-seeking losses would be remiss if this type of critically interacting relationship between them were not taken into account.

Type I DUP Activities

But when we discuss the policy-influencing DUP activities, where policy itself is endogenised, the conceptual problems can be of an altogether different order. Hence, we must definitely avoid confusing these DUP activities with those of the rent-seeking kind. Let me explain.

With the latter as demonstrated in Figure 2.2 on protection, it is straightforward conceptually to show the rent-seeking loss (or gain, if shadow-factor prices are negative). However, when policy itself is endogenous, i.e. the protection is brought about by lobbying DUP activities, and we are then considering the overall cost of protection as the sum of the conventional deadweight loss plus the cost of tariff-seeking lobbying activity, we must pause. We can do it, but is it meaningful?

So, in Figure 2.3, consider an endogenous tariff. Comparing the observed production under such an endogenous tariff at $\hat{P}_{en}$ and the conventional free trade optimum at P^*_{ex}, we then compute the *overall* cost of the protection process as: $CD + DE$, the former being the deadweight loss and the latter being the tariff-seeking DUP-activity loss.

But, while this is in essence the conventional view of the matter, with DUP-activity analysts thus equating (as between Figures 2.2 and 2.3, for instance) the analysis of (exogenous-policy-induced) rent-

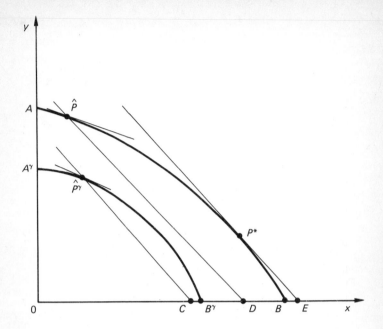

FIGURE 2.2   Rent-seeking DUP activity (type II B): exogenous policy*

* AB is the production possibility curve without rent-seeking. With *exogenous* protection, production is distorted from P^* to $\hat{P}$ and the equivalent-variational cost of protection is DE. But then rent-seeking is triggered, leading to resources being used up in such rent-seeking DUP activity. The production possibility curve, with resources *net* of these wasted resources, is $A^\gamma B^\gamma$. The tariff-equilibrium that is observed then is at $\hat{P}^\gamma$. Therefore, an *additional* rent-seeking loss CD is incurred.

Note: Bhagwati and Srinivasan (1980) showed that this loss CD could be negative, i.e. a gain instead, owing to second-best considerations.

seeking with that of endogenous-policy DUP activities, I am afraid that there is now a key conceptual difficulty.

For, with policy endogenous, I find it difficult to see what legitimacy P^*_{ex} has as a reference point any more. If the policy choice is fully endogenised, then $\hat{P}_{en}$ is the policy that emerges as part of the equilibrium solution to the augmented politico-economic system. You lose the freedom to vary policy at will, that you have in traditional economic theorising with its puppet government with no role other than as a sounding board for the economist.[4] This is the

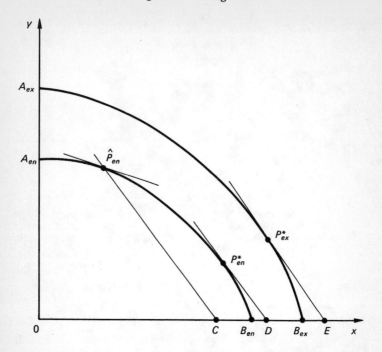

FIGURE 2.3   Tariff-seeking DUP activity (type I): endogenous policy*

* $A_{ex}B_{ex}$ is the production possibility curve (ppc) with all resources and $\hat{P}_{ex}$ is the production if the tariff is exogenously specified. With tariff endogenously determined, through tariff-seeking DUP activity, $A_{en}B_{en}$ is the ppc. The actual, observed tariff-inclusive equilibrium production therefore is at $\hat{P}_{en}$. At given world prices, P^*_{ex} and P^*_{en} are the optimal production points on the two ppcs. Therefore, CD is the deadweight loss of protection and DE is the DUP tariff-seeking loss (Bhagwati, 1982) if we take P^*_{ex} as the reference point (see text, however).

Determinary Paradox (developed in **Bhagwati**, Brecher and Srinivasan, 1985).

In this case, I have suggested that it is not meaningful to talk of the cost of DUP activities in the manner of Figure 2.3. Rather, one wants to regard the DUP activities as part of the total, augmented politico-economic system and ask instead *variational* welfare questions around the observed equilibrium (at $\hat{P}_{en}$ in Figure 2.3). For example, if terms of trade improve, what will be the new, changed $\hat{P}_{en}$ and then its welfare relative to that at the old $\hat{P}_{en}$? Such variations can come from changes in either the political or the economic side of the system.

One then changes the way questions of measurement of costs of distortions are raised. None of this fundamental questioning arises, of course, if only (exogenous-policy-triggered) rent-seeking DUP activities – of type IIB – are considered.

CONCLUDING REMARK

There are other questions that can be raised, for example it is hard to segregate activities into productive and unproductive, as our analysis presumes. But so is it hard to fill empty boxes such as 'externalities', as we are repeatedly reminded by Chicago-trained economists. In my view, such difficulties do not destroy the utility of the conceptual distinction being made.

Notes

1. An early draft of this paper was presented to the American Economic Association meetings in Chicago, 28–30 December 1987. It has profited from the comments of David Colander, Mancur Olson, Gordon Tullock and Warren Samuels. In addressing an important new development in the theory of economic policy, I trust that the paper provides a fitting tribute to Nurul Islam, whose dedication to policy has always been matched by an unusual intellectual curiosity and scholarship.
2. See, in particular, Krueger (1974), Srinivasan and Whalley (1986), and Grais, de Melo and Urata (1986). The fine *World Development Report* (1987) also contains a valuable discussion of DUP activities.
3. I have developed this theme further in the context of recent developments in the theory of commercial policy in the Bernhard Harms Prize Lecture (Bhagwati, 1988).
4. The implications of the new theory of political economy for the theory of economic policy are explored more fully in Bhagwati (1987b), where the phrase 'puppet government' is also introduced.

References

Bhagwati, J. (1982) 'Directly-Unproductive Profit-Seeking (DUP) Activities', *Journal of Political Economy*, 90 (October), pp. 988–1002.
Bhagwati, J. (1983) 'DUP Activities and Rent Seeking', *Kyklos*, 36, pp. 634–7.

Bhagwati, J. (1987a) 'Directly Unproductive Profit-Seeking Activities,' *The New Palgrave*, London: Macmillan.

Bhagwati, J. (1987b) 'The Theory of Political Economy, Economic Policy and Foreign Investment', Discussion Paper Series no. 386, Columbia University Department of Economics, to be published in D. Lal and M. Scott (eds), *Essays in Honour of I.M.D. Little*, Oxford: Oxford University Press.

Bhagwati, J. (1988) 'Is Free Trade Passé After All?' Bernhard Harms Prize Lecture, in *Weltwirtschaftliches Archiv*, 1989.

Bhagwati, J. and T.N. Srinivasan (1980) 'Revenue Seeking: A Generalization of the Theory of Tariffs', *Journal of Political Economy*, 88 (6), December, pp. 1069–87.

Bhagwati, J., R. Brecher and T.N. Srinivasan (1984) 'DUP Activities and Economic Theory', in D. Colander (ed.), *Neoclassical Political Economy*, Cambridge, Mass.: Ballinger, pp. 17–32.

Buchanan, J. (1980) Chapter 1 in Buchanan, J., G. Tullock and R. Tollison (eds) *Towards a General Theory of the Rent-seeking Society*, College Station: Texas A & M University Press.

Desai, Padma (1986) 'Soviet Growth Retardation', *American Economic Review*, 76, 175–80.

Desai, Padma (1987) *The Society Economy: Problems and Prospects*, Oxford: Basil Blackwell.

Grais, W., J. de Melo and S. Urata (1986) 'A General Equilibrium Estimation of the Effects of Reductions in Tariffs and Quantitative Restrictions in Turkey in 1978', in Srinivasan and Whalley (1986).

Hillman, A. and J. Riley (1989) 'Politically Contestable Rents and Transfers', *Economics and Politics*, 1 (1) March.

Krueger, Anne (1974) 'The Political Economy of the Rent-Seeking Society', *American Economic Review* 66 (May), pp. 1–19.

Panagariya, A. (1989) 'The parallel Market in Centrally Planned Economies', *Economics and Politics*, 1(2), July.

Srinivasan, T.N. and J. Whalley, eds (1986) *General Equilibrium Trade Policy Modeling*, Cambridge, Mass.: MIT Press.

Tullock, Gordon (1967) 'The Welfare Cost of Tariffs, Monopolies and Theft', *Western Economic Journal*, 5.

Varian, H. (1989) 'Measuring the Deadweight Costs of DUP and Rent-seeking Activities', *Economics and Politics*, 1(1), March.

Wellisz, S. and R. Findlay (1986), 'Central Planning and the Second Economy in Soviet-type Systems', *Economic Journal*, 96, pp. 646–58.

World Development Report (1987) The World Bank, Washington, DC.

3 On Some Unresolved Issues in Optimum Tariff Theory

Wahidul Haque

INTRODUCTION

J.S. Mill[1] conjectured that a country may gain, compared to a free-trade position, by imposing an optimum tariff. The conjecture, of course, has been verified by Bickerdike[2] and Edgeworth[3] for the case of two goods. The general case for two goods is still open: although it is generally believed that optimal tariff must be non-negative, J. de V. Graaff[4] has argued that optimum tariff would be negative if Giffen effects are sufficiently strong in the tariff-imposing (home) country. Murray Kemp[5] has objected to Graaff's position by saying that 'any peculiarities of home demand are irrelevant to the determination of the sign of the optimal tariff' although, he thought, Giffenness abroad could affect this sign. Graaff also said (without proof) that some optimal tariffs may be negative if there are more than two goods.

Kemp[5] has posed these unresolved issues in the form of three open questions in the case of more than two goods. The questions are:

(1) Can optimum tariff rates be all zero, i.e. can free trade be optimal?
(2) Can net optimum tariff revenue be negative?
(3) Can all tariff rates be negative?

Question (1) is, of course, a re-statement of Mill's original question concerning more than two goods. Answers to these questions are some twenty years due. In this note, I shall try to tackle them. As in the two-good literature, I shall assume 'smooth' economies, i.e. the utility and product-transformation functions in the home country and the excess-demand functions (the offer curves) in the foreign countries are continuously once-differentiable. The findings briefly are as

27

follows. Mill's conjecture is verified for the general case, i.e. Kemp's question (1) is answered in the negative. His second question is answered in the negative too. The third question on the sign of tariff rates is given a more-or-less complete discussion here.

As to Kemp's opinion on the sign of the tariff rate being independent of peculiarities of home demand, he seems to overstate his case. We shall show formally the intuitively obvious fact that optimal tariff rates must be determined on the basis of both domestic and foreign peculiarities. His scepticism on the overriding importance of domestic Giffenness attributed by Graaff is well made. I have seen no such overt influence.

In the next two sections, a formal model on optimum tariff is developed which has been lacking in the literature on the subject, and the questions are answered and discussed. The secret lies in Walras's Law: differentiate Walras's Law and use the result in an 'optimum tariff equation' and the answers fall out therefrom.

THE FORMAL MODEL

Assume m consumers and n producers in the home country. There are ℓ commodities which are all 'formally' traded – reciprocal demand for non-traded goods being identically zero. P stands for the set of vectors in the Euclidean space R^ℓ having strictly positive coordinates. ω_k^i is the ith consumer's initial endowment of commodity k. We write $\omega^i = (\omega_1^i, \ldots, \omega_\ell^i)$, $\omega = |\Sigma \omega^i$. $u^i\colon P \to R$ is the utility function of consumer i in the home country. u^i is assumed to be strictly monotone-increasing and continuously once-differentiable. The production set of the jth producer in the home country is

$$Y^j = \{y^j \ \varepsilon \ V^j \mid G^j(y^j) \leqslant 0\} \tag{3.1}$$

where V^j is the union of an open subset of R^ℓ and the origin and $G^j\colon V^j \to R$ is a strictly-increasing continuously, once-differentiable function. The foreign countries as a whole present an excess-demand function $f\colon P \to R^\ell$ satisfying Walras's Law

$$pf(p) = 0, \ V \, p \ \varepsilon \ P \ \ldots \tag{3.2}$$

It is assumed that f is continuously once-differentiable. Then the foreign 'offer curve' is parametrically defined as the graph

$$G = \{(p, z) \mid z = f(p), pz = 0, p \ \varepsilon \ P\} \qquad (3.3)$$

It may be that for some good k, $f_k(p) = 0$, $V \ p \ \varepsilon \ P$. This will force the home country to exhibit zero excess-demand for this good though such an act may not be optimal for any country at all.

The foreigners may or may not have hidden a tariff vector underneath their excess-demand function. But the home country, on the prescription of J.S. Mill[1], wishes to impose an 'optimum tariff' on its net imports. In other words, it has to choose vectors $x^i \ \varepsilon \ P$, $i = 1, \ldots, m$; $y^j \ \varepsilon \ V^j$, $j = 1, \ldots, n$ and $p \ \varepsilon \ P$ 'optimally' such that

$$\omega + \sum y^j - \sum x^i - f(p) \geq 0 \qquad (3.4)$$

$$G^j(y^j) \leq 0 \ , j = 1, \ldots, n \qquad (3.5)$$

The question for us now is the sense of the optimum. The optimum tariff theory so far developed in the literature uses 'community indifference curves' which means that all consumer preferences have been aggregated into a single utility function. We could, following this tradition, simply assume the number of consumers m to be precisely 1 and conduct an 'ordinal' exercise of maximising this function subject to the constraints (3.4, 3.5). Alternatively, we could invoke the basic theorem of welfare economics (Debreu,[6] Theorem 6.4, pp. 95–6), and identify a favourite Pareto-optimal vector $\bar{v} = <(\bar{x}^i), (\bar{y}^j), \bar{p}>$ and a domestic price system $\bar{\pi}$ such that $\bar{v}$ is an 'equilibrium relative to the price system $\bar{\pi}$'. This view will simply require us to take the 'trade-set' $-f(P)$ as an additional production set on top of $Y^1, \ldots, Y^n$. However, no such *a priori* identification is possible. Willy nilly, we have to go cardinal and borrow a strictly-increasing Scitovsky welfare function $W(u^1(x^1), \ldots, u^m(x^m))$ which we will maximise subject to the constraints (3.4, 3.5). In particular, this will cover the 'community indifference' case. It will also cover the utilitarian case of the sum of the individual utilities – a case whose 'partial comparability' aspects have been analysed by Amartya Sen in a masterly contribution.[7]

Because of the monotonicity assumptions on u^i and G^j, equality will prevail in (3.4, 3.5) if an optimum exists. Also, due to the monotonicity assumptions on W, u^i and G^j, (3.4) and (3.5) will hold with equalities. Our problem, then, is to maximise

$$W(u^1(x^1), \ldots, u^m(x^m)) \qquad (3.6)$$

subject to the constraints

$$\omega + \sum y^j - \sum x^i - f(p) = 0 \qquad (3.7)$$

$$G^j(y^j) = 0 , j = 1, \ldots , n \qquad (3.8)$$

We need a technical discussion at this point of our analysis. Write the left-hand side of (3.7) and (3.8) as $F(x, y, p)$. Because the gradient $DG^j(y^j)$ is positive r, the Jacobian $DF(x, y, p)$ at any point (x, y, p) satisfying (3.7, 3.8) will have full rank $\ell + n$, the number of equations in (3.7, 3.8). To see this, take an arbitrary ℓ-vector α and an arbitrary n-vector β and consider the linear system of equations:

$$DF(x, y, p)(\hat{x}, \hat{y}, \hat{p}) = (\alpha, \beta) \qquad (3.9)$$

We are done if a solution $(\hat{x}, \hat{y}, \hat{p})$ of (3.9) exists. In full, (3.9) reads

$$\text{(a)} \ \sum \hat{y}^j - \sum \hat{x}^i - Df(p)\hat{p} = \alpha$$

$$\text{(b)} \ DG^j(y^j)\hat{y}^j = \beta_j, j = 1, \ldots , n \qquad (3.10)$$

Since $DG^j(y^j)$ is positive, (3.10b) has a solution $\hat{y}^j$ which can be fed into (3.10a) to obtain an infinity of solutions $((\hat{x}_i), \hat{p})$. One solution is: $\hat{p} = 0$, $\hat{x}^i = 0$, $i \neq 1$, $\hat{x}^1 = \sum \hat{y}^j - \alpha$.

With the fact that $DF(x, y, p)$ is non-singular, we can invoke the Lagrange method for solving our problem. Let

$$\Phi(x, y, p, \lambda, \mu) = W(u^1(x^1), \ldots , u^m(x^m))$$
$$+ \lambda(\omega + \sum y^j - \sum x^i - f(p)) + \sum \mu^j G^j(y^j)) \qquad (3.11)$$

where $\lambda = (\lambda_1, \ldots , \lambda_\ell)$, $\mu^j, j = 1, \ldots , n$ are the Lagrange multipliers. If a solution to the optimization problem exists, then it must satisfy the following first-order conditions.

$$\frac{\partial \phi}{\partial x_k^i} = \frac{\partial W}{\partial u_i(x^i)} \frac{\partial u^i(x^i)}{\partial x_k^i} - \lambda_k \quad = 0, \quad \begin{matrix} k = 1, \ldots , \ell \\ i = 1, \ldots , m \end{matrix} \quad (3.12)$$

$$\frac{\partial \phi}{\partial \lambda} = \omega + \sum y^j - \sum x^i - f(p) = 0 \qquad (3.13)$$

$$\frac{\partial \phi}{\partial y_k^j} = \mu^j \frac{\partial G^j(y^j)}{\partial y_k^j} + \lambda_k = 0 \qquad \begin{matrix} k = 1, \ldots, \ell \\ j = 1, \ldots, n \end{matrix} \qquad (3.14)$$

$$\frac{\partial \phi}{\partial \mu^j} = G^j(y^j) \qquad\qquad = 0$$

$$\frac{\partial \phi}{\partial p_k} = - \sum_{k'=1}^{\ell} \lambda_{k'} \frac{\partial f_{k'}(p)}{\partial p_k} = 0 \qquad k = 1, \ldots, \ell \qquad (3.15)$$

Then (3.12) and (3.14) give the familiar marginal rates of substitution equals-price ratio conditions:

$$\frac{\partial u^i(x^i)/\partial x_k^i}{\partial u^i(x^i)/\partial x_q^i} = \frac{\partial G^j/\partial y_k^j}{\partial G^j/\partial y_q^j} = \frac{\lambda_k}{\lambda_q} \qquad (3.16)$$

where λ_k is the domestic price of good k in 'welfare units' (the shadow price). The optimum tariff rates τ_k are defined by

$$(1+\tau_k) \frac{p_k}{p_q} = \frac{\lambda_k}{\lambda_q} \quad , \ldots \qquad (3.17)$$

$$\text{i.e. } \tau_k = \frac{\lambda_k/\lambda_q}{p_k/p_q} - 1 \qquad (3.18)$$

Obviously, $\tau_q = 0$. The tariff rates (3.18) thus depend on the choice of the numeraire q; they vary with the numeraire. (3.15) is the 'optimum tariff equation'. Applying (3.17) in (3.15), we get

$$\sum_{k'=1}^{\ell} (1 + \tau_{k'}) \, p_{k'} \frac{\partial f_{k'}}{\partial p_k} = 0 \, , \, k = 1, \ldots, \ell \qquad (3.19)$$

which will prove to be the basic tool for our purpose.

THE ISSUES AND QUESTIONS

Kemp's second question regarding the possible negativity of the optimum tariff revenue is hard to answer – I will leave it open. The first question can be given a full answer – the third more-or-less a full one. We employ equation (3.19) for this purpose with the vital assistance provided by Walras's Law (3.2).

Differentiating Walras's Law (3.2) with respect to p_k, we get

$$\sum_{k'=1}^{\ell} p_{k'} \frac{\partial f_{k'}(p)}{\partial p_k} + f_k(p) = 0 \qquad (3.20)$$

Add $f_k(p)$ to both sides of (3.19) and use (3.20) to get

$$\sum_{k' \neq q} \tau_{k'} p_{k'} \frac{\partial f_{k'}}{\partial p_k} = f_k(p), \, k = 1, \ldots, \ell \qquad (3.21)$$

Let $(\bar{x}, \bar{y}, \bar{p}, \bar{\lambda}, \bar{\mu})$ be an optimal tariff policy and $\bar{\tau}$ the implied optimal tariff.

Suppose free trade is optimal. Then $\bar{\tau}_{k'} = 0$ for all k' and (3.21) implies that $f_k(\bar{p}) = 0$ for all $k = 1, \ldots, \ell$. We get the trivial case: if free trade is optimal, it must be autarkic. If free trade involves non-zero trade, it cannot be optimal. This then verifies Mill's conjecture in the case of more than two goods. Mill's conjecture thus becomes

PROPOSITION 1: Free trade is non-optimal in general in a many-goods world.

To answer Kemp's second question, bear (3.18) in mind and notice that the optimum tariff revenue equals

$$-\frac{1}{\bar{p}_q} \sum \bar{\tau}_k \, \bar{p}_k \, f_k(\bar{p}) = -\frac{1}{\bar{\lambda}_q} \, \bar{\lambda} f(\bar{p})$$

Now refer to (3.12). Since $\bar{p}$ maximises $\phi(\bar{x}, \bar{y}, p, \bar{\lambda}, \bar{\mu})$, it clearly maximises $-\bar{\lambda} f(p)$ so that

$$-\bar{\lambda} f(\bar{p}) \geq -\bar{\lambda} f(\bar{\lambda}) \equiv 0$$

This yields

PROPOSITION 2: Optimum tariff revenue cannot be negative.

Let us now examine Graaff's statement that in the two-goods case if the import is a domestic Giffen good, then tariff on it must be negative. In this two-good model, export is the numeraire. Say that good 1 is export and good 2 is import. Then from (3.21):

$$\bar{\tau}_2 \bar{p}_2 \; \frac{\partial f_2}{\partial p_2} = f_2(\bar{p}) \qquad (3.22)$$

Now $f_2(\bar{p}) < 0$ since good 2 is imported by the home country. Graaff's statement will be false if this good is normal abroad because the left-hand side of (3.22) will be non-negative with $\bar{\tau}_2 < 0$ while the right-hand is negative. Graaff ought to have located Giffenness abroad, not at home. Indeed, if this good is Giffen abroad, i.e. $\partial f_2 / \partial \bar{p}_2 > 0$, then the tariff $\bar{\tau}_2$ must be negative.

The above is generalised in the l-good case as follows.

PROPOSITION 3: If all goods are gross-substitutes abroad and a non-numeraire foreign-Giffen good is imported, then there will be at least one negative tariff rate (not necessarily on the Giffen good).

The proposition follows from (3.21) by noticing that $f_k(\bar{p}) < 0$ and $\partial f_{k'} / \partial p_k \geqslant 0$ under hypothesis.

We now examine Graaff's other point that in an ℓ-good world, some optimal tariff rates may be negative without the qualification of Giffenness. This proposition was not proved by Graaff. On this, Kemp[5] (p. 171) says: 'To prove it, or to produce a counter-example, is a major outstanding intellectual challenge'. Without taking up the gauntlet, let me offer the following:

PROPOSITION 4: Assume all goods are gross substitutes abroad. If the numeraire good is exported, in an optimum tariff regime, then all tariff rates cannot be negative; if it is imported, then all tariff rates cannot be positive; if it is not traded, then at least one tariff rate is positive and at least one other tariff rate is negative.

The proposition follows from (3.21) with $k = q$. I now state another result.

PROPOSITION 5: Optimal tariff is equivalent to an optimal quota.

Proof: An optimal tariff policy (x, y, p) implies tariff τ from (3.18) and quota $f(p)$ from (3.7). On the other hand, fix the quota $f(p)$ and solve (3.6–3.8) for (x, y) which will lead to τ via (3.18) again.

Some comments are in order. Answers to Graaff's question depend on which good is chosen as the numeraire. If optimal tariff is not autarkic, then the home country must export at least one good and import at least one good. Take the imported good as numeraire. Then there must be at least one negative tariff rate. On the other hand, taking the exported good as numeraire, at least one tariff rate must be positive. If a non-traded good exists, as is in general the case, then taking this good as numeraire, we see that at least one tariff must be positive and at least one negative. All this of course is under the assumption that all goods are gross substitutes abroad. One can draw just the opposite conclusions if all goods are gross complements. Be that as it may, the blunt message of the above propositions in this: some restricted trade is better than free trade.

CONCLUDING REMARKS

It should be obvious to the reader that all the dependent variables (x^i), (y^j), p, (μ^i), (λ_k) are solutions of the equations (3.4–3.7) where the functions W, u^i, G^j, f and the endowment ω are the independent variables. It can be shown that the dependent variables are upper semicontinuous correspondences of the independent variables and indeed, if some more smoothness is assumed, for almost all values of the independent variables, the dependent variables take finite numbers of values, locally, as solutions of (3.4–3.7) and move continuously with the independent variables. These considerations have far-reaching implications for the tariff retaliation process involving some new results in differential topology.[8] I hope to report on this matter elsewhere.

From the above paragraph, it should be evident that the value, and hence sign, of the optimal tariff rates depend both on home and foreign conditions. Kemp overstates his case in this sense.

Notes

1. Mill, J.S. *Principles of Political Economy*. London: Longmans, Green, 1909.
2. Bickerdike, C.F. 'The Theory of Incipient Taxes', *Economic Journal* 16 (1906), 529–35.
3. Edgeworth, F.Y. *Papers Relating to Political Economy*, II. London: Macmillan, 1925.

4. Graaff, J. de V. 'On Optimum Tariff Structures', *Review of Economic Studies*, 17 (1949–50), 47–59.
5. Kemp, M.C. 'Notes on the Theory of Optimal Tariffs', *Economic Record*, 43 (1967), 395–404. (Also, chapter 12, in the author's 'Three Topics in the Theory of International Trade'. Amsterdam: North Holland, 1976.
6. Debreu, G. *Theory of Value*. New York: Wiley, 1959.
7. Sen, A.K. 'Interpersonal Aggregation and Partial Comparability', *Econometrica*, 38 (1970), 393–409.
8. Haque, W. 'Transversal Mappings and Disequilibrium Analysis', Working Paper Series No. 8506. Institute for Policy Analysis, University of Toronto, 1985.

4 Comparative Advantage and Free Trade

Paul Streeten[1]

INCREASING RETURNS

In reply to the question whether there exists in economics a set of propositions that is both true and non-trivial, the great M.I.T.-WIT (the opposite of NIT-WIT) Paul Samuelson is reported to have said: the doctrine of comparative advantage. In spite of its venerable age, there are many politicians, officials and common men and women who have not grasped it. Even that great institution of trade liberalisation, the General Agreement on Tariffs and Trade, approaches trade negotiations as if admitting more imports were a concession and removing protection a sacrifice.

The doctrine of comparative advantage forms the basis for the recommendation of free trade. It is generally held to be one of the few recommendations on which the overwhelming majority of economists agree. Rousseau wrote: Man is born free, and everywhere he is in chains. Similarly, it might be said: Economists recommend free trade and everywhere there is protection. In so far as belief in the doctrine of comparative advantage is undermined, the near-universal recommendation of free trade is also undermined, although it is possible to base the recommendation of free trade on other grounds, often inconsistent with the doctrine of comparative costs.[1] This paper deals primarily with the doctrine of comparative advantage, but also with consequential modifications of the recommendation of free trade.

Clearly the doctrine of comparative advantage is 'valid' in the sense that its conclusions follow with inexorable logic from its premises. But the primary question raised in this paper is: 'Is it true?' Do its premises correspond to the real world? A secondary questions is: 'If the doctrine is not true, are government interventions with foreign trade justified?'

In a much praised and at the same time much neglected article Allyn Young demolished the doctrine of comparative advantage.[3] By adding to Adam Smith's theorem that the division of labour depends upon the extent of the market, its reverse, viz. that the extent of the market also depends upon the division of labour, he destroyed the analytical foundation of comparative advantage. While Adam Smith thought mainly of the geographical extent of the market, of area and population, Allyn Young saw that the size of incomes, the buying power and the capacity to absorb a large annual output of goods, is also an important dimension of the size of the market. And the size of incomes is clearly determined by the division of labour and the degree of specialisation. And while Adam Smith thought of the division of labour as specialised tasks and labour-saving inventions, Allyn Young thought of it in terms of roundabout methods of production, machinery to make more consumption goods, machines to make machines, the division of labour between industries, and what we would today call the formation of specialised human capital. It is on this interdependence between specialisation (including economies of roundabout methods of production) and market, between power to produce and power to buy, that economic progress depends.

The doctrine of comparative advantage must assume either constant unit costs (in its Ricardo version) or increasing unit costs (in its Heckscher-Ohlin-Samuelson version). But increasing returns are ubiquitous and are Allyn Young's starting point. The division of labour depends on the division of labour. Allyn Young showed that this is not a tautology, but at the root of economic progress. Increasing returns within a firm are, however, not compatible with either perfect competition or competitive equilibrium, or the recommendation to all countries to adopt free trade. It may lead to the wrong kind of specialisation, early starters gaining superiority in lines in which late starters would have had a comparative advantage, had they come earlier. It may lead to monopoly, where the increasing returns are internal to a firm. There will be no tendency to factor price equalisation.

If one country has a comparative advantage in increasing unit cost industries, and another in decreasing unit cost industries, it has been argued that the increasing cost country will suffer. It will expand its increasing cost industry and contract its decreasing cost industry, and face rising costs in both. This will not be the case if the decreasing costs are internal to the firms, and are anticipated, so that the firm will borrow to move down its cost curve. But if the decreasing costs are external to the firm, and not internal to any other firm, the wrong type of specialisation may occur. Another qualification, however, is needed. The external economies would have to depend on the size of the domestic industry only, and not on the size of the world industry. In those conditions free trade cannot be recommended, although the optimum policy may be a subsidy to the decreasing cost industry, rather than protection.

But this is not the world of Allyn Young. It is a rather academic world in which wrong specialisation occurs because one country specialises in increasing cost industries, another in decreasing cost industries. In Allyn Young's picture increasing returns prevail everywhere, and change becomes progressive and propagates itself in a cumulative way. Change in the use of resources (the reorganisation of productive activity) creates the opportunities for further change. International trade in this picture has also great benefits to offer, greater benefits than those promised on the assumption of diminishing returns. They lie in the extension of markets and greater specialisation. But it is the result of a series of disequilibria, not of a tendency towards an equilibrium. And, although Allyn Young did not say this, the lines of specialisation are determined by those who are first in the field, those who have the new technology, and those who can capture a large market. Whether such a world of growing specialisation and regional uniformity of production is desirable, or whether more diversified activities are worth the cost of reduced specialisation, is another question.

Large indivisibilities and consequential economies of scale are part of Allyn Young's world of increasing returns. But he did not foresee the growth of supercomputers and modern aircraft, which require very costly and large investments, and the mobilisation for which will be confined to a few countries. Whoever establishes an early foothold and expands rapidly gains advantages over competitors. Differences in comparative advantage have little to do with who produces what. This does not mean that the first comers are bound to dominate the field for ever. After a time, diseconomies of management, fatigue, or innovation elsewhere, may cause a decline and give others an opportunity to move up.

There are, of course, other good (and some bad) reasons for adopting free trade than the doctrine of comparative advantage. This section discussed the case for trade based on economies of scale and increasing returns, reaped in export industries or in import substitutes. Among other reasons for free trade are the following:

1. the encouragement of greater competition;
2. the encouragement of the growth of institutions, attitudes, or skills conducive to greater efficiency;
3. the political advantage of simple rules, compared with the complexity of permitting all exceptions permitted by economic theory;
4. the political case for yielding to self-interested pressure groups who stand to gain from more trade.

In the absence of trade, markets are monopolistic. Trade reduces imperfections in competition. The first point raises questions about the optimum degree of exposure to the winds of competition. Too little exposure can foster cosy monopolies; too much may wither delicate seedlings. The argument from competition is also inconsistent with the argument from scale economies (and of course, with the argument from comparative advantage). The second point is an empirical one. On the face of it, a strong basis of a domestic technological capacity in the form of a capital goods industry, technical education, and learning by doing seem to be stronger candidates for learning innovative and efficient production than just opening up trade.

The third point (and possibly the fourth), the political advantage of simple rules has, as Paul Krugman and Gerald Helleiner have pointed out, stood the traditional approach on its head. Political pressures used to be blamed for the inability of governments to pursue free trade. The Invisible Foot trampled on the beautiful work of the Invisible Hand. Now political forces are invoked to defend free trade against the modern arguments for intervention. In complex situations, in which the new sophisticated arguments for trade intervention are difficult to implement, yield uncertain returns, and may be captured and abused by special interests, and in a world whose politics are as imperfect as its markets, simple rules are best.[4] But it should be remembered that there are other simple rules, if simple rules are needed, such as that a country below a certain level of development should be allowed to put up a 20 per cent tariff, etc. Moreover, the principle of simple rules is not applied to other spheres subject to political pressures, such as our tax system. Those (like Paul Krugman) advocating 'simple' rules as a way of avoiding prisoner's dilemma outcomes resulting from the pressure of special interest groups may be confusing simplicity with universality. The rules should not relate to uneliminable individual cases, but universality can, indeed must, allow for differences in countries and circumstances.

COMPARATIVE ADVANTAGE CREATED, ARBITRARY AND TEMPORARY

The textbooks speak of factor endowments. It is these and other God-given natural phenomena such as climate, that are said to determine comparative advantage. In the Ricardo version, different countries have different production functions, but the same endowment with a single factor. viz. labour. In the Heckscher-Ohlin version, production functions are the same everywhere, but factor endowments vary between countries. Ricardo's production possibility curve exhibits constant unit costs, Heckscher-Ohlin's increasing unit costs. Both are given and unchanged over long periods. Several authors have extended the Heckscher-Ohlin model to the long run, allowing for the production of a capital good, for savings and investment, and growth.[5]

This model has dominated the minds of trained economists for a long time. But with the growing importance of science and technology, the capacity to form human capital, and the increasingly systematic relation between expenditure on research and development, and commercial results, comparative advantage has become something created and manipulated. At the same time scientific research expenditure and human capital formation are outstanding cases of activities subject to scale economies and increasing returns. These economies of scale are not God-given but accrue to whoever is first in the field and has sufficient resources to wait for the 'lucky strike'. The same goes for cost reductions from learning by doing. Textiles may initially have been a labour-intensive industry. But a fully automated textile plant uses hardly any labour. The direction of R & D expenditure can shift the comparative advantage of different countries in growing different crops. Japan's strategy has been to build up one industry after another behind protective barriers, and then to sell the products in excess of domestic requirements abroad at low prices.

In the world just described government intervention in the form of export subsidies or import restrictions can play the role of cost-reducing technological innovations by the firm, and give it the initial advantage required to establish its comparative advantage in the chosen field. It may, of course, be that these incentives are better given through subsidies to research and development expenditure, education, training, credit, employment or production than through direct interventions in trade.

X-INEFFICIENCY

The doctrine of comparative advantage as the basis for the recommendation of free trade assumes that all economies are on their production frontier, so that producing more of one good is possible only by producing less of another. All factors of production are fully and optimally employed. The two axes normally represent importables and exportables, but they may also represent welfare derived from different products or for different groups. Any point on this transformation curve which does not lie where the international terms of trade are equal to the domestic transformation ratio permits us to raise welfare by moving to this point: the point of free trade.

In fact no economy is ever at this frontier, and many are deep inside it. The reason for this is the existence of various inefficiencies, 'distortions', organisational flaws, wrong incentives, etc. But it may at first be thought that from a point inside the frontier *any* move towards the frontier is an improvement. It is true that any move towards the frontier must be an improvement. But it is often not possible to know whether the removal of one or several distortions is in fact such a move. In a distorted economy, the removal of only one or a few distortions may move the economy away from, rather than towards, the optimum. As Henry Bruton has suggested, the path to the production frontier should be considered as a maze, some ways leading away from the frontier.[6] But, being inside the production frontier (or the welfare possibility frontier), there is no presumption that reducing protection and moving from the production of importables behind protection towards the production of exportables without, or with less, protection is always the correct policy. The more efficient production of import substitutes may be just as good as that of exports. It is probably this fact more than any other that gives rise to the divergent perceptions of the correct trade policy of the practical man and the economist referred to in the first paragraph.

It could, of course, be that certain institutional and organisational forms make movement in one direction speedier than in the other. An open trade policy, moving towards exportables, would be

favoured by contact with foreign competitors, with world-wide capital markets, and the pressures on reducing costs resulting from the
bracing winds of foreign competition. On the other hand, it could be
that learning by doing, and even learning by doing without (viz.
imports) and building an indigenous technological capacity are
favoured by some protection and closing in. These links would have
to be established empirically.

CREATIVE AND ALLOCATIVE FUNCTIONS OF MARKETS

Nicholas Kaldor distinguished between the allocative and the creative functions of the market.[7] Before him, Schumpeter, in his
analysis of creative destruction, made a similar distinction and explained how a system, that at any given moment performs below its
full potential, can yet perform much better than one that achieves
higher allocative efficiency. The allocative function is the one usually
described in textbooks and underlies the doctrine of comparative
advantage. It is reflected in movements along the production frontier, e.g. in response to a tariff removal, from import substitutes to
exports.

The creative function consists in pushing outward the production
frontier; creating new and more efficient opportunities for production. It may be the result of investment or of a financial, technical,
organisational, managerial or institutional innovation. The conventional way of dealing with this is to say that savings/investment ratios
determine growth, and that these can be raised by shifting a lower
total income (as a result of a sacrifice in allocative efficiency) to
groups with higher savings ratios. This assumes that there are no
better ways of raising savings, such as fiscal policy (raising the budget
surplus by increasing taxation or reducing public consumption).

There are, however, many other forces responsible for growth than
the investment ratio. Among these are the spirit of enterprise,
attitudes to risk and venture, technical and institutional innovations,
organisational arrangements that permit this spirit and these attitudes
to be expressed, the role of the government in encouraging or
impeding economic activity, etc.[8] It is possible to be inside the
production frontier at any given time, but to push out the frontier
continually at a rate that more than compensates for the static
inefficiency: to have the wrong balance between toothbrushes and
nailbrushes, but have more of both.[9] The gains from the creative

function then exceed the losses from the allocative function. Alternatively, being nearer or on the production frontier may push the whole frontier out faster. The relation between X-efficiency or allocative efficiency, discussed in the previous section, and creative efficiency (of either markets or their substitutes) can work in either direction.[10] But, as in the case above, when we were inside the frontier and moved the system towards the frontier, there is no presumption that the international terms of trade provide the optimum incentive for the most rapid dynamic move outwards.[11]

It does not, of course, follow that the best way of moving towards the frontier is a deviation from free trade. It may be domestic interventions of the tax/subsidy kind. In most cases, only if such interventions are ruled out is intervention in trade justified.

CAPITAL FLOWS

The doctrine of comparative advantage assumes that there is a mechanism which translates comparative real advantage into absolute cost and price advantage. For businessmen and traders, as we have seen, do not understand the doctrine. Even if they did, it would not concern them. They are interested in making money. That means buying in the cheapest and selling in the dearest market, as indicated by market prices. Under the gold standard the mechanism of translation was specie flows and differential changes in the general price level. Under a regime of fixed exchange rates, the mechanism works through domestic monetary and fiscal policies that change price and employment levels. Under flexible exchange rates, the mechanism is the exchange rate, together with fiscal and monetary policies, through which comparative real advantages are translated into absolute price advantages.

Some international capital flows are consistent with this mechanism. If a country wishes to invest abroad because it expects the investment to yield over a long period higher returns than could be got at home, its demand for foreign currencies will lower the exchange rate and tend to generate the export surplus to provide the capital flow for the foreign investment.

The situation is, however, quite different if vast amounts of speculative capital slosh around the world in response to actual or expected differentials in interest rates, forward rates or exchange rates. Today's capital flows are perhaps twenty times trade flows. In such a situation the exchange rates no longer reflect real comparative cost advantages. The translation mechanism has broken down. Prices, subject to large and sudden changes, are no longer a guide to the optimum allocation of resources. The events of 18 October 1987 are an extreme example of violent fluctuations in prices, not founded on new, relevant information. Forward exchange contracts are not an adequate insurance against these uncertainties.

A QUIET LIFE

Sir John Hicks said that the reward of a monopolist is often a quiet life. The effort to maximise profits by equating marginal returns is itself subject to diminishing psychic returns. The free trade gospel, based on the doctrine of comparative advantage, bids us always to strive for higher incomes from the international division of labour. But adjustments in response to changing comparative advantage are costly. They involve changing occupations, often changing residence, periods of unemployment and uncertainty, and generally upheaval and disruption. In an international environment in which comparative advantage changes rapidly, trade policy can become a policy for tramps. The citizens of an already fairly rich country may say: We have already many earthly goods. We wish to forgo some extra income from international trade for the sake of a quieter life; for not having to learn a new trade, for not being uprooted from our community. There is nothing irrational or 'non-economic' in such a choice.[12]

It will, of course, depend upon how important international trade is in the economy of the country. It must avoid suffering reductions in income resulting from having opted out, even only at the margin, of remaining internationally competitive. It will also depend on not permitting the vested interests benefiting from the protection (which include capitalists and managers, as well as workers) to become so powerful as to drive the economy beyond the point where forgone income from international specialisation just balances the benefits of a somewhat less disruptive life. It is probably true that most countries have sought protection beyond this optimum point, and the real costs to the community of keeping workers employed in industries that should be shrunk, greatly exceeds the benefits that could be reaped by a redeployment of labour.

The qualification introduced above for countries heavily dependent on international trade would, in turn, have to be qualified if international cooperation could be implemented on the optimum rate of technical progress where such progress involves disruption. In most other lines of advance we accept the application of some form of benefit/cost calculus, but only where advances in knowledge and its technical and commercial application are concerned do we not ask questions about its social and human costs. When technological progress in synthetics knocks out lines of raw-material exports on which a poor country is heavily dependent for foreign exchange, the costs of adjustment may greatly exceed the benefits to buyers, quite apart from the evaluation of the distributional impact. It would then be reasonable to ask for some form of international agreement to slow down the pace of scientific and technological progress. The issue here is not a quiet life, but the avoidance of impoverishment, through deteriorating terms of trade or growing unemployment, by international cooperation.

There is a literature on the so-called 'non-economic' objectives of policy-makers, and on how to modify free trade policy to accommodate them. But my point is not really a non-economic one. Leisure is part of conventional economic objectives, as are both psychological and financial costs of disruption; the costs of resettlement, of rehousing, of retraining, etc. My point is that these benefits and costs are entirely within the domain normally surveyed by economists and have been largely ignored, but lead to a modification of the doctrine of comparative advantage as a basis for free trade.

UNEMPLOYMENT

The doctrine of comparative advantage assumes full employment. Only then do prices reflect marginal costs. In conditions of general unemployment, the shadow wage of labour is lower than the wage rate. It may even be negative. If the unemployment is the intended result of government policy (say in order to reduce inflationary pressures, or in order to redeploy labour), the conclusion has to be modified; similarly, if the unemployment is for other reasons consistent with a move towards an optimum allocation of resources. This would be the case if unemployment in one group of industries is accompanied by excess demand for labour in another.

Unemployment in trading partners is irrelevant for the trade policy of a given country. Like other forms of foreign obstacles to the efficient allocation of resources, it is a given fact for the country deciding upon its policy. To impose trade restrictions because other countries suffer unemployment is like the much-quoted attempt to cast rocks into your own harbour because others suffer from rocky harbours. This is not true of domestic unemployment, to which the considerations in the previous paragraph apply.

Even if the unemployment is domestic and is not the result of intended policies (e.g. against inflation, or to reduce the bargaining power of labour), but the result of market failure, it does not follow that trade interventions are the best method to cure it. Policies to raise aggregate demand, or subsidies to wages or adjustment assistance are likely to be better.

EXTERNALITIES OF CONSUMPTION AND INDUCED TASTES

Economic welfare is not just a matter of command over resources; the greater the command, the higher the welfare. It is a matter of command in relation to wants. Gains from international trade have to be assessed in relation not only to additional income (and output) but also to additional wants, expectations and aspirations generated by the extra income. It is then quite possible, indeed likely, that gains in income are accompanied by losses in welfare, because wants grow faster than command over resources. The appetite grows faster than what it feeds on. This is not largely because of advertising and sales promotion, but is mainly the result of the unequal division of the gains from trade. Even with an equal division between countries, there can be greater inequalities within countries. The lower income groups take as their reference group the higher income groups. When the lion's share of the gains goes to these higher income groups, the poorer are worse off. It is then possible that the countries with large gains from trade fail to benefit because internal inequalities are great, and the others (often the developing countries) do not benefit because international inequalities are great. It is, of course, possible to define welfare in a different way, such as a widened range of choice. But this definition has been disputed by psychologists. Moreover, it is a well-known fact that disagreements over the distribution of additional income can be just as acrimonious and divisive as disputes over the distribution of a constant income, implying absolute lowering of some people's income.

The classical advocates of free trade, and most explicitly J.S. Mill, wished to bring out the educational effects of free trade and did not assume constant tastes: the receptivity to new ideas and new techniques; the stimulus to the creation of new wants, new incentives to work and save, and new rewards; the growth of new forms of organisation. It is worth quoting J.S. Mill at some length to show that he believed in the possibility of learning by trading.

There is another consideration, principally applicable to an early stage of industrial advancement. A people may be in a quiescent, indolent, uncultivated state, with all their tastes either fully satisfied or entirely undeveloped, and they may fail to put forth the whole of their productive energies for want of any sufficient object of desire. The opening of foreign trade, by making them acquainted with new objects, or tempting them by the easier acquisition of things which they had not previously thought attainable, sometimes works a sort of industrial revolution in a country whose resources were previously undeveloped for want of energy and ambition in the people: inducing those who were satisfied with scanty comforts and little work, to work harder for the gratification of their new tastes, and even so save, and accumulate capital, for the still more complete satisfaction of those tastes at a future time.

But the economical advantages of commerce are surpassed in importance by those of its effects, which are intellectual and moral. It is hardly possible to overrate the value, in the present low state of human improvement, of placing human beings in contact with persons dissimilar to themselves, and with modes of thought and action unlike those with which they are familiar. Commerce is now, what war once was, the principal source of this contact. Commercial adventurers from more advanced countries have generally been the first civilisers of barbarians. And commerce is the purpose of the far greater part of the communication which takes place between civilised nations. Such communication has always been, and is peculiarly in the present age, one of the primary sources of progress. To human beings, who, as hitherto educated, can scarcely cultivate even a good quality without running it into a fault, it is indispensable to be perpetually comparing their own notions and customs with the experiences and example of persons in different circumstances from themselves: and there is no nation which does not need to borrow from others, not merely particular arts or practices, but essential points of character in which its own type is inferior.[13]

The argument can easily be reversed if it is decided that the generation of tastes, wants and incentives should be restrained, or of a different nature and in a different direction. Developing countries may see a danger in opening trade too indiscriminately to a world in which demand and production patterns are different from the ones they would like to pursue. They may choose as their model specific other cultures and open their trade ralations selectively to these countries. But the assumptions of contemporary economic theory are not sympathetic to this approach.

INTRA-FIRM TRADE

A large and growing proportion of world trade is conducted between affiliates or branches of multinational or transnational firms. At least one third of world trade in manufactured goods is now intra-firm trade. The considerations that guide these firms in their pricing, output and investment decision are likely to be different from those guiding arm's-length transactions. It could be argued that the allocation of real resources will still be governed by the doctrine of comparative advantage (assuming prices reflect real costs), but the allocation of shown profits between countries will be quite different. It will be guided by considerations of taxation, of trade union pressures, of price controls, of insistence on joint ventures, on public image, and all other considerations that give rise to transfer pricing.

Analogous arguments apply to the growth of public enterprises conducting international trade. If efficiently managed, they will produce in the lowest cost conditions. But extraneous considerations of power, national prestige, or social objectives also enter, and comparative advantage goes by the board.

Trade policies and exchange rate policies are greatly weakened by the ability to locate firms abroad. If Japan wishes to maintain its export surplus to the USA, in spite of a depreciating dollar, its firms put their manufacturing plants into Korea and Taiwan, whose currencies have depreciated with the dollar. In this way the reduced comparative advantage of some Japanese industries resulting from the relatively appreciating yen is frustrated. As direct foreign investment by the multinational firm is increasingly replacing arm's-length trade transactions, the rules that apply to trade will apply less and less.

UNCERTAINTY

Even if the doctrine of comparative advantage were otherwise fully applicable, what would guide investment and production decisions is not current comparative advantage, but future comparative advantage (assuming these are reflected in prices and costs) when the output and sales materialise. But the future is uncertain. Economists deal with this by assuming insurance and contingency markets for all possible future states of the world. But even economists do not claim realism for these assumptions. Attitudes to shouldering the risk of being wrong about the best estimate (or range of estimates) will therefore shape these decisions. Businessmen will make their guesses, and will estimate the benefits from being right, compared with the costs of being wrong.

This will have two results. First, provision will be made for action which might show a higher cost for the best estimated outcome, but lower costs for deviations from it. Among these may be spare and flexible capacity, reserves of various kinds, whether in the form of inventories, or foreign exchange, or lines of credit, and similar provisions.

If full commitment has to be made to a certain investment, the damage suffered from alternative courses will be estimated and the lowest-cost course be adopted. If, for instance, the decision turns on whether to embark on a higher-cost import substitute or a lower-cost export, but there is uncertainty whether the export can be sold, the higher-cost import substitute may be adopted, the excess costs representing a form of insurance against being too optimistic about exports.

On the other hand, it has been observed that the more outward-orientated economies of East Asia have been more successful in responding to shocks such as high interest rates on debt, slowly-growing world demand, rising protectionist barriers and deteriorating terms of trade. It could therefore be the case that flexible and diversified exports are a better insurance against uncertainty than is import substitution. In either case, the strategy with respect to comparative advantage will deviate from the course that would be indicated if uncertainty were absent.

OLIGOPOLISTIC GOVERNMENT RELATIONS AND INTERNATIONAL COOPERATION

Much of trade theory and the theory of policy takes the interest of the nation state as its starting point. Thus the textbook trade theory says that the only legitimate exception to free trade is the optimum tariff argument for intervention, according to which a country that can influence its terms of trade can improve them by import or export restrictions. But retaliation by others can land every country in a worse position than if it had not sought to snatch this advantage at the cost of others. It has become a truism to say that the world is now more interdependent. But interdependence has been scutinised much more in the relations between multinational corporations, financial markets, and activities in the market than between policies adopted by the governments. The challenge, then, is to formulate both a positive and a normative trade theory of government interaction in an interdependent world.

The positive theory would apply the theory of oligopoly, especially aspects of game theory, to the relations between government policies. This is a relatively unexplored area. Yet there are clear analogies between the way governments react to each others' tariff, subsidy and exchange rate policies, and the way oligopolistic firms react to each others' price and output policies. For example, whether a duopolistic firm will match a rival's price reduction or price increase will depend on whether it is faced with excess demand or excess capacity. Similarly, whether a government will match a rival's devaluation will depend on whether it has large foreign exchange reserves, whether it is faced with inflationary pressures or large unemployment. It is easy to think of other similarities.

The normative theory would analyse the gains from tacit or explicit international cooperation, and the principles for the distribution of these gains. It would be concerned with the avoidance of prisoner's dilemma situations and free-rider problems and would formulate the incentives for moves towards an efficient and equitable allocation of resources from a global point of view. It should be accompanied by an exploration of the political economy of reform; how can interest groups be mobilised to move towards desirable outcomes? How can coalitions or constituencies be formed to promote the policies that the normative theory indicates? What are the present obstacles and inhibitions, and how can they be removed? Such alignments will normally be across national frontiers, such as independent retail chains or consumers' associations and labour-intensive exporters, or advanced country banks and developing debtor countries, or even economists, the 'guardians of rationality', as well as the 'trustees for the poor',[14] and the global community. In the past, the self interest of the dominant power – Britain in the nineteenth century and the USA for a quarter century after the last war – ensured that some rules of international conduct were obeyed. With the disappearance of a single dominant power, we have, for the first time, to formulate rules and create institutions for a pluralistic world. Such an approach would be a far cry from the doctrine of comparative advantage with its assumption of atomistic agents and a specified government's action in the face of fixed policies by other governments, but it would be a step towards our present reality.

In spite of its great intellectual attractions, the doctrine of comparative advantage cannot provide the basis for either predicting the flow of trade, or recommending free trade.

Notes

1. I am grateful to Mohan Rao and Elliott Morss for helpful comments.
2. See Paul Streeten. 'A Cool Look at "Outward-Looking" Strategies for Development', *The World Economy*, vol. 5, no. 2, September 1982, pp. 162–5. I contend there that arguments for freer trade that are based on (i) the doctrine of comparative advantage, (ii) economies of scale, and (iii) increased competition, are mutually inconsistent. Yet they are often presented as if they were additive.
3. A.A. Young, 'Increasing Returns and Economic Progress', *Economic Journal*, December 1928.
4. Paul Krugman, 'Is Free Trade Passé'? *Journal of Economic Perspectives*, vol. 1, no. 2, 1987, p. 143; and G.K. Helleiner, 'Trade Strategy in Medium-Term Adjustment', June 1988, paper prepared for the UNU/WIDER project on medium-term strategies for adjustment.
5. See, for example, Ronald Findlay, 'Factor Proportions and Comparative Advantage in the Long Run', *Journal of Political Economy*, 78, no. 1 (January/February 1970) pp. 27–34.
6. See Henry Bruton, 'The Search for a Development Economics', *World Development*, vol. 13, nos 10/11, October/November 1985, pp. 116–18. Bruton does not make use of the maze to illustrate the theory of the second best, according to which partial liberalisation may be a move away from the optimum. He writes only about obstacles and inhibitions. But this seems a legitimate extension of his diagram.
7. Nicholas Kaldor, 'The Irrelevance of Equilibrium Economics', *Economic Journal*, 1972, and H.W. Arndt, 'Market Failure and Under-development', *World Development*, vol. 16, no. 2, February 1988.

8. Jagdish Bhagwati, in his book *Protectionism*, MIT Press, Cambridge Massachusetts, 1988, pp. 99 and 100 shows by means of two diagrams that 'prescriptive' government interventions of the East Asian type are capable of pushing the production frontier out faster (or pushing it inward less fast) than the proscriptive types common in India.

9. Peter Wiles, 'Growth Versus Choice', *Economic Journal*, September 1956.

10. By specifying the reasons for being inside the production *possibility* curve (e.g. high transaction or information costs, or risk aversion, or political constraints) and contrasting it with a production *feasibility* curve, the analysis in terms of X-efficiency approaches that in terms of the creative effects of markets. The distinction between moving towards the frontier and moving the frontier itself disappears. Whether the two approaches become identical depends on whether one thinks that deviations from maximising behaviour occur, or whether these apparent deviations can always be accounted for in rational, maximising terms. The moves towards the frontier or of the frontier itself should be thought of not as moves in free space, but more as moves in a labyrinth or maze. If everything is for the second-best in this best of all feasible worlds, the removal of only one constraint does not necessarily bring us nearer to the Pareto optimum.

11. The question whether better substitutes for the market in its creative function can be found, such as some forms of government intervention, raises additional issues, not discussed here.

12. Another option would be to train a force of workers who must be ready to move to new places and learn new skills in response to the changing international scene. These commandos would get higher pay and better conditions than the ordinary work force in return for accepting these disruptions. The life might appeal to young bachelors or people keen on frequent change.

13. J.S. Mill, *Principles of Political Economy*, London: Longmans, Green, 1902, pp. 351–2. It is interesting to note that the demonstration effect, applied in the postwar years to consumption, was thought by Mill to apply to work and savings.

14. See G.M. Meier, *Emerging from Proverty; The Economics That Really Matters*, Oxford University Press, 1984. Introduction.

5 The Governance Gap

Just Faaland and Jack Parkinson

It is almost ten years since we were prompted by the inspiration of Professor Islam to think collectively of the relations between Bangladesh and the many aid donors, countries and institutions, which furnished aid in the first few years of independence. Much of what we said was familiar to the large number of people from other countries who had participated in trying to help Bangladesh in those early years as well as to those involved in negotiations with donors but we hope that in putting facts before a wide audience we succeeded in documenting a side of international aid transactions which for many commentators goes largely unsuspected. In this essay we reflect a little more on the conditions that enable outside pressures to be brought on those developing countries that have decided that it is in their interests to seek external assistance, and how some of the pitfalls which we described in our study[1] may be avoided.

The warning that we felt we should convey was of the danger of interference in almost every aspect of the determination of economic policy when dependence on aid is all-pervasive and apparently inescapable. 'The World Bank will seek to participate both by discussion and by studies of its own in the making of national plans . . . the Fund in turn pronounces on the government's financial policies and delivers its verdict on exchange rate policy', while the British design two-thirds of the industrial sector, the French the airport and the Russians the power supply. 'The attention of foreigners is not confined to material welfare. Health, education and family planning pass under their scrutiny as they analyse, criticise, advise, innovate and experiment in areas where they cannot have any certain knowledge of the consequences of the policies they advocate'.[2] Since we wrote there have been other studies of the influence of aid on Bangladesh, not least that of Professor Rehman Sobhan who wrote with feeling and conviction of the damage that aid and foreign interference were doing to the economy, people and national interests of Bangladesh. He, too, emphasised the loss of sovereignty resulting from aid dependence:

Bangladesh's policy-makers continue to wait on decisions in Washington, London, Tokyo, Bonn and Paris before they formulate their annual development budgets, announce an import policy, formulate a food policy or even decide how many children should be born. The decision makers of the developed world hold the lifeline of any regime in Bangladesh in their hands and can visit havoc on the life of a country in a way which was inconceivable two decades ago. The sovereignty of the Bangladesh nation state, in its prevailing social configuration, is therefore likely to remain a polite fiction as long as Bangladesh does not challenge their current strategic assumptions and ideological preconceptions.[3]

This is, of course, no less true today than it was a decade ago. Bangladesh is an extreme case but the issues we were writing about apply in a wider context and affect other countries also if they become too highly dependent on aid, accumulate unmanageable debt or fall victim to violent economic change that affects their external position adversely. This prompts some reflection on the process that leads to progressiveness in the unfolding of influence, the form that influence may take and the ways in which this may be minimised, given that some involvement with donors is desired.

AID INDUCED STRUCTURAL CHANGE

It is not easy to put the theme of aid and influence into a theoretical setting. A natural starting point might be the two-gap model introduced into the discussions of economic development in the 1960s.[4] It will be recalled that in its simplest and unelaborated form the model focused on two obstacles to development. The first of these was the scarcity of resources which restricted savings and investment, the savings gap; the second was the inability to earn foreign exchange to finance imports in sufficient amount to realise the volume of production and investment which could otherwise be undertaken, the import gap. In either case, aid might bring relief but the dynamics of this lay imperfectly explored. While indeed the magnitude of gaps in the end would necessarily be equal once all forces impinging on the economic system had actually worked themselves out, the value of this analytical approach lay in the attention it gave to the mechanism of adjustment that brought about such equality, as well as in the attention it gave to the identification of the *binding* constraint on development.

Schematically one line of argument would run as follows: A poor underdeveloped country, perhaps stagnant for a long period, may have development potentials which are not realised because the economy by itself cannot, or at least in fact does not, bring forth the savings necessary to invest in such development; the country is too poor to develop and the resource gap constrains development. This gap can then be closed through the import of savings from other countries to allow investments to go ahead and development potentials to be realised. For this critical additional resource to be made available, an equivalent balance of payments deficit would have to be created, and thus an import gap follows as a necessary consequence of meeting the resource gap. Once this process has been started and assuming it is maintained over a period of years, the domestic structures of production and of resource development are altered and so are balance of payments, import and export structures. As these new structures are developed and maintained, they become ingrained in the economy of the country and any decision or need to shift back to the old structure of no resource and import gaps (or even to shift partly back to more equal balances) becomes difficult and can only be achieved over time. In other words, the developing country has become aid dependent both in terms of resource gap and import gap.

Moreover, once this process of aid dependence has started, unintended consequences follow which do not lend themselves to the neat textbook or theoretical analyses often advanced. In such constructions, there is a predetermined formal adjustment path in terms of national income entities. The process of adjustment is supposed to take the form of structural changes having the effect of increasing domestic savings to close the savings gap and other changes in output or demand which will achieve a balance of payments without the need to rely on aid. This is the end to which all developing countries may be expected to strive and in terms of macroeconomic analysis it is readily portrayed. It might be expected that the savings gap would diminish under its own volition. Incomes will increase; per capita incomes, in particular, will increase and, perhaps, the distribution of income will initially become more unequal, with the effect of increasing the propensity to save (although we accept that this may be uncertain); there may also be an increase in government revenues with the same effect, and the same qualifications, as well as other favourable structural changes. Whatever the precise mechanism, it is generally to be observed that increases in per capita incomes lead to higher savings. At the same time, economic activity will expand and develop and change its structure in such a way as to make the expansion of import requirements slower and the promotion of exports faster (or possibly to reduce both or any other combination that will bring the balance of payments into equilibrium, including the flow of private capital).

It is our contention that the adjustment process is not likely to follow the smooth progression often supposed and will be prolonged by aid dependence and distorted by foreign influence. The analysis cannot be conducted solely in terms of economic forces and changes but has to take account of social and political circumstances that may retard attempts to reduce dependence on foreign savings and forgo the use of resources provided from abroad. Very often the binding constraint will not be economic but political, even if it finds its expression in economic magnitudes.

The absence of determination to wean the economy from dependence on aid as quickly as possible has its consequences. Further dependence, it seems, can develop organically, leading to a wide-ranging shift of authority and effective decision-making power from national authorities and bureaucracies to aid providers. This shift opens up a third type of gap which cannot be subjected to easy measurement; it is essentially a political gap occupied by foreign influence inserting itself into the functions of government in the recipient country. The government is no longer the undisputed master in its own house; the situation is one of ambivalence; two sets of influence are now at work. As we expressed it earlier, 'a country as heavily dependent on aid as Bangladesh on foreign assistance, cannot escape continuous participation by donors in the formulation of its policies. It may prepare its five year and annual plans, its minister of finance may draw up his budget, the ministries may make their programmes, but all do so with the consciousness that dominant aid agencies are looking over their shoulder.'[5] Dependence on aid which started as an effort to fill material gaps finishes with a considerable surrender of control and authority. This we describe as the *governance gap*, measured by the degree of involvement of foreign powers in setting policy.

As we begin to reflect on this process, it becomes apparent that the process of ultimately eliminating the need for aid is not a simple one. There may be a whole host of different sets of strategies that might bring ultimate equilibrium into sight. Some might, for example, include import substitution on a substantial scale; others might lay stress on export promotion; still others might emphasise structural adjustment, or private enterprise or nationalisation. The possibilities are legion. But the choice between such strategies – or rather the balance between them – and the course of their implementation are all subject to the exercise of outside influence. In the real world one is led far from the simple equilibria structures of classical economics and, one might reasonably fear, into many types of models with different structures which would lead not to equilibria but to disequilibria, and again to many different outcomes that might favour one class of society or another, generate alternative financial structures, or favour consumption over investment and, in short, produce radically different outcomes. Couple all this with the effects of random and unpredictable disturbances and where do we stand?

In an age of economic modelling and all the sophistication of econometric science with the incorporation of stochastic processes into theoretical analysis, it might seem superfluous to stress the need to take account of the uncertainty of economic outcomes; but this is not really the point. What we are concerned about is the unpredictability of events which cannot be foreseen but which may make a nonsense of any preconceived views of how economies should be organised and how they function. This is all the more evident at the interface of economics and political organisation. Many of the major issues of economics are unresolved: many debates of the time do not produce determinate results, and many, perhaps well founded, views defy acceptance. What might have convinced the committed planners of Russia that they could be wrong, or the equally committed protagonists of capitalism that their answers might be unacceptable? Where monetarists and Keynesians jostle in indeterminate confusion who should be so bold as to say that one is right and the other wrong, or to seek to rationalise the discussion by remarking 'Horses for courses'? Still another aspect of this discourse is that maximisation subject to real life constraints is very different from maximisation in some abstract environment. The best is the enemy of the good and may be largely irrelevant in an unfavourable environment.

This raises the fundamental question of the right of outside bodies to offer advice or exert influence on the economic policies of recipient countries. While donor legislatures and administrators do have the responsibility of ensuring that public money is wisely spent this does not, by itself, confer any moral authority or political right on the donor to dominate the decision-making of the recipient country. Yet it often happens.

AREAS OF INFLUENCE

It is helpful to distinguish a number of different categories of influence. The first of these is concerned with setting objectives which will determine the priorities of development. Although disagreement about major objectives is always a possibility, there may be shared preoccupations that lead to a meeting of minds. In some cases these may concern common political objectives, as might apply to assistance given to Egypt or Pakistan, and these objectives may find some of their expression in the provision of economic support as well as military help. If objectives can be agreed, the exercise of influence is less likely to give rise to deep concern and this may extend to agreement on economic objectives removed from political ones; if so, a possible source of dissension will have been removed.

A second category of influence lies in attempts to intervene in the determination of general policy issues, even in a situation where there may be accord on major objectives. If, for example, the virtues of planning or the free market are strongly urged and ideological issues surface, there may be recurrent efforts to make the country see reason. Such pressures may be exerted by powerful donors or by international institutions.

A third category of influence is to do with implementation of assisted development programmes. This may take objectionable forms but it stems from the accountability of donor agencies to their controlling bodies and as such is understandable. If properly exercised, it may be viewed in relation to agreed objectives and the need to see that the assistance given is effective in the attainment of those objectives. This requires evaluation and it may be appropriate for the donor agency to carry this out even though most aspects of this function might be delegated to the receiving country if donors have confidence that it can be relied upon to carry out the necessary checks.

Finally, there is a subtle form of influence which takes place within accepted programmes and consists of the efforts of public or private interests within donor countries, and to some extent institutions, to realise their own objectives or ambitions, sometimes with the connivance of interests within the recipient country itself.

Ensuring acceptable returns from the provision of aid funds or other resources is among the more legitimate objectives of donor concern and influence. However, the area of legitimate influence of this nature depends on the type of the transaction, as may be illustrated by reference to the operations of private banks as against multilateral institutions such as the World Bank and the IMF. A private bank is generally concerned with the viability of the project that it is financing (lending to some individual or corporate body). Whether its loans will be serviced or not depends on the performance of the borrower within the economic framework of the country, as this may be determined by the government or economic forces. The lender's surveillance tends, therefore, to be limited to the entity to which the capital has been lent; there is little recourse beyond this. For the World Bank it is different. Lending is not so much to one specific entity, although the funds are destined for this, but to the government of the country. Not all the projects for which funds are made available will be revenue producing even if they are wholly beneficial in relation to their costs. In such cases, recourse for the sevice of debt cannot be solely to the entity benefiting from the loan since there is no strictly earmarked flow of funds from which payment can be demanded and from which payment is restricted. Following a similar line of reasoning, it follows that the Fund also is in the position of having to distrain on a borrowing country's resources and revenues and so it strives to influence events so that funds can be made to flow into its hands. It may, of course, take this process a stage further by endeavouring to get a debtor country to create conditions in which not only obligations to the Fund can be met but also the demands of other lenders, including some who have deftly insured themselves against loss by demanding government guarantees on their loans. These processes are to be seen at work in many countries, not only in those as economically down and out as the Sudan.

It follows that, unlike private banks, the World Bank and the Fund are rationally concerned with the total performance of the economy as it affects what is, in effect, a floating charge upon its assets and future performance. This gives a rationale for the great concern of international organisations with the performance of a borrowing country's economy as a whole, and not just those parts of it with which they are immediately involved. If such international institutions were constrained to lending only to specific entities from which, alone, they could demand repayment, there would be less justification for taking an interest in the overall performance of the economy. The overpowering lien on the resources of the country has also to be seen in relation to IMF's and the World Bank's demands always to be seen as a preferential creditor from which there is no escape.

Of course, differences between lending by private institutions and lending by international organisations can be over-drawn. On the one hand, private banks have lent massively indeed to governments of developing countries, not only to individuals and private corporate bodies, and therefore they now depend heavily on the economic and financial health of the borrowing countries; hence they have a direct interest in the success of governmental policies. On the other hand, international financial institutions, and the World Bank in particular, see themselves in a role of institutions for development, not merely as intermediaries in the transfer of resources to developing countries. In the pursuit of this wider objective the Bank clearly will be concerned with development strategies and policies in its member countries. However, while the Bank can reasonably claim an advisory role, this hardly gives legitimacy to the exercise of other types of influence, in particular to the linking of the level and composition of one or other agency's resource transfers to the acceptance of advice on issues of general development approaches.

It might appear that there should be a clear distinction between making commercial loans, including loans from the World Bank, and furnishing ODA (Official Development Assistance) or IDA (International Development Association) credits, which are free of most, if not all, interest charges. With concessional aid or IDA money, even very modest returns from a project would be sufficient to service it, and it might, therefore, appear inappropriate to ensure that some imaginary and commercial conditions of repayment should be met. This is not really the case. It is necessary to look beyond this to securing, in terms of social benefits, at least an equivalent return and by implication using the money to the best advantage in the face of the opportunity cost represented by some other project forgone. All these considerations are reinforced if the administrative and technical skills available in the borrowing country are weak or unsuited to the design, organisation and operation of a project that is being considered for financing. Satisfactory rates of return need to be insisted upon to ensure that a project is to be well executed and profitable in the widest sense.

Attempts by donors to determine the objectives of a developing country are potentially much more oppressive. In the determination of macroeconomic policy there are both internal and external objectives to consider and as usual in economic relationships they may be closely related. Intervention in policy formation may be more justified if there is a serious imbalance in the external payments position and this could apply to a large surplus as well as to a large deficit, although the former is hardly likely to apply very frequently in the case of a developing country which, even in surplus, would be unlikely seriously to inconvenience the rest of the world or even individual countries trading with it. A serious deficit is another matter, for financing it makes a call on the resources of other countries which they may not be willing to provide, or only on a temporary basis, without some assurance that the situation will be brought under control.

The balance of payments is not always a thing of particular concern in a developing country. If aid and capital inflows on acceptable terms serve to balance the payments position, pressure from donors to interfere in the determination of domestic policies will be much reduced. The justification for interference would have to be on other grounds, such as ensuring the maximum return on investments, as we have already suggested. It may be in some cases that there is a better understanding of economic forces and the selection of policies to control them by donor countries, or more likely institutions, than is available in the recipient countries, although this is by no means always the case; yet, even when it is not, the flow of recommendations is unlikely to be stifled. We can easily imagine Professor Islam in the position of a World Bank official; he was also the first Deputy Chairman of the Planning Commission in Bangladesh. In the latter role, the World Bank did not hesitate to offer him advice and to suggest changes in the policies he was advocating and supporting. One might be excused for wondering what advice Mr Islam, of the World Bank, might have offered Minister Islam, of the Planning Commission, if he had been able to change his hat with sufficient rapidity, and what Professor Islam might have said to both of them, which one may suspect would have been both pointed and tinged with a touch of sardonic humour. What, perhaps, should be grasped from this imaginary exchange of roles is that most administrators are not advancing the views they themselves advocate so much as putting forward the policies adopted by the institutions they represent.

When two strong decision takers confront each other in the way described above, there is the prospect of a battle for supremacy which may prove to be counter-productive. To force acceptance of external institutional views may lead to later economic disruptions of a different kind. In the case of Zambia, for instance, acceptance of the IMF's policies was followed by a reversion to ones that could be made politically acceptable. It is a telling fact that when oil prices were raised by the OPEC countries, the change was viewed with dismay by politicians, economists and financial journalists alike and that when oil prices began to fall, the same groups of observers again expressed anxiety. What was really of concern was not so much the changes themselves as the process of adjustment that would have to be undertaken in response to altered economic circumstances. Given that the success of economic policies can seldom be guaranteed it is as well to be cautious in advocating one course of action or another. If outside agencies are to advocate changes in government policies, it might be best to think of them as modifications to existing policies rather than as total reversals, and to remember that change is frequently difficult to assimilate.

In contentious matters, there is a very real danger that the advice offered to a country by an outside agency will align it with one or more contending factions, so involving it in matters of political controversy. It may be suspected that this is usually the case for there is often a political reason for apparently unsatisfactory economic policies and the most effective way to promote change may be to support those advocating it. To take but one example, and there are many more, in the Sudan there have been strong differences of opinion about the policies advocated by the IMF in recent years, so that institution has had both its supporters and opponents within the country and in consequence has inevitably become embroiled in domestic dissension and politics. Such differences may be reflected in the attitudes of the international civil servants who have dealings with developing countries, for institutions are not monolithic in the opinions of their officials. Alignment with a particular faction is not just a macro phenomenon, it occurs at the micro level also and sometimes in unexpected forms. There may be a common professional interest shared between government officials in a recipient country and businessmen in a donor country; the one may wish to operate certain types of equipment and the other to supply them with their preferences but this may not represent an optimal use of aid from the point of view of the recipient country and may be opposed by other organs of government such as the Planning Commission or the Ministry of Finance. Instances of this kind were brought out by Professor Islam in our previous study and they extended to pressures to carry out projects that were really not desirable or of low priority, although this did not prevent them from being supported by government departments within the Bangladesh government system.[6]

While donor countries may prefer to leave macroeconomic discussion to the Bank and the IMF, they have their own objectives for the exercise of influence. Some of these are concerned with their own national interests, tied aid being a typical example, but others are concerned with objectives that they think recipient countries should adopt. Very often these stem from the ethos of the donor country in question and represent a concern not primarily with a concept or judgement of objective efficiency so much as with a set of values that it is felt should be uniformly observed. These objectives may be entirely praiseworthy but they may not be those that recipient countries have most in mind. The so-called like-minded countries are very much concerned with helping the very poor within the countries with which they deal and their aid programmes are fashioned with this intention. While most donor countries would maintain that their objective in providing assistance was to combat poverty they would certainly differ in their approaches in the selection of groups to concentrate on and in the most desirable time-profile of the effects that they wished to create. By comparison with other donors, the approach towards poverty alleviation of the like-minded countries is more direct and immediate, at the present time, with packages tailored specifically to the needs of the poor. Here, as elsewhere, such programmes are not to be forced upon developing countries, however laudable they may be; cooperation, not coercion, must be the guiding light. It must also be recognised that programmes to help the poor are often difficult to identify and have a more than average risk to failure; and it may be suspected that programmes designed to benefit the most disadvantaged groups are frequently the most difficult and costly to implement and, if undertaken prematurely, prove to be largely unrewarding, involving disproportionate costs, not only in money, but also in the use of scarce administrative ability. The design of development programmes involves, above all, the achievement of balance between many competing objectives even if all of them are directed to the mitigation of poverty, and it involves a scrutiny of the development path over a period of time. Here, again, costs and benefits have to be balanced out at the margin so that the effort to relieve immediate poverty has to be restricted. Thus, it could well be wrong for donor countries to press programmes for the relief of immediate poverty too far, unless they are prepared to meet all the cost of doing so, including the effects of such programmes on other development activities. The exercise of influence, however well-be a helpful thing if it fails to recognise that in assessing the balance between needs, local administrators are likely to have a more certain economic and political touch.

If poverty-orientated policies as advocated by donors are to succeed, there has to be the fullest accord between donors and recipients or, as Norway puts it, between the cooperating partners. There is one country where this meeting of minds and intentions has been almost fully achieved: we refer to Botswana. This is an unusual country in almost every respect. It has a large area although much of it borders on desert and a small population of rather more than one million. It is a multiracial society with the political power in the hands of Africans who are fortunate to have a large number (although never enough) of competent administrators, many with European origins. Botswana is totally exceptional in having a considerable surplus on the balance of payments, largely generated by the sale of diamonds, one commodity that it is rather satisfactory to mine in present conditions. It is arguable that it has very little need for aid and that the very substantial amount that it has obtained has, in arithmetic terms, gone only to swell its reserves of foreign currency. A meeting of minds on objectives and approaches has proved surprisingly easy to attain in such circumstances and aid programmes have been administered with commendable success and relatively few cases of failure. In these circumstances the Norwegian approach to economic development has proved to be very successful.

One factor in this success has been the particular approach to the relief of poverty. Although diamond sales give Botswana a high per capita income, much of this income accrues to the government of the country and has been salted away in accretions to foreign exchange reserves of very large dimension. The conservative use of resources is justified on the grounds that the pace of development is determined not by the availability of funds but by the rate at which administrative skills, in business as well as in government, can be developed. Thus, extreme poverty is a continuing feature of the economy with some highly disadvantaged groups remaining outside the development net in many respects. Nevertheless, this has not prevented the very successful implementation of health and educational programmes with a poverty orientation; donor influence and cooperation in this has been very successful and satisfied both the objectives of the donors and the Botswana Government. If such programmes are to reach the poor very often they have to be made all-embracing and to include the rich as well as the poor. A limited programme runs the risk of being deflected to the rich in the first instance through the exercise of internal influence, and only saturation can be counted upon to frustrate this. It is this orientation of poverty programmes that has succeeded in Botswana. Norway's contribution to the poverty programmes has been to assist the development of a decentralised primary health care system by contributing 80 per cent of all bilateral assistance for it and providing medical personnel. In education, much the same process has been followed with, in this case, the assistance mainly of other countries, with the Nordic contribution coming from Sweden, and the United States playing a notable role in developing educational facilities of various types in addition to its other activities.

The next stages of efforts to relieve poverty in Botswana will be more difficult since they involve reaching thousands of remote-area dwellers and creating higher productivity employment opportunities for a large group of rural and urban people who now eke out a living at low levels of income. Again this will be approached by programmes involving cooperation between Botswana and donors working closely together.

It is not only in developing countries that it can prove hard to spread the benefits of material progress; the industrialised countries have the same problem although not to the same degree. The relief of extreme poverty is only one way in which the like-minded countries direct their socially orientated programmes. Norway includes the interests of women and care of the environment as important objectives which should be fostered by its aid programmes. In Botswana, both these objectives have a place but both can be overdone. It is understandable that Norway should attach particular importance to the effects of development on the environment, as it reflects the damage caused to that country from the pollution generated by other countries as well as domestically, but it goes much deeper than this, to a wish to preserve the world's amenities. Such issues do not touch closely on Botswana for there is very little atmospheric pollution that is liable to damage it or its neighbours. Nevertheless, other aspects of care for the environment are of importance and result from the incidence of damaging externalities which economic activities can inflict on the wider interests of the community. The ecology of the country is suffering considerably from the growth in numbers of cattle, which leads to damage to the land and may also constitute some threat to wildlife. These are, to a considerable extent, internal matters, though the preservation of wildlife has its international aspects, and the extent to which other countries should take it on themselves to become involved in such matters is not clear. Nonetheless, the exercise of influence may be justified in an effort to provide a balance of forces between environmentalists and cattle owners and to sustain the government in its efforts to provide for environmental issues in its development strategy, which it is doing in conjunction with internal pressure groups.

The issue of women's affairs is not, perhaps, one in which outsiders should be inclined to meddle in the context of Botswana. The government stoutly maintains that this is not an issue in its country where all citizens are treated equally without distinction. This is not the place to go into the niceties of such discussions but to suggest that some issues may be best left to the countries concerned and not foisted upon them because they have caught the limelight in response to pressure groups in the remote north. What may seem to some observers to be important issues about the status and rights of women arise in much more telling ways in other countries where, perhaps, aid agencies would be ill-advised to meddle. A possible solution to this kind of dilemma is for donor countries with particular interests to reserve part of their aid for the purposes they wish to support and to allocate it not through country programmes but by a more selective mechanism. This might take the form of making the aid available to those countries which support the same objectives as the donors, allocating it as an addition to the normal country programme. In this process there might be an element of competitive bidding. While this solution might commend itself to the Nordic countries and might be effectively implemented by them within firmly established programmes, it might not appeal to other donors which, if their requirements could not be met by particular countries, would be unable to divert their aid elsewhere, so that part of it would, in effect, be lost.

In recent years Norway has been undertaking a major review of the performance of its aid programmes in all the countries that it supports in a major way. The objectives of the Norwegian Government's programmes have been defined in government statements of policy and provide guidelines for aid administrators; they apply in much the same way to different countries and are directed particularly to the relief of poverty. In some cases it has been possible to carry out these intentions with considerable success, but they do not always conform to the recipient government's objectives as is shown in this quotation from the report prepared on aid to Bangladesh which notes that 'The import of Norwegian medicines was against Bangladesh's own drug policy', and that 'the supply of insect sprayers was a most unfortunate case which also conflicted with the country's own policy to protect domestic manufacturers of such sprayers'.[7] More important, perhaps, are programmes launched with the best intentions and aimed at the poor that prove hard to execute effectively. This applied to the Nordic integrated rural works programme in Bangladesh, where objectives of the donors and the government differed and in the event proved to be unrealistic. Nevertheless, the project was judged to have contributed to the development of Bangladesh and helped its mostly very poor people.

FACTORS MAKING FOR VULNERABILITY TO INFLUENCE

The above examples of the exercise of influence and difficulties in attaining the objectives of a particular donor country are insignificant in relation to the extent that influence is exerted in Bangladesh, as our previous study documents in great detail and comprehensiveness in relation to an earlier time. Behind any such discussions lurk a number of complicated and interrelated issues some of which are discussed below. The first of these is concerned with the circumstances that make the exercise of influence possible and where, in practice, influence is likely to be at its strongest. Here both political and economic realities will combine to determine the extent and the form of exercise of influence. A close ally may be more exposed to influence in the interests of political harmony and this will spill over into the economic sphere. There are a number of non-political factors that may make a country anxious to secure assistance. The first of these is backwardness itself. The poor themselves, who might hope to benefit most from economic development, are seldom in a position to influence events, but it is to be expected that pressures to move the country forward will emerge from government, political factions or perhaps some intellectual minority. In the search to promote growth, it is likely that the prospect of securing assistance will be vigorously pursued and that, in the interests of securing rapid growth, there will be pressures to secure large amounts of aid. Poor countries are not only poor in resources but often also in skills and know-how, all of which are readily available in the developed world. Moreover, there will be other handicaps such as exposure to periodic food shortages due to climatic reasons, a major factor in many parts of Africa as well as in Bangladesh; or dependence on the export of one or a few primary products subject to severe market fluctuations; or political interference from other countries inimical to economic progress.

The administrative capacity of government in poor countries can seldom be well developed; there may be neither traditions of central control, trained staff, nor adequate financial resources. All such disabilities can, in some measure, be made good by foreign assistance in the form of goods, personnel or technical assistance, including training. Offers of assistance in such circumstances will be hard to resist and the recipient government may be unable to lay down conditions that would protect from decisions being taken out of its own hands.

The distribution of aid among countries has never followed simple logical criteria. It might be expected, for example, that low-income countries would receive much more in aid than middle-income countries. In 1985, in terms of average, there was in fact very little in it. Excluding India and China, the average for the low-income countries was $16.2 per head (if India and China are included the figure drops to $5.2) against $14.6 for lower middle-income countries and $11.4 for all middle-income countries. What is much more in evidence is that countries with small population can expect to benefit highly in terms of income per capita and that large countries such as India and China with little more than a dollar of aid per head come off very badly. To have a population of over 25 million is almost a guarantee that aid will not exceed $10 per head, although Egypt is an exception as is even Bangladesh, with a population in excess of 100 million. For countries with a population less than this, aid per head can be very high, particularly if political considerations are working in the same direction. Thus, for Israel aid per capita amounted to $467 in 1985 and for Jordan the figure was $157.

For countries with populations the size of India or China the transfer of resources may be of smaller moment than the transfer of know-how. This need not involve the transfer of large amounts of resources which might, in any case, be difficult to do and would carry with it a potential threat to the recipient's control over the use of the imported resources. China seems well placed to avoid this; India has not always been free from the exercise of influence as is well documented.[8] In the 1960s, it was possible for pressure to be exerted on her to devalue in the interests of continuing to receive aid, but it is hard to think that the same scenario could be expected to apply today, for India is both in a strong economic position and has taken a firm stand against accepting unwelcome western interference, even if this means less aid and transference of technology. Moreover, it is one of the advantages of large countries that they can generally mobilise sufficiently capable and experienced politicians and administrators to resist encroachments on their sphere of influence. In this respect, small countries, sometimes with unstable governments, can be highly vulnerable and in no position to avert outside pressures.

For some countries, and particularly those small countries receiving relatively high amounts of aid per capita, dependence on aid is considerable. Several criteria can be used to describe this. For many of the low-income countries, and particularly those with French affiliations, the ratio of aid to GDP is high. In the case of Mali it was 35 per cent in 1985, for Niger it was 20 per cent, for Burkina Faso and Togo 18 per cent, for the Central African Republic 16 per cent and for Bhutan, Ethiopia, Nepal, Burundi, Rwanda, Somalia, the Sudan, Senegal and Zambia 10 to 15 per cent, as also for Bangladesh. Not all of these countries have very small populations. Distress has clearly influenced the amount of aid received by Ethiopia and the Sudan and is a factor in other cases. The objective of aid-flows is frequently to provide the necessities of life or to raise consumption.[9] This is typical of the approach of the Scandinavian countries; where consumption is regarded as inadequate it is considered that a country has a double claim on aid: poverty as it affects consumption and poverty as it limits the development effort. In the case of the relief of distress, aid may come free of strings, or any attempt to use it to influence policy may be totally opposed; in more vulnerable instances, the flow or withholding of aid for the relief of distress may be used as a political counter, as we have illustrated in the case of Bangladesh.[10] Nevertheless, for some countries aid should be making a significant contribution to growth. If it is assumed that the whole of aid had the effect of increasing investment, it could be said to have paid for the entire investment programme in a number of countries. Statistically, in for example Mali or Niger, it is evident that aid is supporting other activities since it is greater than estimated investment expenditure.

We have argued that the extent to which influence can be exercised depends in the first place on the importance of aid to the economy of a particular country. Within the total of aid, the contribution of individual countries and the distribution of the support that is given between donors is likely to be an important factor, although it may be of less significance if a consortium, or similar support group, is in existence. Of the five countries most dependent on ODA, Mali,

Niger, Burkina Faso, Togo and the Central African Republic, it is not surprising to see that France is generally the dominant partner. Even here, however, there is appreciable diversification. In the case of Mali, France provided about 17 per cent of ODA over the four years 1983–6; other important country donors included the United States, Germany and the Netherlands, while among multilateral donors, the World Bank was a major contributor flanked by the African Development Bank and the EC. For Niger the picture is not essentially different with France accounting for about 20 per cent of ODA and the United States, Canada, Germany and, more recently, Italy prominent, with the World Bank, through its IDA wing, the African Development Bank and the EC well represented. In the case of Burkina Faso, France's share is only 16 per cent and there is again a wide distribution of donor countries and institutions. For Togo, France's contribution in 1985 and 1986 was small although it had been large in earlier years, and in 1986 Japan suddenly came into prominence so that the reduction in the French contribution was made good; again there is a fair diversification of receipts with IDA providing large sums. The picture presented by the Central African Republic is more distinct, with the French contribution amounting to 45 per cent over the years 1983–6 and the contribution of other countries being small, although the World Bank in its IDA contribution was prominent.

For the other countries mentioned above, the distribution of aid among donors is of a generally similar pattern. There is often a leading donor and sometimes a cluster of substantial contributors but there is invariably a spread. Concentration among the institutions is greater, as might perhaps be expected, with the World Bank always in evidence.

Other aspects of dependence include reliance on aid to meet balance of payments deficits. This is, of course, at the root of the whole affair: the object of aid is to increase resources and, with the extraordinary exception of Botswana, this can be done only if resources are imported via a balance of payments deficit. Few countries could expect to finance a resource gap of 10 to 15 or more per cent of the GDP for long if they had to service it on commercial terms. In principle the viability of commercial financing would depend on the rate of return that was being obtained on the investment and, within the total increase in production that might result from the use of additional resources, that part of it that could be appropriated for servicing loans, whether in the way of profit or increased (and unspent) tax returns. Since we are talking about aid rather than a commercial inflow of investment, this is not the question. It does, however, recur in another way: what are the consequences of being cut off from aid were that to happen? Bangladesh, in a slightly different context, has experienced this when the very large upward movement of import prices, after the 1973 oil price increase, completely destroyed the basis of the import programme leading to widespread disruption of the development effort and renewed hardships for consumers. And even more dramatically, the withholding of US food aid in 1974 had devastating consequences for the political as well as the economic life of the country.[11]

Government revenues are very much the prey to fluctuation in aid receipts. If aid were given to the private sector of the economy as a gift, government finances would not be directly affected. This is not, however, often the case and aid is either used by the government itself or channelled to the private sector through the sale of foreign exchange with a corresponding increase in government receipts. Few low-income countries raise more than 20 per cent of the GNP in taxation and the use of resources provided under aid is an important source of funds for public expenditure and for implementing the government's strategy. A collapse of external receipts, however it comes about, can have disastrous results, as witness the effects on Zambia from the loss of copper revenues.[12]

It might be concluded from the above survey of aid dependence in relation to major donors that there is little danger of a recipient country becoming dependent on an individual donor to such an extent that exposure to the withdrawal of aid from a single source would have devastating effects. While this may be true, it does not exclude the danger arising from concerted action, as we documented in our earlier study. Such action is very likely if dependence on aid is combined with an unmanageable debt problem or what sometimes will be the same thing, an unmanageable balance of payments position. In these circumstances donor countries may be relied upon to get together and to include in their pressures the interest of banks and other financial institutions that may be owed money. Even when this is not the case donors are likely to come together to pool information and exchange views, often in the country in question at regular meetings and sometimes more formally when the World Bank has organised a consortium with attendant meetings on Bank premises.

This process may go further than national boundaries; it extends also to the selection of targets for the development effort of United Nations countries; attempts to fix aid at 0.7 per cent of GDP for donor countries, which fortunately has not functioned as a maximum among countries generously disposed, or specification of broad objectives, such as attainment of health targets. This process is not confined to the majesty of full United Nations' resolutions but extends to the aspirations of the individual agencies, pushing basic needs, employment, the environment. Moreover, it may carry with it particular ideologies, fortunately not always the same ones.

CONCLUSION

It seems to us to be inevitable and unavoidable that aid donors will attempt to exercise influence on the countries that they assist. In some cases such influence could be beneficial but, whether it is beneficial or not, it is bound to be resented in most cases. Influence is exercised by individual donors acting independently as well as collectively, and the untrammelled influence exerted by multilateral institutions is pervasive. How then might a country seek to resist the pressures of influence from whatever quarter it may come?

The first maxim might be to strive to avoid too great a dependence on aid. To limit aid to not more than 10 per cent of GDP might be a sensible rule to apply. The five most exposed countries in our list appear to us to be in no position to resist advice from donor countries and agencies, particularly if the latter combine their approaches to some degree.

The second maxim might be based on the principle of divide and rule. The wider the net can be spread to attract donors, the greater the opportunity to play one off against another. Specialisation and administrative convenience may appear to dictate the assignment of different roles to different donors and, of course, this happens to some considerable extent; but it might be good practice always to think in terms of an understudy in order to offer the prospect of some competition in particular sectors. For some recipients, it may be possible to reinforce this if donor countries of different ideologies can be involved. In the same vein, coordination of the aid effort by donors should be discouraged when and where it goes beyond what can be effectively controlled and guided by the host country. For this strong institutions are needed in the recipient country so that it can be seen to be capable of conducting the government's business efficiently, including coordinating the use of aid.

A third maxim might be to try to arrange affairs in such a way as to limit potential damage in the event of aid being cut off or reduced. Apart from attaining self-sufficiency in the production of food, this might include raising exports, or replacing imports, to an extent sufficient to ensure that the economy could continue to function at an acceptable level if aid were to be cut off. Indirectly this might represent a return to the initial conception of aid or lending serving to build up productive capacity and in the process to provide the means to service loans by expanding exports. It might also involve using external financing for projects that could be divided into a series of stages, all of them self-contained and capable of yielding benefits on completion: construction of schools might fall into this category, billion-dollar dams would not. The ability to do this will depend on the maintenance of national sovereignty; if the governance gap has opened widely the recipient country will be at the mercy of donors in the determination of national policies well beyond the direct deployment of aid resources themselves.

A fourth maxim might be to do everything possible to improve the administrative ability of those in the public service. It is a constant complaint of donors that it is impossible to get things done and while this may reflect physical problems in some instances, frequently it is a case of administrative failures. Improvement of administrative capacities is a long drawn out business and the ability to do it depends on the availability of persons of sufficient educational attainments. Even in the best of circumstances administrative talent is likely to be very scarce. Relief may be given by the use of expatriate personnel, although this is a far from ideal solution. If it is to be fully successful and not itself an instrument of foreign control, the use of administrators from other countries has to be carefully regulated. Few countries could hope to do this with the success achieved by Botswana, particularly because administration in a small country is a very different thing from attempting to provide for the needs of a population of 100 million or more.

Fifthly, and ultimately most importantly, to resist undue influence the government needs to know its own mind and be prepared to stand up to donors. It is much easier as well as more tempting for donors to exercise undue influence if the government is in doubt, undecided and vacillating in its approach to development.

Finally, we return to a weakness we discussed in our earlier study: the power of large well-organised donor countries to gang-up on individual countries highly dependent on aid and the inflow of foreign capital. The developed countries are very powerfully organised in support of their interests. The World Bank and the IMF are regarded as institutions of the donors; they meet in many closed groups to discuss their economic interests, and in the Organisation for Economic Cooperation and Development (OECD) and the Development Assistance Committee (DAC) to concert their policies and attitudes to the developing world. The round-table meetings led by the United Nations Development Programme (UNDP) may be much better as a forum for discussion for they permit a dialogue between donors and recipients. The attempts of the LDCs to build up countervailing institutions have achieved only moderate success; the New International Economic Order is a dead letter and crucial decisions can be taken in institutions in which the developing countries are not represented or have little power. Is it possible that we are beginning to see an effective move towards a more balanced dialogue with the emergence of the South Commission under the guidance of Nyerere? In a less ambitious way, it may still be possible to do something. Any country facing a consortium or donor meeting is in the potential position of being a defendant facing a number of critics, maybe a score or more. Would it be possible to expand such meetings and include some representatives of other developing countries, not donors, involved with the recipient country, to provide both moral support and a more understanding outlook, and capable of exercising some pressures on the donor countries to expand their efforts and support the objectives of the recipient country?

Notes

1. Just Faaland (ed.), Nurul Islam, Jack Parkinson, *Aid and Influence*, London: Macmillan, 1981.
2. *Op. cit.*, pp. 11–12.
3. Rehman Sobhan, *The Crisis of External Dependence*, Dhaka: University Press, 1982.
4. See, for instance, H.B. Chenery and Alan M. Strout, 'Foreign Assistance and Economic Development', *AER*, 1966, pp. 679–773.
5. *Aid and Influence*, p. 11.
6. *Aid and Influence*, Chapter 6.
7. Ole David Koht Norbye, ed., *Bangladesh Country Study and Aid Review*, Bergen: Chr. Michelsen Institute, pp. 118–19.

8. Edward S. Mason and Robert E. Asher, *The World Bank since Bretton Woods*, Washington DC: Brookings Institution, pp. 196–7 and 455.
9. Gustav Papanek, 'The Effects of Aid and other Resource Transfers on Savings and Growth in Less Developed Countries', *Economic Journal*, vol. 82 (1972), p. 937.
10. *Aid and Influence*, Chapter 7.
11. *Aid and Influence*, Chapter 7.
12. For a discussion of this see *Zambia Country Study and Norwegian Aid Review*, Chapter 2, Bergen: Chr. Michelsen Institute, 1986.

II Planning and Development

6 Participatory Development: Some Perspectives from Grassroots Experience

Dharam Ghai

INTRODUCTION[1]

In recent years, especially since the early 1970s, there has been increasing interest in participatory approaches to development. This interest is manifested both at the national and international levels and appears to be shared by individuals and institutions of widely divergent ideologies and backgrounds. At the international level, most multilateral and bilateral agencies have recognised the importance of participation both as a means and as an objective of development. Likewise, national plans in many countries pay a great deal of attention to the need for a participatory pattern of development. However, as tends to happen in situations of this sort, this growing consensus owes much to certain ambiguities in the concept of participation. Different authors and organisations give different interpretations to this concept. Often these differences are a reflection of differences over the concept of development itself.

The notion of participation may be examined from different levels and perspectives. One distinction relates to participation in the public domain, work place and home. The first aspect refers to all matters discussed and decided in public institutions – local organisations, national governments, parliaments, parties, etc. The second concerns factories, offices, plantations, farms and other work places. The third dimension refers to family relations and work at home. The latter is largely neglected in most discussions on participation. Yet, in relation to the time spent in different places, 'home democracy' is at least as important as 'work democracy' and is a crucial determinant of the welfare of some members of the family, especially the women and children.

A different but slightly overlapping distinction concerns participation at local, national and international levels. Although there has
been a good deal of discussion of participation promotion at the local
and national levels, much less attention has been given to the implications of a participatory approach at the global level.[2] In view of the
linkages and interrelationships between developments at these different levels, a satisfactory analysis of participation should be based on a
recognition of interdependence among the different levels of aggregation. This is, however, a complex and daunting undertaking. This
article has a more limited, modest purpose – namely, to shed some
light on the participatory approach to development through a study
of selected grassroots initiatives in a few Asian and African countries.
This is done in the belief that these experiences yield fresh and
exciting perspectives of the meaning and processes of development
and contain within them elements of a self-reliant, egalitarian and
participatory approach to development. They therefore offer a rich
field from which to draw lessons, with a view to strengthening the
quality of development efforts in rich and poor countries alike.

In the light of the preceding remarks, the paper begins with a
discussion of some alternative concepts of development and participation. This is followed by a brief description of nine grassroots
initiatives whose experiences are used subsequently to illustrate some
aspects of participatory approaches to development. The paper then
examines the themes of participatory processes and institutional
framework, and of self-reliance and the role of outside assistance.
There is then an analysis of these initiatives as economic enterprises,
agencies of social reform and schools for democracy. The concluding
section focuses on their strengths and limitations as alternative development models. The gender issues are discussed in various sections
of the paper.

ALTERNATIVE CONCEPTS OF DEVELOPMENT AND PARTICIPATION

The notion of development is an ambiguous one and is subject to
different interpretations.[3] We may distinguish here three interpretations. First, development is often treated synonymously with economic growth and is thus interpreted to mean increases in labour
productivity, declining share of agriculture in total output, technological progress, and industrialisation with the consequent shift of

population to urban areas. While these structural changes are generally associated with economic growth, equating them with development shifts the focus to economic aggregates and away from living standards and human dimensions.

The second interpretation of development seeks to remedy this deficiency by concentrating on such indices of living standards as poverty, income distribution, nutrition, infant mortality, life expectancy, literacy, education, access to employment, housing, water supply and similar amenities. This way of looking at development brings it closer to the common-sense view and endows it with greater human reality. Nevertheless, the emphasis continues to be on economic and social indicators and individual human being and social groups tend to be off-stage passively supplied with goods, services and materials.

In contrast, the third view of development puts the spotlight on human potentials and capabilities in the context of relations with other social groups. According to this view, development is seen in such terms as greater understanding of social, economic and political processes, enhanced competence to analyse and solve problems of day-to-day living, expansion of manual skills and greater control over economic resources, restoration of human dignity and self-respect, and interaction with other social groups on a basis of mutual respect and equality. This notion of development does not neglect material deprivation and poverty but the focus shifts to realisation of human potential expressed in such terms as human dignity, self-respect, social emancipation, and enhancement of moral, intellectual and technical capabilities.[4]

The three ways of looking at development are not, of course, mutually exclusive. Indeed, the optimal pattern of development should embody elements of all three: the growth of human capabilities and potentials must be accompanied by progressive reduction of material deprivation and social inequalities which, in turn, should flow from structural change and modernisation of the economy. But in practice, these aspects of development seldom evolve in a harmonious relationship and typically emphasis on one or the other would have different implications for organisation of economic activities, patterns of investment and design of programmes and projects.

As with development, the concept of participation is also riddled with ambiguities. Once again, it may be useful to distinguish between three different interpretations. One common usage of the term refers to 'mobilisation' of people to undertake social and economic

development projects. Typically the projects are conceived and designed from above and the people are 'mobilised' to implement them.
Their participation thus consists in their contribution of labour and
materials, either free or paid for by the authorities. The projects
which generally tend to be of an infrastructural nature are meant to
benefit the rural poor. But in many cases the benefit may accrue
mainly in the form of employment generated during the construction
phase. The distribution of the benefits from the assets and facilities
created would depend on a variety of factors such as the patterns of
ownership of productive resources, the distribution of political power
among social groups and the nature of the project. At their best, such
projects may result in a widespread diffusion of benefits both in the
construction and the subsequent phase. At worst, 'participation' may
result in free provision of labour and materials by the poor to create
facilities which are of benefit primarily to the affluent groups.

The second interpretation equates participation with decentralisation in governmental machinery or in related organisations. Resources and decision-making powers may be transferred to lower-
level organs, such as local officials, elected bodies at the village or
country level, or local project committees.[5] While this may make
possible local-level decisions on the choice, design and implementation of development activities, there is no presumption that this
need imply any meaningful participation by the rural or urban masses.
Indeed, the distribution of political and economic power at local
levels in many countries is such that decentralisation may well result
in allocation of resources and choice of development activities which
are less beneficial to the poor than when such decisions are taken at
the central level.

The third view of participation regards it as a process of empowerment of the deprived and the excluded (Gran, 1983; Oakley, 1987;
Oakley and Marsden, 1984). This view is based on the recognition of
differences in political and economic power among different social
groups and classes. Participation is interpreted to imply a strengthening of the power of the deprived masses. Its three main elements
have been defined as 'the sharing of power and of scarce resources,
deliberate efforts by social groups to control their own destinies and
improve their living conditions, and opening up of opportunities from
below' (Dillon and Steifel, 1987). Participation in this sense necessi-
tates the creation of organisations of the poor which are democratic,
independent and self-reliant (Advisory Committee on Rural Development, 1979; International Labour Organisation, 1976).

One facet of empowerment is thus pooling of resources to achieve collective strength and countervailing power. Another is the enhancement of manual and technical skills, planning and managerial competence and analytical and reflective abilities of the people. It is at this point that the concept of participation as empowerment comes close to the notion of development as fulfilment of human potentials and capabilities. This view of participation and development may best be illustrated through the experience of some grassroots initiatives, to which we now turn.

SOME GRASSROOTS PARTICIPATORY INITIATIVES

In recent years, there has been a huge expansion of small-scale development projects focusing on the rural and the urban poor and involving some sort of group action (Commission on the Churches' Participation in Development, 1981; Economic Commission for Latin America, 1973; Food and Agriculture Organisation, 1979; Hirschman, 1984; United Nations, 1981; Wasserstrom, 1985; World Health Organisation, 1982). These projects show a great deal of variation with respect to activities, organisational framework, financing arrangements, the sponsoring agencies, the role of outside assistance and the nature and extent of popular participation. They range from outstanding to disastrous, judged by the criterion of participation as empowerment of the people. In this section we give a brief description of nine grassroots experiences which, while displaying a great deal of diversity in respect of some aspects mentioned above, nevertheless share some characteristics as participatory initiatives. The nine initiatives considered here are the Grameen Bank (GB), the Small Farmers' Development Project (SFDP), the Self-employed Women's Association (SEWA), the Working Women's Forum (WWF), Sarilakas, Participatory Institute for Development Alternatives (PIDA), Se Servir de sa Saison Seche en Savane et au Sahel (Six-S), the Organisation of Rural Associations for Progress (ORAP), and Action pour le Développement Rural Intégre (ADRI).

Although they have several points in common, it is convenient to group them into four categories in accordance with their central characteristics. The first category, comprising GB and SFDP, illustrates innovative programmes to extend credit to the rural poor. SEWA and WWF represent pioneering efforts to organise poor women working in urban slums as vendors, home-based workers and casual labourers into trade-union type associations. The third category, illustrated by Sarilakas and PIDA, comprise initiatives to promote peasants groups and rural workers' organisations to struggle for their rights and to undertake collective initiatives to appropriate a larger share of the surplus generated by their economic activities. The fourth category, comprising Six-S, ORAP and ADRI, represents efforts to promote social and economic development through mobilisation and pooling of labour and other resources, drawing inspiration from traditional self-help and mutual aid groups.

Promoting Participation through Credit Programmes

The *Grameen Bank* was started in 1976 by a professor of economics at Chittagong University as an experiment to provide credit to poor landless men and women in rural areas (Fuglesang and Chandler, 1986; Ghai, 1984; Hossain, 1984; Yunus, 1982). Initially supported by funds from some commercial and nationalised banks, it became an independent bank in 1983. At the present time, the government has 25 per cent of the initial paid-up share of the capital with the remaining 75 per cent being held by borrowers of the bank. The GB has received funds from a number of donor agencies including the International Fund for Agricultural Development (IFAD), Asian Development Bank and the Ford Foundation. The membership is restricted to the poor defined by a net worth criterion.

Members organise themselves into groups of five persons and ten such groups constitute a circle. The loans, which are quite modest in size, are given for a one-year period and the principal is repaid in weekly instalments over this period. The banking operations take place in weekly meetings held in the locality of the groups. The loans are granted for a wide range of economic activities such as trading, transport, processing, handicraft, cattle raising and simple manufacturing. There are separate groups for men and women with the latter now accounting for two thirds of the total. The bank has experienced a rapid expansion in its activities with the number of members increasing from less than 15 000 in 1980 to nearly 250 000 in 1988. The members have established a variety of social programmes such as family planning, schools, nutrition, sports and music, and have sought to promote social reforms.

The *SFDP* in Nepal is also a credit programme for the rural poor but, unlike the GB, it extends loans to small and marginal farmers (Agricultural Projects Services Centre, 1979; Ghai, 1984; Ghai,

Lohani and Rahman, 1984; Mosley and Prasad Dahal, 1987; Rokaya, 1983). It evolved from a pilot project launched in 1975 by the Agricultural Development Bank of Nepal (ADB/N) with financial and technical support from FAO/UNDP. The basic objectives of the project were to increase the incomes and standard of living of the rural poor, promote participation and self-reliance, and adapt local delivery mechanisms of government agencies to the needs of the rural poor. The approach adopted was to encourage the rural poor to organise themselves in small groups with the assistance of a group organiser to receive credit for individual and joint activities. The credit was provided on a group guarantee basis without any collateral.

The membership has expanded from around 440 in 1976 to about 25 000 in 1984 and perhaps 50 000 in 1988. It has attracted funds from a number of bilateral and multilateral sources. The programme comprises a wide range of economic, social and community activities which are supported by an expanding training component. Economic activities include cultivation, livestock, horticulture, irrigation, cottage and rural industry and marketing. Social activities comprise health, education, family planning, maternal welfare and child care and sanitation. Community projects comprise construction of roads, bridges, schools, meeting halls, water facilities, irrigation, biogas and social forestry. The bulk of economic activities are undertaken on an individual basis with, however, growing importance of group ownership and management in cottage industry, orchards and irrigation.

Organising Poor Self-Employed Women in Urban Slums

SEWA represents a pioneering effort to organise self-employed poor women in urban slums in Gujerat, India, into a trade-union type organisation (Self-employed Women's Association, 1984). Until they formed a trade union in 1972, self-employed women were not recognised as workers by legislation or by society. Thus their struggle related as much to their desire for recognition as legitimate workers as to improvements in income and working conditions. The initiative in forming SEWA was taken by an experienced woman trade unionist who previously worked with the long-established Textile Labour Association. SEWA's membership is drawn from three categories of women workers: petty vendors and hawkers, homebased producers, and providers of casual labour and services. Started primarily as a movement for poor urban women, it has now spread to cover also women agricultural labourers and home-based workers in rural areas.

As a trade union for self-employed women, it has worked to secure higher wages for casual workers, for those on contract work such as home-based workers and for suppliers of services such as cleaning and laundering, with a gradual extension to such workers of protection and benefits provided by labour legislation to organised workers in modern enterprises. It has also instituted a credit scheme for vendors, hawkers and home-based workers to finance working capital and purchase of raw materials and tools. Credit was originally arranged through nationalised commercial banks but soon the women decided to form their own savings and credit cooperative. The cooperative has expanded rapidly in terms of shareholders, deposits and loans.

Further benefits have accrued to vendors, craftswomen and home-based workers through the formation of producers' cooperatives for vegetable and fruit sellers, bamboo workers, hand block printers, spinning-wheel and handloom operators and dairy workers. The economic capacity of the members has also been enhanced by the provision of training courses in a wide range of skills such as bamboo work, block printing, plumbing, carpentry, radio repairs, simple accounting and management. Finally SEWA has sought to solve some of the urgent social problems of their members through a maternal protection scheme, widowhood benefits, child care and training of midwives.

The *Working Women's Forum* was started in 1978 at the initiative of a woman activist with considerable previous experience in social and political work. It operates in the southern Indian states of Tamil Nadu, Andhra Pradesh and Karnataka (Arunachalam, 1983; Azad, 1985; Chambers, 1985; Chen, 1982). Its membership of nearly 50 000 is drawn largely from poor urban women but there is also increasing representation from rural areas. It covers similar occupational groups to SEWA, such as street hawkers, craft producers, home-based workers, and fisherwomen and dairy workers in rural areas. It arranges loans for members from the commercial banks and increasingly from the Working Women's Cooperative Society – the savings and credit scheme set up by the members themselves. The WWF has also initiated a wide range of training schemes. It has organised extensive family planning and public health programmes, group insurance schemes, night schools for working children, campaigns against caste prejudice and discrimination, petty harassment and bureaucratic abuse suffered by its members, and educational sessions on workers' rights and minimum wages.

Promoting Peasant Groups and Organisations of Rural Workers

Sarilakas in the Philippines evolved out of an attempt by the Rural Workers' Office, Ministry of Labour, to organise the unorganised rural workers. The initial attempts to promote rural workers' organisations suffered a series of setbacks due to inadequate preparation, faulty approach and excessive economic expectations engendered by the 'facilitators' (Rahman, 1983). With assistance from the ILO and exposure of the organisers to participatory initiatives in Sri Lanka, India and Bangladesh, the project adopted a different approach with emphasis on group discussions and analysis of their socio-economic situation, reflection on the sources of their impoverishment and identification of feasible initiatives in a self-reliant framework. The new approach proved more successful in establishing durable participatory organisations in several villages, resulting in a series of different initiatives such as the institution of collective savings schemes for purchase of inputs by marginal farmers, joint ownership and operation of agricultural machinery and rice mills, rehabilitation of irrigation facilities, enforcement of legislation on change from sharecropping tenancy to fixed-rent liability, protection of the fishing rights of small fishermen, land rights of sugarcane growers, etc.

In 1982, the project was taken over by a non-governmental organisation – PROCESS. Subsequent activities have included community communications, legal assistance to the poor and education and training. The organisation is now working in nine provinces, 49 municipalities and around 260 villages.

PIDA in Sri Lanka was established in 1980 as a non-governmental organisation for the promotion of grassroots participatory groups. It is an action research collective with a membership of 15 or so animators working in 40 villages in various rural locations (Tilakaratna, 1985). It grew out of the UNDP-sponsored Rural Action Research and Training Project initiated in 1978. Its main objective is to promote participatory and self-reliant organisations of the rural poor which in turn can become the main vehicle of their economic and social advance. The key role in this process is played by animators who encourage the villagers with similar background to come together for informal discussion of their socio-economic situation, the problems they face and the steps they might take to ameliorate

their living standards and working conditions. After initiating the
process of group discussion and reflection, the animator attempts
progressively to reduce his or her role, leaving it to the villagers
themselves to conduct their inquiries, form groups and take initiatives to strengthen their economic position.

The initiatives can take a variety of forms. Some groups focused
their attention on possible savings from purchases of consumer goods
in village stores. They expanded their activities to procure and
distribute a whole range of basic consumer goods and start thrift and
credit societies, thus evolving cooperatives of the rural poor. The
groups, which started from the production front, cut down their
cultivation costs through a series of collective efforts, used their spare
time to cultivate a common plot of land as a means of increasing their
collective fund, initiated actions to develop irrigation facilities and
diversify crop patterns, established links with banks and obtained
bank credit by demonstrating their credit-worthiness, thus eliminating their dependence on usurer credit, and bargained for improved
access to public services.

Some groups began their activities in produce marketing. They
devised collective marketing schemes, explored and discovered new
market outlets, delinked from village traders and intermediaries and
retrieved the surpluses hitherto extracted by them, stored a part of
the crop to take advantage of better prices and increased the value of
the produce by processing. In the case of wage labourers, attempts
were made to check leakages from their income streams by forming
informal cooperatives for consumer, credit and thrift activities, and
to obtain access to land or other productive assets, thus switching
over from the sale of labour to farming either on a part-time or
full-time basis.

Mobilising Resources through Self-Help and Cooperative Efforts

Six-S was started in 1974 in Burkina Faso at the initiative of a local
agronomist working with some foreign volunteers. The original motive was to take advantage of the long dry period from October to
May to undertake a series of self-help social and economic activities
to improve the living standards of the rural people (Egger, 1987a;
Rahman, 1988; Sawadogo and Ouedraogo, 1987). The practice until
then had been for the young people to migrate to urban areas and to
neighbouring countries in search of employment. One feature of this
initiative was reliance on traditional mutual help and cooperation

groups to promote a large-scale, self-help movement with numbers running into 200 000 and extension into other Sahelian countries such as Mali, Mauritania and Senegal.

The groups undertake a variety of income-generating, community and social activities. The first set includes vegetable gardening, stock farming, handicraft, cereal banks, and the production and sale of horse carts. Communal activities comprise construction of water dams and dikes, anti-erosion works, wells, afforestation, etc., while social projects include rural pharmacies, primary health care, schools, theatres, etc. Six-S provides credit to partially support such projects. Activities of communal benefit are subsidised through limited cash remuneration and food for work, and the free supply of needed equipment. In turn, Six-S gets funds from members groups' contributions and external donors. All Six-S groups have a savings fund built with member subscriptions and receipts from income-generating activities.

There has been a rapid multiplication of groups in the region. The established groups assist new ones in a variety of ways. Farmer-technicians are employed by Six-S during the slack season to advise the groups and assist their activities. When some members of Six-S groups carry out an innovation or master a technique, they form a mobile school to transmit it to other groups. Thus new ideas and innovations spread rapidly throughout the Six-S movement.

ORAP was started in 1981 by a group of concerned people in Matabeleland in Zimbabwe to initiate a new approach to their development problems. It sees itself essentially as a support organisation for self-reliant development in rural areas. Its first priority is the encouragement and support of autonomous organisations among rural people and their ability to analyse their own situation. (Chavunduka and others, 1985; Nyoni, 1986). As with Six-S, it also relied on traditional groups and practices of mutual help and cooperation. The basic units are village groups which federate into 'umbrellas', and higher up to associations and finally to the Advisory Board of ORAP.

After a period of deliberation and analysis, the groups undertake a variety of economic and social activities, combining their skills and labour with material and financial assistance from external donors through ORAP. The activities comprise carpentry, netwire-making, sewing, building, basketry, wood-carrying, livestock-grazing, vegetable-gardening, poultry-keeping, baking and grinding mills.

Considerable emphasis is put on training and development

education activities. The prolonged drought in the region led ORAP to develop a food relief programme and subsequently to give priority to food production, with stress on recourse to traditional seeds and fertilisers, diversity of food produced, improved food storage and cereal banks in the villages, and improved water storage and local irrigation schemes. Recently new emphasis has been put on organising activities at the family units – a collective of five to ten families – to meet their immediate needs such as wells for drinking water, sanitary latrines, improved baths, improved kitchens, as well as cultivation, food production, harvesting and threshing corn.

Another recent innovation has been the construction on a self-help basis of development centres. These are multipurpose centres for meetings, workshops, organisation of training courses in various technical fields, such as bakery, building, blacksmithing and marketing outlets.

ADRI is an organisation of peasant groups in Rwanda. It owes its origin to an initiative taken in 1979 by a local agronomist to undertake 'animation' work with peasant women in the Kabaye district in 1979 (Action pour le development rural intégre, 1987; Egger, 1978b). As in Six-S and ORAP, the basis of organisation was traditional groups of mutual help. Some other groups sprang up in the area leading to the formation of an inter-group organisation, Impuzamiryango Tuzamuka Twese (ITT). Activities undertaken by the group include collective cultivation of cash crops, social forestry, grain storage, consumer stores, livestock rearing, furniture making, brick making, beer brewing and grain mills.

Dissatisfaction with the Banque Populaire led the peasant groups to form their own savings and credit society called Caisse de Solidarité (Solidarity Bank). This society plays a particularly important role in the management of external funds for group activities. All the groups assume responsibility for these funds which serve both as a guarantee to donors and to generate collective interest in the repayment of funds by each group. Several groups have evolved into multipurpose cooperatives covering farming, marketing, artisan production and collective savings schemes. In one area, several groups have come together to form a fund with contributions from peasants, particularly at harvest time, in cash or kind. The fund serves as a social security scheme for members, covering death, fire, natural disasters, accident, sickness and finance of secondary education.

ADRI was formed to stimulate the expansion of such peasant

groups to all parts of the country. It is a development NGO which assists peasant groups and associations through animation work, and exchange visits, promotion of a wider federation of associations and provision of direct support to base groups on funding and implementing collective social and economic projects.

PARTICIPATORY PROCESS AND INSTITUTIONAL FRAMEWORK

Contrasting Conventional Projects and Participatory Initiatives

It is no caricature to say that a conventional development project is conceived and designed from outside by national and international experts together with the paraphernalia of prefeasibility and feasibility studies, appraisal reports, specification of inputs and outputs, calculation of internal rates of return and sophisticated cost-benefit analysis. The people for whom all this is supposed to be done exist only in the abstract as numbers whose output and productivity are to be enhanced and whose 'needs' are to be satisfied. Their participation in the preparatory phase, if they are lucky, may at best consist of some hastily organised meetings with the 'experts' and bureaucrats where they are 'briefed' about the objectives and activities of the planned projects. In the implementation phase they are expected to carry out their pre-assigned roles.

Participatory development is radically different in approach, methodology and operation. As implied earlier, its central concern is with the development of the moral, intellectual, technical and manual capabilities of individuals. A development project is therefore regarded as a process for the expansion of these capabilities. This implies that the initiative in establishing the activities must be taken by the people themselves who should also be firmly in charge of their implementation and evolution. This in turn calls for an entirely different methodology in initiating and sustaining development activities.

Social organisations and leaders of grassroots initiatives worldwide are working with many different approaches and methodologies for participation promotion. There is no single blueprint. Indeed, such a concept would be contradictory to the very spirit of participatory development whose central purpose is the awakening of people's dormant energies and unleashing of their creative powers.

The grassroots experiences described in the preceding section like-wise reveal diversity of approaches to participation promotion. It may be useful to discuss separately two dimensions of this theme, namely methodologies and the institutional framework for partici-pation promotion.

Methodologies for Participation Promotion

Whatever their differences, the nine experiences considered here have one aspect in common: the initiation of development activities is preceded by a preparatory phase involving interaction with and among the people concerned. The purpose, duration and intensity of this interaction have tended to vary from one initiative to another. At one extreme, the interaction phase may consist only of understanding and acceptance of the basic objectives and operation of the project by the people before their enrolment as members. At the other extreme, this phase extending over long periods may involve intensive dis-cussions and dialogue, analysis and reflection and conduct of field work and social inquiry, thus using the methodology of participation promotion associated with 'conscientisation' and 'participatory action research'.[6] Depending on its scope and intensity, the preparatory phase may serve to instil discipline, build confidence, 'indoctrinate' or socialise members to the underlying philosophy and objectives of the initiative, raise consciousness, develop critical and analytical abilities, and promote group solidarity and democratic practices. Furthermore, these processes of participation promotion are not considered once-for-all events preceding the initiation of develop-ment activities, but an integral part of the style of work within the association.

The initial phase in the establishment of peasant groups in Rwanda consists of animation and conscientisation (Action pour le développe-ment rural intégre, 1987). It is only after this phase that the peasants decide to form associations. The process also generates the array of activities to be undertaken by the group. Likewise the Six-S puts a great deal of emphasis on animation work and group meetings. The emerging pattern of activities is seen as a reflection of people's situation, knowledge, experiences, capacities and wishes.[7] The WWF relies on spearhead teams and group organisers to initiate interaction with the potential members.

In ORAP, any material development work must be preceded and/or accompanied by continuous discussion and analysis of the reasons for undertaking a development activity. In principle, all groups must go through a discussion process to determine what their problems are, where they come from and how they can solve them. This approach is summarised graphically in the words of a member of a local group: 'Before coming to ORAP, I didn't know how development started. Now I know that before development, there must be thoughts in mind'. (Chavunduka and others, 1985).

SFDP and GB are first and foremost credit programmes. Before any activities are initiated, the group organisers in the former and bank workers in the latter undertake a socio-economic survey of the villages concerned. The 'tenant' groups are then encouraged to come together for discussions among themselves and with the development workers. Out of this process emerge the groups which are the basic units around which the credit programme is organised. In GB, for example, the basic unit consists of a group of five landless persons. Before receiving loans, the groups go through an intensive 'instruction' of one to two weeks on the philosophy, rules and procedures of the bank. The group members have to pass a 'test' before they are granted recognition. During this test the members must satisfy the bank staff of their integrity and seriousness, undertanding of the principles and procedures of the GB and ability to write their signatures.

The methodology of 'conscientisation' and applied action research is perhaps applied most systematically in the activities organised by PIDA. A brief illustration of its work in a village may convey the flavour of PIDA's approach to participation promotion (Tilakaratna, 1984). In 1978, a four-member team of development workers (DWs) visited a village to explore the possibility of initiating a grassroots participatory development process. The first step was to make a preliminary study of socio-economic conditions in the villages. The workers visited all households and initiated discussions with the people individually as well as in small informal groups on the problems at village level. The main poverty group was identified as betel producers. The DWs continued discussions about the source of their poverty. Soon, however, they reached the stage where further progress called for more information on production and marketing of betels than they possessed. Two village groups volunteered to undertake the investigations and collect information on the working of the betel industry – a women's group to examine production and a youth group to explore the marketing aspects.

This investigation enabled the peasants to see for the first time the reality of betel farming, in particular how an impoverishment process had been created by the loss of a sizeable economic surplus at the marketing stage to the village traders who in turn sold betel leaves to state-exporting firms. A group of betel producers then met to explore alternative marketing possibilities. An action committee formed by the group spent two months visiting various traders in the vicinity and exporting firms. After a series of setbacks and negative responses, the committee found one exporting firm which was prepared to buy directly from them provided the sales were channelled through the registered village cooperative. This immediately resulted in a doubling of the prices received by peasants for their betel leaves and greater price stability. The group grew in number and the incomes of the members expanded threefold due to better prices and higher production. Subsequently they formed their own multipurpose cooperative.

The underlying approach of participatory development has been described in these words by PIDA's co-ordinator:

> The central element of a participatory process was identified as conscientisation which was seen as a process of liberating the creative initiatives of the people through a systematic process of investigation, reflection and analysis, undertaken by the people themselves. People begin to understand the social reality through a process of self-inquiry and analysis, and through such understanding, perceive self-possibilities for changing that reality . . . Conscientisation leads to self-organisation by the people as a means of undertaking collective initiatives. Each action will be followed by reflection and analysis generating a process of praxis as a regular ongoing practice. These interactive elements . . . were seen as the heart and soul of a participatory process. (Tilakaratna, 1985)

A Sri Lankan peasant summed it all up in these simple words: 'the rust in our brains is now removed' (Tilakaratna, 1985).

The Institutional Framework

While discussions, analysis and reflection constitute the methodology of participation promotion in most of the initiatives considered here, the institutional framework provides the vehicle for the practice of participation. As might be expected, there is a great deal of variation in the organisational arrangements they devise to conduct their work.

However, one common characteristic they share is that in all cases members are organised into base or primary groups. Participatory development is inconceivable in the absence of such groups. The process of conscientisation presupposes the existence or creation of small groups with a homogeneous socio-economic background. Beyond that the organisation of small farmers, rural workers and urban poor in groups serves a number of crucial functions. First, it provides a forum for dialogue, analysis and reflection, thereby contributing to the capacity of the members to understand and find solutions to their problems. Second, membership in a group reduces individual insecurity and dependence and builds confidence. This is a vital function especially in societies characterised by social oppression, economic polarisation and status hierarchies. Third, the groups provide a mechanism for discussion, choice and elaboration of social and economic activities to be undertaken on individual or joint basis. Fourth, they constitute appropriate structures for the launching, ownership, management and operation of some projects. Fifth, the groups serve to increase the effectiveness of government social and economic services by acting as receiving mechanisms. Sixth, the formation of groups enables the poor to transform their individual weaknesses into collective strength thus enhancing their bargaining power vis-à-vis other economic groups and exerting countervailing pressure against local power structures.

The group structure of some of the initiatives discussed here illustrates these points. In the GB, groups and the centre hold weekly meetings for banking transactions, as also for discussions on other social and economic activities. Although the loan is given to the individual and he or she has ultimate responsibility for it, it must be approved by the group chief and the centre chief. The groups, therefore, assume responsibility for its repayment. The choice of activity financed by the loan is left to the individual and the group. Group pressure plays an important role in ensuring the nearly perfect loan repayment record achieved by the bank. The Group Fund consisting of personal savings and Group Tax for emergency and social security purposes is operated by the groups. Joint enterprises such as shallow and deep tubewells, weaving and rice hullers are owned and managed at the level of individual groups, collection of groups, or centres. Construction, management and running of schools, community halls and other social activities would typically be organised at the level of individual or several centres.

In the SFDP, the group plays a key role in investment decisions.

The decisions on individual and joint loans are taken through group discussion and consensus, and the group provides the guarantee for the loan. The monthly meetings of the group also provide occasions for discussion and approval of annual and longer term plans for social and economic activities.

In ORAP, the new emphasis is on base units comprising three to five families. A few of the family units come together to form production units. The activities to be undertaken emerge from discussions within these groups. Some of the projects are of a family nature such as cultivation, latrine and kitchen improvement, but others involve larger units such as irrigation, grain mills, food storage and community buildings. Mutual help and cooperation are organised through the family units or production groups. The Naam groups in the Six-S form the nucleus of a myriad of activities such as water catchment and storage schemes, reforestation, soil preservation, cereal banks, artisanal production and collective farming. They also operate credit and savings societies, provide guarantees for individual and collective loans, and organise a variety of welfare schemes and social activities. The peasant associations in ADRI constitute the core of the movement. A number of family, community and income-generating projects by peasant groups are gradually transforming themselves into multipurpose cooperatives.

The village groups promoted by PIDA and by Sarilakas seek to raise the living standards of their members through collective action designed to improve wages, secure access to land, reduce the burden of usury, and retain a larger share of surpluses through joint purchase, elimination of middlemen in marketing, etc. In SEWA also exertion of pressure through collective power has been an important element in the benefits derived by its members. In addition to its function as a trade union of self-employed women workers, SEWA has organised members in cooperatives based on occupations. Social insurance, welfare and training programmes have also been organised.

While SEWA and WWF are exclusively women's organisations, GB and SFDP have separate groups for men and women, although SFDP also has a few mixed groups. On the other hand, in the other initiatives, while there may be some separate groups for men and women, the common pattern is to have mixed groups. This has served to break down stereotypes of gender roles and to promote solidarity and cooperation between sexes and generations.

While participation of members in the activities of the organisation through base groups is a feature common to all these grassroots initiatives, there is a great deal of variation concerning higher level entities. Sarilakas and PIDA essentially act as promoters of self-reliant participatory organisation of the rural poor. The organisations thus formed may cooperate in a variety of ways including joint projects, exchange of visits, information, etc., but so far no attempts have been made to federate them into regional or national associations, although federations have emerged at municipality and provincial levels in Sarilakas and across villages in PIDA. The parent body of the SFDP is the Agricultural Development Bank which does not have any representation from the small farmers in its policy-making organs. While the original intention was to encourage regional and national associations of SFDPs, this has not materialised, although individual groups cooperate in a variety of ways. Essentially, the same remarks apply to the GB with the crucial difference that now 75 per cent of the paid-up share capital belongs to members and the 12-member Board of Directors includes four persons, including preferably two women, elected by the borrower shareholders.

The other organisations have ascending layers of bodies with representatives chosen from lower-level entities. For instance, in ADRI, the peasant groups come together into regional associations which federate into a national organisation. Likewise, the ORAP organisational structure moves up from village groups to 'umbrellas', to association and the Advisory Board. WWF and SEWA have representative or general assemblies at the apex. The higher-level bodies consist of representatives elected from the lower ones. Some activities and services may be carried out at higher levels, e.g. the development centres in ORAP are operated at the level of associations and the Solidarity Bank in ADRI is run at the apex as are the savings and credit cooperatives run by SEWA and WWF. Thus in all these cases the organisational structure provides for participation in decision-making by the rank-and-file members of the movement.

SELF-RELIANCE AND THE ROLE OF OUTSIDERS

These initiatives have a diversity of origins. SFDP, PIDA and Sarilakas originated as government programmes with support of international agencies. But PIDA and Sarilakas moved away from their official links to convert themselves into development-orientated non-government organisations (NGOs). SFDP continues to be run as an Asian Development Bank (ADB) project but the bank operates in an independent manner. Although GB started as an experiment by an academic, it has been converted into a bank with joint ownership by the government and the borrowers. It is also run independently of the government ministries. All the other initiatives originated with concerned professionals and social activists independently of official agencies. It is noteworthy that the key figures in the initiation and consolidation of these initiatives were nationals of these countries. This is an aspect of self-reliance which already sets them off from the great majority of development projects which are often conceived and designed by outsiders.

A key characteristic of these initiatives both in their establishment and subsequent expansion is the role played by development workers variously described as social activities, change agents, facilitators, group organisers, catalysts and animators.[8] The success of these initiatives is in no small measure due to the approach and style of work adopted by these development workers. They do not possess any special technical skills but their human qualities are vital to the success of their mission. These include a deep understanding of the economy and society of the impoverished groups, compassion and sympathy with their plight, ability to inspire trust and confidence and to motivate and guide them, not in a paternalistic and authoritarian way, but in a manner to enhance their confidence and self-reliance. While many initiatives such as for instance the GB, the SFDP and SEWA, continue to rely on a core of professional and administrative staff to run their activities, others such as PIDA and Sarilakas regard their primary objective as being the stimulation of self-reliant participatory organisations. The animators who perform this role are expected to phase out gradually, and internal cadres and animators selected from within the village population progressively to take over their functions. Likewise, it is the policy of WWF to have members of that organisation steadily take over as group and area organisers. It was noted earlier that Six-S increasingly relies on peasant-technicians and advanced groups to transmit knowledge and innovations to other members and groups.

Self-reliance has many other aspects and several of these are illustrated by the experiences of the participatory initiatives discussed here. In some ways, the most important element is growing control over economic resources and social environment, resulting in greater confidence and reduction in insecurity and dependence, brought about on the one hand by the strength derived from membership of a group and on the other by a steady increase in individual intellectual, moral and technical capabilities. Indeed it is this aspect of their experience that is repeatedly emphasised by members in discussions and evaluations of the impact of the initiatives. Another dimension of self-reliance concerns the mobilisation of labour and other resources to launch income-generating activities and infrastructural and service projects. This feature is common to all initiatives but is central to the African experiences.

Provision of credit is the cornerstone of GB and SFDP but plays a role of varying importance in other initiatives as well. It should be noted here that in most cases funds are made available on a loan basis to be repayable over a specified period and at commercial rates of interest, although the rates are lower than charged by private money-lenders. In cases where a credit programme is a major component of their activities, such as SFDP, GB, SEWA and WWF, the default rate is astonishingly low by any standards. This is an eloquent testimony to the self-reliant spirit of these initiatives.

Furthermore, practically all initiatives have instituted other schemes which reinforce their self-reliance. The organisation of collective savings for consumption and production loans and for emergency purposes is a common element in all initiatives. The Six-S, ADRI and ORAP have initiated various types of cereal banks to enhance food security. Some groups in ADRI have started schemes which represent the beginnings of a social security system. Similar schemes covering childbirth, death, widowhood, etc., have been launched by SEWA and WWF financed completely or partly by the members' contributions.

The high rates of saving and accumulation achieved by many groups in these initiatives is further evidence of their self-reliant approach. In GB, for instance, together with interest payments, Group Fund and Emergency Fund, the members save a minimum of 25 per cent of the income generated by the bank loans. If to this is added savings for special projects and members' personal savings and investment, the savings rate in many cases may well amount to 50 per cent of the additional income. In an extremely poor community where meeting subsistence needs is an everyday struggle, such rates of saving can only be considered phenomenal.

Initiatives such as PIDA and Sarilakas push the concept of self-reliance to extreme limits. PIDA regards its role as assistance in the mobilisation of efforts by the rural poor as animation work. It does not provide any technical assistance, extension services, grants or loans. The villagers themselves are expected to enhance their incomes and production and social welfare through collective actions of the type discussed earlier and through staking a claim for their share of resources from the commercial banks and government social and economic services. Even the animation and facilitation work done by external animators is for a limited period to be taken over at the earliest opportunity by internal cadres.

Most of the initiatives discussed here have been recipients of assistance from national, multilateral and bilateral sources. No conventional type of analysis has been undertaken of the effectiveness of this assistance. Except for the two major credit programmes, the assistance received has been relatively modest. It has consisted for the most part of funds to start loan schemes, grants for training programmes, financing of workshops and occasional grants for equipment for production or infrastructural projects. No foreign experts have been attached to these movements nor have they 'benefited' from technical cooperation and consultancy missions. These initiatives thus represent truly authentic indigenous attempts at self-reliant development at the grass roots level.

PARTICIPATORY INITIATIVES AS ECONOMIC ENTERPRISES

The initiatives we have been considering cannot be looked at as conventional development projects. They respond to the multifarious needs of their members. Efforts to improve the living standards of the members are certainly at the core of their concerns and often provide the motivation for the creation of the movement but both the leaders and the participants also stress objectives which go beyond material achievements. In this section, we discuss some economic aspects – leaving for later sections the social and political dimensions of the work of participatory initiatives. The pattern of economic activities undertaken by them has already been discussed in earlier sections. The intention here is to analyse briefly the nature of these activities and to make a rough assessment of their economic impact.

Economic Benefits to Members

Provision of credit to individual members or to groups, directly or indirectly, plays an important role in all initiatives. Credit facilitates the purchase of stock-in-trade, raw materials, equipment, tools and agricultural inputs. Especially in densely populated poor countries, capital is an extremely scarce factor of production and carries high potential returns. Its value is further enhanced to the poor as institutional credit is largely unavailable to them and they must rely for urgent needs on moneylenders who impose five to fifteen times the rates charged by commercial banks. The provision of credit thus contributes to increases in the incomes of the members by financing higher turnover of their stock, improvements in tools and equipment, access to raw materials and inputs, and by substitution of institutional for moneylenders' loans.

While detailed evaluation of economic activities of other initiatives is not available to the author, several surveys have attempted to quantify the economic impact of the credit programme of the GB and SFDP.[9] There is naturally a good deal of variation in returns on individual activities but overall the investment programme financed by loans generated rates of return in the region of 30 to 40 per cent. Apart from the factors mentioned earlier, the contributory factors in the GB have been that the activities undertaken are familiar to members; the skills and technologies are known and are relatively simple; the clients are not dependent – except in a few cases – on extension services or inputs from the government. Furthermore, the participants themselves select the activities for which they seek loans. It may be assumed that they would select activities which they are confident of carrying out successfully. Group dynamics, emulation, competition and peer pressure are additional factors which have played a positive role in all initiatives of the type considered here.

Similar factors have been at work in the SFDP with the additional point that high yields in its projects have been possible in part because the credit programme has brought within reach of small and marginal farmers the Green Revolution package of improved seeds, irrigation and fertilisers. Impressive income gains to women hawkers and home-based workers in SEWA and WWF have also been made possible essentially through access to credit. As indicated earlier, the mere substitution of institutional for moneylenders' credit – even disregarding higher turnover, better prices and improved technology – is a source of substantial gains in income. Rough estimates made for SFDP members showed that income gains from this source alone equalled those brought about by increased production.

Another way in which these initiatives have helped increase income, production and employment is through pooling of labour and other resources under collective projects such as irrigation and water catchment schemes, soil conservation, reforestation, construction of access roads, cultivation of common plots, mutual help in ploughing and harvesting, food storage, cereal banks, transport, marketing and joint purchase of agricultural inputs. This list of such efforts is long and impressive. In Africa especially, activities of this nature have contributed to stability and increase in incomes and production, reduction of food insecurity and generation of fuller employment through breaking of infrastructural bottlenecks, overcoming of labour shortages and introduction of improved techniques. Cooperation in pooling resources facilitated by institutional innovations inspired by traditional practices has been at the heart of gains achieved through these initiatives.

The third and related source of gains has accrued from the exertion of collective pressure and power to secure higher wages for jobs and contract work, enforcement of land and tenancy reform, fishing and forestry rights, implementation of the provisions of labour legislation, improved prices for raw materials and for processed foods. These gains have been the result of stronger bargaining and countervailing power as well as of institutional reforms such as service and production cooperatives, collective funds, credit and thrift societies, consumer stores, etc. These aspects have been especially important in the work of PIDA, Sarilakas, WWF and SEWA. This is a reflection of deep-seated social cleavages and economic polarisation prevalent in many Asian countries.

Finally, some of these initiatives – especially in South Asia – have contributed to increased incomes through reduction of excessive expenditure on ceremonial occasions. These include dowries, thread, birth and death ceremonies, and festivities of various kinds. Group discussions, solidarity and demonstration provide the necessary support from members to make the radical break from ancient practices. The gains accrue not only from direct reductions in expenditure but, even more importantly, from the savings in servicing of loans incurred by poor people at exorbitant interest rates from moneylenders and landlords – a debt trap from which they are unlikely to escape during their lifetime. Although no precise estimates are available of gains to disposable income from these sources, the rough estimates I made for SFDP members show that – even disregarding the interest charged by moneylenders – the average annual reduction in ceremonial expenditures was equivalent to Rs.600–700 – somewhat more than the gains realised from increases in income due to production loans.

Wider Economic Impact of the Initiatives

The final theme under this heading concerns the wider economic impact of the initiatives. It is possible for a programme to confer significant socio-economic benefits on its members while simultaneously generating strong negative effects on other segments of society. Likewise a project with a mediocre rating in terms of the direct impact on intended beneficiaries may nevertheless generate beneficial indirect and side effects for the poor. All the initiatives considered here are doubly blessed: they bring significant social and economic benefits to members while simultaneously generating positive spill-over effects on the poorer segments of these societies. These wider economic effects may be considered under three heads: the 'macro-economic' impact of project activities, assistance given by members to the fellow poor in their area or 'technical cooperation at the grassroots level', and the impact on national programmes and policies.

Although in aggregate terms most of these programmes are of negligible importance, they exercise significant influence at local and regional levels. The macro-economic effects may extend to markets for labour, credit, and goods and services. As far as the labour markets are concerned, the impact of activities undertaken under most initiatives is to intensify utilisation of family labour and shift labour allocation from wage to self-employment. This may be due to more intensive cultivation, non-farming activities, access to land, work on infrastructural projects and participation in training and social programmes. The effect is that, while the demand for labour goes up, the supply of wage labour goes down. Other things being equal, this should contribute to an increase in wages for the poor and the unskilled. This indeed seems to have happened in the areas in which SFDP, GB, WWF and SEWA have been active.

Many of the activities launched under these initiatives result in the diversion of bank credit to the rural poor, creation of new credit and savings schemes and substitution of institutional for moneylenders' credit. Thus, by increasing the supply of institutional credit and reducing the demand for moneylenders' loans, these initiatives exercise a downward pressure on the terms for non-institutional credit. Since the rural and urban poor are the main clients and victims of credit from moneylenders, traders and landlords, this must be counted among the more important benefits to non-members generated by these initiatives.

Productive activities associated with these schemes result in increased output and marketing of goods and services consumed by the poverty groups in rural and urban areas. These include such things as rice, maize, vegetables, fruits, meat, milk, eggs, cloth, household utensils, bamboo products, baskets, simple agricultural tools and services such as transport, storage, marketing, shopping, etc. Typically, these are the goods and services of mass consumption and figure prominently in the expenditure patterns of the poor. Although the rise in the incomes of the members results in increased consumption of many of these goods and services, the net effect for most goods is to increase their availability. This in turn, by keeping the relative prices of such commodities lower than they might otherwise be, contributes to an increase in the real incomes of the poorer segments of society.

The benefits from these initiatives also spread to other poor people through assistance rendered to them by members in a variety of ways. The pioneer groups must be looked upon as constituting a social vanguard whose impact radiates through the neighbouring communities. The members assist the fellow poor to form their own groups. This may happen at the initiative of the members of the established groups or at the request of the non-members who spontaneously wish to emulate their efforts. It is possible to quote instances from all the initiatives discussed here of the pioneer groups and animators being besieged by requests from others in the same or neighbouring villages for help in starting similar activities. This is perhaps the most important explanation of the rapid expansion of the membership of many of these organisations. Even where the entire set of activities is not replicated, some aspects of their valuable experiences are quickly disseminated to the neighbouring communities. Indeed the 'bush telegraph' is the most effective vehicle of transmission of new ideas, techniques and practices among the peasantry and rural workers. To give some examples, SFDP members helped others with group formation, initiation of social activities and community projects, credit and technical advice. In Khopasi and Jyamire villages, community irrigation projects were started at the initiatives of the SFDP groups but non-members in the catchment area were invited to participate in the scheme through donation of labour and cash. The example of betel and coir yarn producers in establishing new marketing channels was swiftly followed by several neighbouring villages.

Likewise, the pioneering efforts of Six-S, ORAP and ADRI have spread rapidly to other parts of the country through demonstration effect and emulation. For example, the Groupement Naam de Somi-aga in Burkina Faso helped set up eleven groups in six other villages. For their part 42 villages assisted this group in the construction of a dam. Six-S has developed original methods for transmission of skills through peasant-technicians who are paid by the organisation to train other members and groups in new technologies, social innovations and management techniques. The principal vehicle for this is 'chantiersécoles' (training camps) organised on a regular basis during the dry season at the request of the groups. These range from soil conservation techniques to management of maize mills, from water-pump maintenance to fenced livestock, and from cereal banks to nutritional centres. Each group assumes the responsibility to pass its special skills to others.

The impact of these initiatives is spreading further afield. Six-S is already operating in four Sahelian countries and plans are afoot to extend its activities to Niger and Chad. WWF is working in three states in southern India. Sister organisations to SEWA have been set up in about ten other Indian cities such as Bhopal, Delhi, Lucknow, Mithila and Bhagalpur. Many international seminars, study tours and workshops have been organised around these initiatives. SWAPO cadres have visited ORAP, the GB has attracted visitors from several Asian and African countries and has given technical assistance for organisation of credit programmes for the rural poor in Malaysia, Sri Lanka and Malawi. Perhaps the most dramatic example of the international impact of these initiatives is the role played by the managing director of the Grameen Bank in establishing small-scale credit schemes for the urban poor in Chicago and Arkansas – the latter at the request of the governor of the state. That the leader of a credit programme for the impoverished masses of one of the poorest countries in the world should be advising on establishing similar programmes in the metropolis of one of the richest countries in the world is indeed a paradox of extraordinary proportions!

Each of these initiatives contains valuable lessons for official development programmes, projects and policies. It is one of the tragedies of the development efforts in our countries that these creative and original efforts at self-reliant development through mobilisation of the limited resources of the impoverished groups should have had so little impact on official development thinking and practice, both at national and international levels. Fortunately there are glimmers of hope. By way of example, we may mention that in Nepal the basic concept of credit for the rural poor based on group guarantee has been extended by the Agricultural Development Bank of Nepal (ADB/N) to other villages where the SFDP is not operating. Likewise many elements of the SFDP – formation of groups, channelling of credit for individual and group activities through the group, investment decisions by the groups – have been incorporated partially in several integrated rural development projects in the country. Several women's programmes have also drawn upon the experience gained in the SFDP. Its existence has enhanced the effectiveness of some support services and has put pressure on other institutions such as cooperatives and the Agricultural Inputs Corporation to improve their performance.

Another example: the success achieved by SEWA in projecting the problems of poor self-employed women at the national level. The efforts of the organisation have had some impact on thinking and action concerning self-employed workers. After prolonged pressure from SEWA, the Gujarat government set up the Unorganised Labour Board in 1980. The National Planning Commission added a chapter on the self-employed in the Sixth Five-Year Plan and the Prime Minister has set up a Commission on Self-Employed Women which appropriately is chaired by the originator and leader of SEWA.

PARTICIPATORY INITIATIVES AS AGENCIES OF SOCIAL REFORM

The preceding sections have already touched on the role played by the participatory initiatives as instruments of social change. We discuss here four aspects of social progress: provision of social services and cultural amenities, change in family relations, emancipation of women and reform of antiquated and harmful customs and practices. Unlike many other development projects, the initiatives discussed here have integrated social and economic activities in their programmes. In this respect as in others, the leaders and organisers of these associations have simply followed the wishes of their members. ORAP, Six-S and ADRI have a wide range of social and cultural activities such as literacy, schools, nutrition, child care, help for the old and the handicapped, village clinics, personal hygiene, music and dances. WWF organises literacy classes, night schools for working children, family planning, and nutrition education. SEWA has pioneered social assistance and welfare schemes for maternity, death, widowhood, etc. The social activities of the GB comprise sanitation, health care, nutrition, education and family planning. The performance of the SFDP members has been superior to those of their neighbours in terms of literacy, education, family planning, sanitation and access to health services. It should be remembered that except perhaps for SFDP, the bulk of these social services are organised by the members themselves with contributions in cash and kind.

The second aspect relates to the effect on family solidarity. As mentioned earlier, it is a collective of three to five families which contributes the base units for many of ORAP activities. The involvement of all members of the family on projects of direct benefit to them, serves to promote family unity and harmony. In Six-S, the traditional Naam groups have brought together the old and the young thus reducing generational tensions and promoting harmony among members of different age groups.

All the initiative provide for full participation by women in all their activities either in mixed or in their own groups. This is leading to slow but profound changes in the social status and economic position of women, especially in South Asia. Membership in SEWA and WWF has given women, long subjected to subordination and oppression, a new sense of pride, dignity, personal worth and economic independence. All the South Asian initiatives have enabled women to increase incomes and acquire some organisational and management skills in planning and implementing group activities. In many households, the participation of women in income-generating activities has created a new division of labour and a new pattern of relationships. In some of the households with women members of the GB, it was found that the male members had begun to partake of some of the tasks traditionally done by women, e.g. looking after the children. It was also noted that the economic activities undertaken by women in turn created new opportunities for male members of the family. The women may, for instance, husk rice, make bamboo and cane products, or look after milch cows, while the husbands complement the household economy by buying raw materials, selling processed rice, handicrafts, milk or meat. This has enhanced women's economic independence and social status within the extended family. The husbands and other male members in the household have accepted the new situation willingly and, in some cases, even enthusiastically.

Finally, participation in these organisations is leading to a reform of ancient but antiquated customs and practices. Reference was made earlier to the role played by these organisations in reducing burdensome ceremonial expenditures. More impressive is the progress being made by the initiatives in South Asia in combating the age-old practice of dowry and child marriages, and caste and ethnic prejudice and discrimination. There is also evidence of decline in drunkenness, gambling, crime, wife-beating and similar types of anti-social behaviour. All this casts an interesting light on the determinants of social attitudes and behaviour. It may be noted that government policies and programmes in many countries have sought for long to bring about precisely this type of change but without much apparent success. The experience of these initiatives shows that once the people are organised in voluntary, cooperative groups and are given the necessary motivation, they decide on their own to carry through social changes of far-reaching significance.

PARTICIPATORY INITIATIVES AS SCHOOLS OF DEMOCRACY

Grassroots participatory organisations may be regarded as foundations of a democratic society. They promote the democratic cause in at least three ways. First, a representative and pluralistic democracy presupposes that all major social and economic groups in the country have a voice and a role in shaping national policies. For this to be possible, such groups should be able to articulate and press their views on vital issues of concern to them. Typically in most poor countries, and in many rich ones for that matter, the weaker and impoverished groups represented by the landless and marginal farmers in rural areas and the unemployed, casually employed and the poor self-employed in urban areas, have little voice and limited role in influencing government policies on social and economic matters. Given their individual weaknesses, they can exercise pressure and influence only by forming their own organisations.

None of the initiatives considered here has articulated its role in political terms. But it is clear that in practice some at least have come close to representing the interests of their groups in the political and economic processes of their countries. SEWA and WWF have served as pressure groups in the struggle against certain vested interests which have opposed the reforms proposed by them. They have also sought to influence legislation on matters of interest to their members and have deployed their strength in relation to bureaucracy and political parties to promote the interests of their members. Likewise, Sarilakas and PIDA have enabled poor peasants, landless workers and fishermen to exercise their collective strength to enforce legislation, renegotiate contracts and generally enhance their bargaining power.

In some cases the members of these organisations are beginning to play a more direct political role. In Nepal, for instance, it is rare for the small farmers, tenants and sharecroppers to hold offices in cooperatives and ward *panchayat* (local government) bodies. It is, however, a common sight now in all project areas for SFDP members to be seen participating in such organisations at the village level. To give just one example, in Khopasi, thirty-two SFDP participants served as ward members and nineteen as *panchayat* members. Also three out of nine members of the executive committee of cooperatives were SFDP participants. Likewise in areas where the GB has opened its branches, there has been a perceptible increase in the influence and power exerted by its members in village affairs.

The second way in which these initiatives serve the democratic cause is simply by providing an example of an embryonic democracy at work. In the section on the institutional framework of grassroots initiatives, it was noted that base groups constitute the core of their organisations. The groups are generally run in an open democratic manner. The style of work is through discussions and dialogue and decision is reached through consensus. Some of the groups have devised original solutions to the problems faced by the organisations as democratic entities at all levels, namely those of accountability of leadership, prevention of concentration of power in the hands of office-holders and active participation by all members in the management of group activities. The betel producers, for instance, decided to limit the size of their membership to ensure that all members participate actively in and effectively control the economic activities of the group. The requests for additional membership were handled by assisting them in forming new groups of their own. The insistence on keeping the members of the group to a manageable size is also characteristic of other initiatives. The Six-S and ADRI groups seek to prevent perpetuation of hierarchical division of labour by rotating the tasks among members. Office-bearers are chosen by election for limited periods. Some groups elect a different person to preside at each meeting. These organisations, therefore, promote the habit of group discussion, consultation, planning and implementation of joint activities, and resolution of conflict through debate – qualities which constitute the foundations of a participatory democracy.

Thirdly, the grassroots initiatives aid the democratic processes in poor countries by developing the intellectual, moral, managerial and technical capabilities of their members. This aspect has been discussed at length above. Suffice it to say here that in the last analysis it is these human capabilities that are the ultimate determinants of the vitality and creativity of a truly democratic society.

SOME CONCLUDING OBSERVATIONS

In this paper we have attempted to analyse the significance, processes and characteristics of participatory development through an examination of the experiences of a few grassroots initiatives in Asian and African countries. In the concluding section we touch on the strengths and limitations of participatory grassroots initiatives as models of development. But before addressing this issue it is necessary to make some qualifying remarks on the initiatives analysed in this paper.

The analysis presented here has necessarily been selective, highlighting distinctive features and notable achievements of nine participatory initiatives. As such it has undoubtedly given an optimistic, perhaps idealistic, picture of the functioning of such initiatives. It is necessary to emphasise first that the initiatives considered here are among the most successful of numerous similar efforts under way in Third World countries. Secondly, there is a great deal of variation in the quality of performance between and within the different units of the initiatives discussed here. Thirdly, the account presented above has not discussed the many difficulties, setbacks and frustrations suffered by these initiatives. It is necessary to point out that these movements had to overcome a wide variety of problems at some stage or another and continue to face difficulties of organisation, finance, know-how, staff and opposition or indifference from certain vested interests.

Despite these difficulties, the grassroots initiatives considered here have achieved a wide measure of success. It may be useful to summarise what appear to have been the major contributory factors to their success. There are three elements in the participatory character of these initiatives which probably have contributed strongly to their good performance: work in the preparatory phase prior to initiation of activities, an institutional frame which allows for an assertion of members' priorities in the unfolding of the activities undertaken, and the formation of groups as a basic unit in the organisation. These features in turn owe much to the approach and human qualities of the leaders of these movements and their band of dedicated development workers.

Relatively quick positive results in terms of the satisfaction of the psychological and material needs of the members have been important in sustaining interest and commitment. The material achievements in the Asian initiatives flowed in large measure from provision of credit and the wresting of a larger share of surpluses through enhanced bargaining power and cooperative activities, and in African experiences from cooperation in mobilisation of internal resources and attraction of outside funds for production diversification, infrastructural development and technological innovations. The organisational framework adopted facilitates mobilisation of labour and other resources, institution of schemes for collective savings, social security, and provision of social and economic services. At the same time, it allows for the initiation of activities of different sizes and with different modes of production and systems of management. Finally, these experiences demonstrate that a pattern of development rooted in grassroots participatory organisations, while giving full play to individual and group initiatives, promotes a relatively egalitarian distribution of incomes and access to common services and facilities.

Despite its promising potential, the participatory approach to development has made little headway in official programmes and policies at the national or international levels. Even among the non-governmental initiatives, the success rate is relatively low. A full discussion of this apparent paradox cannot be undertaken here, but some of the relevant considerations may be noted. In the first place, the participatory approach to development is relatively new and few in the 'development establishment' have proper knowledge or full understanding of it. Secondly, as noted above, many apparently participatory programmes provide little more than token representation of the 'beneficiaries' and thus fail to arouse their interest or commitment. Thirdly, participatory approach, especially in its empowerment version, tends to be mistakenly equated by the dominant groups with subversive or revolutionary doctrine. As such many participatory initiatives have to contend with hostility, harassment and attempts at suppression. Certainly, relatively few attract resources of the type and amount reserved for more conventional development projects.

There are some additional difficulties which are perhaps inherent in a participatory approach. The pace and pattern of activities may evolve slowly and haltingly and in directions different from those envisaged initially. The initiatives are often of a limited size and dependent for their success on the leadership of an exceptional person and a small band of dedicated social activists. It is therefore difficult to replicate them on a nation-wide basis. Furthermore, while successful in handling simple operations, they lose their effectiveness when confronted with large-scale complex activities. Their expansion beyond a certain size is likely to provoke the antagonism of more powerful forces. There is some validity in these charges but the experience of some of the initiatives has refuted a few of them. It would, however, require a separate paper to do full justice to these issues.

Notes

1. This article represents an effort to introduce to a wider audience a little known but particularly interesting and promising approach to development. Its knowledge and discussion has so far been confined to a narrow band of 'insiders'. Being myself an outsider to the 'movement', it is perhaps necessary to enter a personal note at the outset. My interest in the participatory approach to development goes back at least to the mid-1970s when I was in charge of the preparatory work for the World Employment Conference convened by the ILO in 1976. Subsequently, as Chief of the Rural Employment Policies Branch, I initiated work on participatory organisations of the rural poor (PORP). This work at ILO was coordinated by Md Anisur Rahman.

   The United Nations Research Institute for Social Development (UN-RISD), which I joined in September 1987 as Director, has also undertaken an impressive research effort on participation with emphasis on 'the nature of people's participation, the conditions conducive to participation and the organisational structures which evolve to sustain it'. The research programme has resulted in the publication of 12 books and a large amount of related material on social movements such as peasant associations, trade unions, protest groups, women's organisations and cooperatives. Currently an effort is under way to provide a synthesis of this vast material. The present article, however, is based largely on the work carried out under the PORP project in ILO.

   Although an 'outsider', I have been fortunate over the past decade and a half to visit and hold discussions with peasant groups, their leaders, social activities and sympathetic government officials in at least 17 countries in Asia, Africa and Latin America. Of the nine grassroots initiatives examined here, I have visited the Small Farmers' Development Project, the Grameen Bank, Sarilakas and the Working Women's Forum. In addition, I have been privileged to have discussions with the leaders or key figures of all the initiatives.

I acknowledge my debt to the numerous but anonymous peasants and landless workers, both men and women, leaders of peasant groups, social activists and sympathetic officials who have deepened my understanding of the social reality of the impoverished masses in rural areas of the Third World. My greatest intellectual debt is to Anisur Rahman and colleagues who participated in the PORP programme. These include S. Tilakaratna, Orlando Fals Borda, Ela Bhatt, Philippe Egger, Justin Maeda, Alula Abate, Muhammed Yunus, Jaya Arunachalam, Nandini Azad, Ponna Wignaraja, Santiago Roca, Edel Guiza, Sithembiso Nyoni, Bernard Ledea Ouedraogo and Shriram Upadhyaya.

For comments on an earlier draft, I am grateful to Mohiuddin Alamgir, Orlando Fals Borda, Michael Cernea, Philippe Egger, Keith Griffin, Edel Guiza, Albert Hirschman, John Knight, Peter Oakley, Anisur Rahman, Amartya Sen, Fredj Stambouli and Paul Streeten. I alone am responsible for the views expressed here.

2. At least one author has made the brave effort to explore the implications of participatory development at all these different levels: see Gran (1983).
3. Among numerous treatments of this subject, three may be mentioned here: Dag Hammarskjold Foundation (1975), Sen (1983), Haque and others (1977).
4. A more restricted definition but along similar lines has been given by Sen (1983): 'The process of economic development can be seen as a process of expanding the capabilities of people'.
5. For an extended discussion of the role of local institutions in development projects, see Uphoff (1986).
6. The classic work on conscientisation is Freire (1972); see also Rahman (1985) and Fals Borda (1985).
7. Sawadogo and Ouedraogo (1987) described this approach in these words: 'C'est ainsi que nous animons les groupes-cibles en fonction de ce qu'ils *sont*, de ce qu'ils *savent*, de ce qu'ils *vivent*, de ce qu'ils *savent faire*, et de ce qu'ils *veulent*.'
8. The issue of self-reliance in relation to animators is addressed in Tilakaratna (1987).
9. These have been summarised in my evaluations of GB (Ghai, 1984a) and SFDP (Ghai, 1984b). All subsequent information on these initiatives is taken from these sources.

References

Action pour le développement rural intégre (1986) *La dynamique des organisations paysannes au Rwanda: le cas de l'intergroupement Tuzamke de Kabaya* (mimeo), Geneva: ILO.

Advisory Committee on Rural Development (1979) *Rural Employers' and Workers' Organisations and Participation*, Geneva: ILO.

Agricultural Projects Services Centre (1979) *Impact Study of Small Farmers' Development Project*, Kathmandu.

Arunachalam, Jaya (1983) *Alternative employment Options for Indian Rural Women*, Manila: IRRI.

Azad, Nandini (1985) 'Improving Working Conditions for Rural Women through Creation of Alternative Employment Options', in Shimwaayi Muntemba (ed.), *Rural Development and Women: Lessons from the Field*, Geneva: ILO.

Chambers, Robert (1985) *The Working Women's Forum: A Counter-culture by Poor Workers*. Brighton: Institute of Development Studies.

Chavunduka, D.M. and others (1985) *Khuluma Usenza: The Story of ORAP in Zimbabwe's Rural Development*, Bulawayo: ORAP.

Chen, Marty (1982) *The Working Women's Forum: Organising for Credit and Change*, New York: Seeds.

Commission on the Churches' Participation in Development, (1981). *People's Participation and People's Movements*, Geneva: World Council of Churches.

Dag Hammarskjold Foundation (1975) 'What Now? Another Development', *Development Dialogue*. Uppsala.

Dillon, Bridget and Matthias Stiefel (1987) 'Making the Concept Concrete: the UNRISD Participation Programme', *Reading Rural Development Communications*, Bulletin 21. Reading University, Berkshire.

Economic Commission for Latin America (1973) 'Popular Participation in Development', *Community Development Journal*.

Egger, Philippe (1987a) *L'Association Six-S – se servir de la saison séche en savane et au Sahel – et les groupements Naam: note sur quelques observations*, (mimeo), Geneva: ILO.

Egger, Philippe (1987b) *La leçon de Jomba: trois tableaux pour une conclusion sur l'emploi rural au Rwanda* (mimeo), Geneva: ILO.

Fals Borda, Orlando (1985) *Conocimiento y poder popular*, Bogota: Siglo Veintiuno editores.

Food and Agriculture Organisation (1979) *Participation of the Poor in Rural Development*. Rome.

Freire, Paulo (1972) *The Pedagogy of the Oppressed*, Harmondsworth: Penguin.

Fuglesang, Andreas and Dale Chandler (1986) *Participation as a Process: What We Can Learn from Grameen Bank, Bangladesh*. Oslo: NORAD.

Ghai, Dharam, Prakash Lohani and Anisur Rahman (1984) 'The Small Farmers' Development Project of Nepal', in Anisur Rahman (ed.) *Grassroots Participation and Self-reliance: Experiences in South and South-East Asia*, New Delhi: Oxford and IBH.

Ghai, Dharam (1984a) *An Evaluation of the Impact of the Grameen Bank Project*. Dhaka: Grameen Bank.

Ghai, Dharam (1984b) *Small Farmers' Development Project: Mid-term Evaluation*, Rome: IFAD.

Gran, Guy (1983) *Development by People: Citizen Construction of a Just World*, New York: Praeger.

Hirschman, Albert (1984) *Getting Ahead Collectively*, New York: Pergamon.

Hossain, M. (1984) *Credit for the Rural Poor: the Experience of Grameen Bank in Bangladesh*, Dhaka: Bangladesh Institute of Development Studies.

International Labour Organisation (1976) *Employment Growth and Basic Needs*, Geneva: ILO.

Mosley, Paul and Rudra Prasad Dahal (1987) 'Credit for the Rural Poor: a Comparison of Policy Experiments in Nepal and Bangladesh'. *Manchester papers on development*.

Nyoni, Sithembiso (1986) *ORAP since 'Khuluma Usenza': a Review of Self-Assessment* (mimeo), Geneva: ILO.

Oakley, P. and D. Marsden (1984) *Approaches to Participation in Rural Development*. Geneva: ILO.

Oakley, Peter (1987) 'State or Process, Means or End? The Concept of Participation in Rural Development'. *Reading Rural Development Communications*, Bulletin 21. Reading University, Berkshire.

Rahman, M.A. (1988) *Glimpses of the 'Other Africa'* (mimeo), Geneva: ILO.

Rahman, M.A. (1983) *Sarilakas: a Pilot Project for Stimulating Grass-roots Participation in the Philippines*. Geneva: ILO.

Rahman, M.A. (1985) 'The Theory and Practice of Participation Action Research', in Orlando Fals Borda (ed.) *The Challenge of Social Change*, London: Sage.

Rokaya, Chandra M. (1983) Impacts of Small Farmers' Credit Programme on Farm Output, Net Income and the Adoption of New Methods. Kathmandu: Agricultural Projects Services Centre.

Sawadogo, A.R. and B.L. Ouedraogo (1987) *Auto-evaluation de six groupements Naam dans la province du Yatenga* (mimeo), Geneva: ILO.

Self-Employed Women's Association (1984) Ahmedabad: *Self-Employed Women's Association*.

Sen, Amartya, (1983). 'Development: Which Way Now?' *Economic Journal*, London. December.

Tilakaratna, S. (1987) *The Animator in Participatory Rural Development*. Geneva: ILO.

Tilakaratna, S. (1985) *The Animator in Participatory Rural Development: Some Experiences from Sri Lanka*. Geneva: ILO.

Tilakaratna, S. (1984) 'Grass-roots Self-reliance in Sri Lanka: Organisations of Betel and Coir Yarn Producers', in Anisur Rahman (ed.) *Grass-roots Participation and Self-reliance: Experiences in South and South-East Asia*, New Delhi: Oxford and IBH.

United Nations (1981) *Popular Participation as a Strategy for Promoting Community Level Action and New Development*, New York.

Uphoff, Norman (1986) *Local Institutional Development: An Analytical Sourcebook with Cases*. West Hartford, Conn.: Kumarian Press.

Wahidul, Haque, and others (1977) 'Towards a Theory of Rural Development', *Development Dialogue*. Uppsala: Dag Hammarskjold Foundation.

Wasserstrom, Robert (1985) *Grass-roots Development in Latin America and the Caribbean*. New York: Praeger.

World Health Organization (1982) *Activities of the WHO in Promoting Community Involvement for Health Development*, Geneva.

Yunus, Muhammad (1982) *Grameen Bank Project in Bangladesh: a Poverty-Focused Rural Development Programme*. Dhaka: Grameen Bank.

7 The Changing Role of Economic Planning in Japan

Saburo Okita

THE EXPERIENCE OF ECONOMIC PLANNING IN JAPAN

Although the Japanese government has produced several economic plans since the end of World War II and has an economic planning agency, the Japanese economy is not a planned economy. It is a predominantly private-enterprise economy. Occasionally government intervenes in private activities, but the basic nature of the present Japanese economy is a highly competitive market economy.

Contrary to the prevailing image, Japan today is characterised by keen competition among enterprises, large and small. The market share of companies in various branches of industry is still fluid, and a number of firms have been established since World War II, such as Sony and Matsushita. The private sector is very dynamic, and maintains the flexibility of a competitive market system to a large degree.

There are, however, two conflicting trends in government–business relations. One is the historical role of the government. Nearly a century ago Japan, an economically underdeveloped and industrially backward country, began to modernise. The government strongly backed the modernisation and gave protection, encouragement and inducement to new industries. This paternalistic attitude of the government toward private industry has been diminishing gradually as a result of the rapid expansion and strengthening of private industry. Direct intervention by the government in individual private enterprises is practised to a very small extent in present-day Japan.

On the other hand, there are increasing government responsibilities for preventing unemployment and serious business fluctuations, improving social overhead capital, expanding educational and training facilities, maintaining fair competition, promoting social security, and protecting the environment.

In Japan economic planners have avoided introducing strong planning elements into the private sector and have stated explicitly in their plans that the figures for the private sector are only estimates and that the responsibility for making plans and implementing them rests with the private enterprises themselves. Government plans provide only guidelines for the decisions to be made by private enterprises and the broad outlines of the government policies that will influence industry.

In Japan, however, there is general recognition of the usefulness of planning in a free-enterprise economy. The preparation of the economic plans has had an educational effect on the various ministries, on business, on labour unions, and on the general public.

Economic planners in Japan have emphasised the importance of planning as a guide for making current decisions with long-term ramifications. Such an understanding is especially important for Japan because it was undergoing a far-reaching and rapid structural transformation. Japan was changing from a labour-surplus to a labour-shortage economy, from an economy with a low income to one with a high income, and from one with large premodern elements to one with a modernised economic structure.

It is useful to predict in a government plan the direction of major changes in agriculture, industry, foreign trade, and people's living standards; to indicate possible bottlenecks and imbalances that may arise; and to determine the long-term policies necessary to meet these changes.

The plan also helps individuals and enterprises to evaluate how changes in the national economy will affect them in the long run. Thus the plan introduces macroeconomic concepts into personal thinking and has worked to reduce sharp political differences among the various groups in the Japanese society.

In general, economic planning has not been designed to stimulate rapid growth but rather to attain balanced growth and indicate the long-term economic policy.

ECONOMIC PLANS AND THEIR IMPACT

Since the end of World War II several economic plans with a variety of objectives have been prepared in Japan. Indeed, all of these plans were formulated with a view to securing a continuous increase in per-capita income and achieving a full-employment economy, but they put emphasis on different objectives in accordance with the stages of recovery and development of the economy.

THE NATIONAL INCOME DOUBLING PLAN

Among several postwar plans the most important one was the National Income Doubling Plan. In November 1959 Prime Minister Nobusuke Kishi requested the Economic Deliberation Council (the Secretariat of which was the Economic Planning Agency) to draft a new plan for doubling national income. The council worked out a draft and presented it to the government (Ikeda cabinet) in late 1960 after extensive study. Based on this draft, the government officially adopted the Plan for Doubling National Income in December 1960.

This plan aimed to double the national income within the next decade and set a 7–8 per cent annual growth rate as both feasible and realistic. The plan emphasised five points:

1. *Strengthening of social overhead capital*. With a rapid expansion of the private sector, public facilities such as roads, harbours and water supply had become serious hindrances to further economic growth. It was necessary to restore a balance between the private and public sectors by accelerating social overhead investment. The ratio of investment in basic public facilities to enterprise investment was to be raised from one to three to one to two by 1970.

2. *Inducements to industrialisation*. The plan considered secondary industry the leading sector for growth. It emphasised the growth of the heavy metals, chemical and machinery industries as strategic sectors. Although the attainment of these objectives mainly rested with private business, government provided inducements with special tax provisions and the active use of government financial institutions.

3. *Promotion of exports*. The plan assumed a 10 per cent average annual increase in exports. A high rate of growth for exports was needed to finance imports of raw materials, energy and food as well as increase imports due to liberalisation of trade. The plan assumed that the share of machinery products (including vehicles) in total exports would rise from 24 per cent in 1959 to 37 per cent in 1970.

4. *Development of human ability and the advancement of science and*

technology. The plan emphasised the importance of human factors in economic growth. It assumed an increase in public and private research expenditures from 0.9 to 2.0 per cent of GNP. The plan also set targets for the number of university graduates in science and technology, college graduates in engineering, and vocational trainees.

5. *Mitigation of the dual structure and enhancing of social security*. One of Japan's peculiar characteristics is the co-existence of modern and premodern sectors. There have been wide differentials in wages and income among various sectors of the economy. This structure has, in part, supported the competitive strength of Japan's exports and a high rate of savings, but it is also a source of inequality and backwardness. Moreover, as the economy modernised, it had become a hindrance to higher efficiency and technological progress. Therefore the plan emphasised the importance of mitigating this dual structure.

The plan had several other features. It covered the ten years from 1961 to 1970 and described the long-range prospects of the national economy to facilitate the preparation of individual plans by various government agencies. In this connection a long-range investment programme in the public sector was seen as a useful means for attaining the objectives of the plan.

The plan divided the economy into two sectors: the public sector, for which the government is directly responsible, and the private sector, in which private enterprises have responsibilities and initiatives. The plan for the public sector included an allocation of funds for major public works that linked the long-term economic plan with fiscal budgeting.

Since Japanese planning aims principally at providing guidelines for economic activities to be conducted by private enterprise, the plan did not give detailed targets for every sector of the economy but instead emphasised long-term orientation.

For the first time in postwar planning, problems related to income differentials among different groups of people, differentials between large and small enterprises in productivity and wages, and regional differences in incomes, became important. Following this overall national plan, the government worked out a new regional development plan in October 1962, with one of its major purposes to overcome the excessive differentials in income among various regions of the country.

The importance of the human factor in economic development was also emphasised. A Committee for Education and Training was set up as one of the seventeen subcommittees working on the preparation of the National Income Doubling Plan. In April 1961 the Committee for Development of Human Resources was set up in accordance with the recommendation, included in the National Income Doubling Plan, to undertake further studies in this field. In January 1963 the committee submitted its reports to the government and recommended a labour and education policy for economic development.

RECENT TENDENCIES OF JAPAN'S ECONOMIC PLANS

The Japanese economy has shown a number of changes since 1970. Three may be singled out as being particularly important to economic planning.

The first is a slowing of economic growth. Japan maintained a high growth rate, nearly ten per cent in real terms in and after the late 1950s, but growth slowed in the wake of the first oil crisis in 1973, averaging around five per cent in the 1970s (Table 7.1).

There are many reasons for slower economic growth, which include limitations on energy supplies, insufficient work force, intensified environmental problems, greater limitations on plant location and changes in the growth psychology of society.

The second factor is a change in the relationship between Japan and the world economy. Japan's international position has risen rapidly. Japan accounted for only two per cent of the world's GNP in 1955 but nearly ten per cent in 1980 (Table 7.2). With a growing international interdependence, developments linked to overseas trends in oil, fluctuations in exchange rates, and trade frictions came to affect economic performance seriously.

The third factor is a change in policy priority as the level of national income has risen. Economic independence and a higher standard of living were postwar Japan's primary targets. Seeking examples in America and Europe, Japan aimed to introduce technical innovations in the quest for economic progress. As a result of its unusually fast growth Japan's economic power and living standards have improved rapidly, reaching levels close to those of the United States and European countries. Given that background, non-economic aspects such as maintaining a favourable living environ-

Table 7.1 Japan's economic growth rates since 1970

Fiscal year (April–March)	Real	Nominal
1970	8.3	15.8
1971	5.3	10.2
1972	9.7	16.6
1973	5.3	21.0
1974	–0.2	18.4
1975	3.6	10.0
1976	5.1	12.2
1977	5.3	10.9
1978	5.1	9.5
1979	5.3	7.4
1980	4.6	8.5
1981	3.5	5.7
1982	3.3	5.0
1983	3.7	4.3
1984	5.1	6.7
1985	4.4	6.0
1986	2.6	4.2
1987	4.9	4.8

Source: Economic Planning Agency.

Table 7.2 Major economies' shares of world GNP (per cent)

	1955	1960	1970	1978	1980
Japan	2.2	2.9	6.0	10.0	9.0
United States	36.3	33.7	30.2	21.8	21.5
European Community	17.5	17.5	19.3	20.2	22.4
Soviet Union	13.9	15.2	15.9	13.0	11.6
China	4.4	4.7	4.9	4.6	4.7
World total	100.0	100.0	100.0	100.0	100.0
(billion $)	(1,100)	(1,500)	(3,250)	(9,660)	(12,215)

Source: US President's *International Economic Report* (1977) for 1955–1970 figures and US President's *Economic Report* (1980, 1982) for 1978 and 1980.

ment and improving public welfare have come to assume greater importance.

In 1981 the Economic Council set up a Long-Term Outlook Committee. The committee looked at Japan's economy and society from a long-term perspective and considered the options necessary to cope with problems that will arise in the course of change.

In June 1982 the committee which I chaired presented its report

entitled, 'Japan in the year 2000 – Preparing Japan for an Age of
Internationalisation, the Ageing Society, and Maturity'. The report
regards the rest of the twentieth century as a historic turning point for
Japan's economy and society. It points out that Japan must resolve
many problems in the broad trend toward internationalisation of the
economy and society, ageing of the population, and maturing of the
industrial structure.

CHANGING UNDERCURRENT OF ECONOMIC PLANS

Japan is a country with a free economy where resources are distributed by private companies and consumers conduct transactions
through the market-place. Competition is intense, and the market
mechanism is strong. What role does economic planning play against
such a background? In 1969 the Economic Council set up a committee to study the role to be played by economic planning. The
committee singled out three points. The first role is to enlighten the
public by focusing attention on economic projection. An economic
plan shows a blueprint of a future economy: businesses can map out
their own long-term plans using the economic plan as a yardstick.
The second role is to carry out, as a long-term government promise,
specific policy programmes such as investment in social overhead
capital. The third role is to function as a forum for adjusting conflicting interests. The Economic Council that discusses economic plans
consists of businessmen, labour representatives, journalists and economists. These parties have conflicting interests, but in the course of
discussions they narrow the differences of their views on what Japan's
economy and society should look like in the long run.

WHERE ARE LONG-TERM ECONOMIC POLICIES HEADED?

Industrial Policy

Japan has an industrial structure policy, in which MITI (the Ministry
of International Trade and Industry) has played an important role.
The government continuously discusses which industries should lead
Japan's economic activity at every stage of economic development.
Emphasis was placed on the reconstruction of industries producing

basic materials such as steel and coal in the 1950s and on heavy and chemical industries during the high-growth period in the 1960s. The 'Japan in the Year 2000' report points to 'softwarisation' (a combination of knowledge-intensive and service industries) as a direction in which Japan's industrial structure may move. Such a policy of providing a 'vision' of the future, while leaving structural change basically to the forces of the market, seeks to smooth the process of adjustment. It is designed to help develop industries with growth potential and organise an orderly retreat of industries on the wane.

In the future Japan will continue to encounter industrial adjustments in labour-intensive and basic-material industries due to growing competition from newly industrialised countries. Industrial adjustments in the high-growth period were relatively easy to make because the economy was expanding rapidly, permitting workers of decaying industries to be easily absorbed into growth industries. With slower economic growth industrial adjustments may be harder in the future.

Technological Development

Japan adopted a policy of encouraging technology imports in the 1950s, but as it caught up with Western industrial countries, priority has shifted to self-developed technology. In general the government does not play a major role in technological development. As shown in Table 7.3 the Japanese government shoulders a low rate of expenses to total research and development costs, even excluding spending on defence R & D.

Table 7.3 Government share of research and development costs

	Total R & D spending	Defence R & D costs	Government share	Excepting defence
	(billion yen)		(per cent)	
Japan (1979)	4,063.6	27.6	27.4	26.9
United States (1979)	11,896.2	2,661.0	49.3	34.7
West Germany (1978)	3,185.1	181.5	46.7	43.5
France (1979)	2,240.7	481.6	58.4	47.0
Britain (1978)	1,313.0	371.7	49.2	29.2

Source: Science and Technology Agency: *Handbook of Science and Technology Statistics*.

Japan's technological development has been pushed chiefly by the private sector. It is often pointed out that Japan is weak in the development of fundamental technology and strong in application, or that it is good at improving an acquired technique little by little rather than creating original technology. But the conventional practice of growing in applied areas, while depending on technologies introduced from abroad, will reach its limit in the future. Japan will need to develop original technology on its own.

Financial Policy

Japan's financial policy also faces a major turning point. The wave of internationalisation is spreading to the financial front. Japan has a high savings rate, but it is expected to decline gradually in the future along with the ageing of the population. However, Japan is expected to maintain for some years its relatively high savings rate compared with other industrial nations. As the ratio of economic growth has come down from ten per cent in the 1960s to four per cent in the 1980s, there is a structural surplus of domestic savings which is reflected in the large surplus of Japan's balance of payments. This will mean Japan will become one of the important sources of supplying capital to the world. Japan is expected to move into the exportation of capital, and in the course of this shift capital transactions will be liberalised, causing the domestic financial system to change as well.

8 Project Evaluation as an Aid to Planning: How Successful has the Innovation Been?[1]

Azizur Rahman Khan

INTRODUCTION

During the late 1960s and early 1970s development economics came to put a great deal of emphasis on comprehensive methods of social cost-benefit analysis for the appraisal of investment projects. Project planning was seen as a complement to, even a substitute for, economy-wide planning models that had become fashionable in the fifties and sixties. It was widely believed that these models did not provide adequate guidance for investment decisions. In contrast, it was felt, social cost-benefit analysis of projects held out the greatest promise for efficient investment decisions. The application of the method would not only ensure an efficient allocation of resources: it also emphasised growth by permitting an appropriately high valuation of savings, which were relatively scarce. Moreover, the method was able to take equity into account by assigning distributional weights to benefits accruing to different income and social groups. The purpose of this short paper is to argue that the promise that this innovation held out has been less than fulfilled, and to suggest reasons for this.

THE COMPREHENSIVE COOKBOOKS

Long before the development of the comprehensive methods of social cost-benefit analysis, a body of literature on investment criteria and choice of techniques had been in existence. The main argument of this literature was that in making investment decisions in developing countries the market indicators of profit needed adjustment for some well-known structural distortions in the factor market (and externalities). One such distortion was that wages, especially in the modern industrial sector, seemed to be much higher than what labour produced at the margin. Another distortion was that due to the myopia and the isolated decision making of the private savers, the rate of saving was lower than what would be optimal for the society. Social action was needed to correct these structural distortions and other well-known sources of market failure (e.g. the presence of externalities) that led to a divergence between private and social welfare.[2]

Comprehensive manuals for project evaluation in the developing countries, based on social cost-benefit analysis, were developed in the late 1960s and early 1970s. The two most influential documents, authored by some of the most outstanding economists, were published respectively by the Organisation for Economic Cooperation and Development (OECD) in 1968 (written by Ian Little and James Mirrlees) and the United Nations Industrial Development Organisation (UNIDO) in 1972 (by Partha Dasgupta, Stephen Marglin and Amartya Sen).[3] The two manuals take essentially similar approaches to such important issues as the valuation of labour and savings. The Little-Mirrlees method, however, puts much greater stress on the systematic development of a comprehensive set of shadow prices with special emphasis on correction for the distortions due to non-uniform protection. It also appears to us that their method has been more widely used.

By the time the Little-Mirrlees method was developed, attention had shifted to distortions due to intervention by the government rather than distortions needed to be corrected by government intervention. In the factor market intervention-induced distortions resulted from such measures as minimum-wage legislation, arbitrary fixation of wages in the public sector at very high levels, regulation of interest rates and the rationing of credit. Distortions, however, went far beyond the factor market. Physical controls of various kinds were the main sources of these distortions. Foreign trade was usually subjected to widespread quantitative restrictions in the form of almost universal import quotas and occasional physical limits on exports. Frequently the outcomes were very high and non-uniform rates of effective protection combined with an overvalued rate of exchange. Controls on the prices and distribution of domestically produced goods also were widespread. In such a situation, prices of individual goods and services were so distorted that they were useless as indicators of relative scarcities, and market rates of profit were poor guides to investment decisions.

Comprehensive methods of project evaluation of the Little-Mirrlees type argued for the systematic shadow pricing of all factors of production and produced inputs and outputs. Little and Mirrlees provided the most popular cookbook 'for the concoction of a consistent set of shadow prices'.[4] Although 'the work of Little and Mirrlees puts greater stress on the price distortions arising from excessive protection',[5] it is more than an argument for free trade based on static comparative advantage. It adopts a method of shadow pricing of labour that incorporates considerations of intertemporal distribution and is capable of taking into account the issue of the distribution of current consumption. It was hoped by the authors that comprehensive project evaluation would greatly contribute to an improvement in the productivity of investment and overall economic performance.

ACTUAL EXPERIENCE

For a time it appeared that the hope of institutionalising the social cost-benefit analysis of projects might be realised. Both the multilateral development agencies and planning agencies in individual countries showed interest in adopting social cost-benefit analysis based on comprehensive shadow pricing. With the passage of time it now appears, however, that there has been neither a steady progress nor a sustained interest in this endeavour. Today, two decades after the publication of the Little-Mirrlees *Manual*, interest in comprehensive project evaluation appears to be generally on the wane.

Let us elaborate. The World Bank quickly espoused the system of comprehensive project evaluation soon after the major 'cookbooks' became available. Indeed, it made further investment in the preparation of additional cookbooks that are very much along the lines of the pioneers.[6] Writing as members of the World Bank staff in 1975, Squire and van der Tak, authors of the major World Bank cookbook on the subject, said: 'Although our recommendations do not at this time represent established World Bank practice, the Bank is conducting serious experiments in this area, and its appraisal practices are moving in the general direction advocated in this book'.[7] Contrary to this expectation, in the thirteen years since the statement was made the World Bank does not appear to have made any progress 'in the general direction advocated'. The Bank never fully adopted the social cost-benefit analysis for project appraisal. It tries to estimate 'economic rates of return' of projects and for this purpose it uses some shadow pricing which rarely goes beyond labour and capital and is based on anything but careful estimates. Even this ritual is found by the operational staff of the Bank to be very hard to keep up. The overall performance of the Bank in evaluating projects must be judged to be poor. Not only has it been unable to implement its earlier desire to adopt comprehensive social cost-benefit analysis: its estimates of the economic rates of return at the time of appraisal, which serve as the basis for the approval of project loans, have been relatively poorly correlated with the economic rates of return on completion.[8]

It is difficult to know how many developing countries adopted comprehensive methods of project evaluation and shadow pricing. Writing in 1982 Ian Little was able to name seven countries (India, Bangladesh, Sri Lanka, Kenya, Morocco, Korea and Jamaica) for which 'full sets of shadow prices have at one time or another been worked out'.[9] Even in these countries it does not appear that anything like the Little-Mirrlees method was ever fully implemented. In several of them the estimates of shadow prices were the work of unofficial researchers, not the official planning agencies.

The example of Bangladesh may be of interest. Immediately after the independence of Bangladesh (December 1971) a high-level Planning Commission was set up with Nurul Islam as its head. Among the wide range of activities assigned to the Planning Commission was the task of subjecting all significant investment projects in the public sector to proper evaluation. The Commission took this task seriously and set up a system of project evaluation, based on comprehensive shadow pricing, very much along the lines of the Little-Mirrlees method. Officials of the public sector agencies designing investment projects were provided basic training in the application of the method, which was formally adopted in 1973. Within a few months of its adoption, the method was suspended never to be revived again.

Overall experience in the developing countries has not been very different from what happened in Bangladesh. Few countries ever adopted the method in its entirety. Those which made some effort at implementing it were prompted to do so because of the enthusiasm either of the technical staff of the planning agencies or of their counterparts in the donor agencies. Over time, most of the national and international agencies have come to moderate their enthusiasm for the method. Some degree of ritualistic adherence to the method may perhaps continue to characterise the project approval procedure in some developing countries and international development agencies. But these rituals do not even remotely resemble the careful and comprehensive evaluation of projects recommended by the Little-Mirrlees and UNIDO methods.

AN ATTEMPT AT EXPLANATION

One could think of a number of possible explanations for the failure of the comprehensive systems of social cost-benefit analysis of projects to be institutionalised. One explanation might be based on the notion of passing fads that come to dominate a profession for a period before yielding to changes in fashion. In the decades before the comprehensive methods of project evaluation became available, economy-wide planning models were very much in vogue, but gradually became far less fashionable with the passage of time.

A second possible explanation is the difficulty of applying the method. Estimating a complete set of shadow prices and keeping them up to date are difficult tasks. The operational staff of the World Bank argue that the proper implementation of the method requires far more of staff resources than the Bank is currently committing to the task of designing and evaluating projects. In Bangladesh the main reason cited for the suspension of the method was again the difficulty inherent in its application.

A third possible explanation is the unforeseen volatility that came to characterise international trade soon after the comprehensive methods became available. The more popular of the cookbooks, the Little-Mirrlees method, makes much use of marginal import costs and marginal export revenues as indicators of shadow prices of traded goods. During a period of sharply fluctuating import costs and export revenues both the ease and the utility of monitoring these quantities might have appeared to have greatly diminished.

Each of these explanations might be valid up to a point though it is difficult to see that they amount to a full explanation. Unlike economy-wide planning models, project evaluation constitutes a necessary stage in planning that is carried out routinely. One does it properly or poorly. One does not have the option of avoiding the task altogether. An improvement in the method of evaluation would therefore have a much greater attraction for the planners than a passing fad, especially when the benefits of such improvement are clearly very great. The work involved in comprehensive social cost-benefit analysis of projects is admittedly much greater and more difficult than that in calculating market rates of return. But this hardly constitutes a valid argument for the avoidance of the task when the return from it, in the form of avoiding costly mistakes of going ahead with socially unprofitable projects, is so high. Also various cookbooks have made the task quite manageable. The greater fluctuation in international prices was an unfortunate problem. It underlined the increased uncertainty, but did not invalidate the case for making economic calculations. Thus, without completely rejecting the validity of the above explanations, one would want to look for a fuller understanding of the phenomenon.

We would like to suggest that a major explanation for the failure to institutionalise the comprehensive method of social cost-benefit analysis must be sought in an examination of the reasons behind the distortions that make such an analysis necessary. As mentioned earlier, the comprehensive methods of project evaluation put much greater stress on the distortions caused by government policies compared to that in the earlier literature on investment criteria, which called for government action to make corrections for structural distortions. One should try to understand why governments create distortions before trying to get them to correct for the effects of distortions in the evaluation of public sector projects. Why do governments resort to quantitative control of trade, price and distribution, and numerous direct controls that do not appear to serve any rational purpose? Two alternative reasons that we might consider would be (a) ignorance; and (b) the convergence between the *true objectives* of governments and those that would dictate the adoption of the distortion-creating policies.

In reality, the propensity of governments to adopt (socially) irrational policies may be conditioned by a combination of both factors. For example, ignorance may often lead to the mistaken belief that one's objectives can best be reached by adopting certain irrational policies.

It is useful to illustrate these possibilities, with reference to some obviously irrational policy, e.g. a grossly overvalued rate of exchange sustained by import quotas. It may be due to the genuine, but mistaken, belief on the part of the government that the exports (agricultural products, for example) face an international market in which demand is inelastic. Another possibility is that the government is motivated by an objective that is very different from the ones it publicly professes so that the outcome of the (socially) irrational policy is quite consistent with its true, but unspoken, objective. Thus the true objective may be to generate resources in the hands of the politically powerful trading class[10] through the arbitrary distribution of scarce import entitlement and making the producers of exports, the relatively powerless peasants, suffer an income loss. It is not a particularly noble objective to make its public endorsement worthwhile. It is usually prudent to hide, behind arguments of the supposed inelasticity of export demand, the need for the protection of domestic infants and so on.

If the cause behind policies that result in distortions is ignorance, the use of social cost-benefit analysis to rid project selection of its influence should be unnecessary. It should be possible to persuade the government that the assumptions underlying its policies are incorrect. Else why would it be possible to persuade it to use in its calculations of project profitability a surrogate incentive system that is identical with the state of affairs without the irrational policies? Indeed, it would be a better alternative to educate the government and persuade it to dismantle the irrational policies than to get it to use shadow prices in the evaluation of projects. This is because distorted prices and incentives affect a much wider set of economic decisions than the selection of public sector projects, e.g. the choice of private sector projects. It should be noted that the abolition of the distortion-creating policies would still leave the structural distortions in place. The need for social cost-benefit analysis would therefore remain; but shadow pricing would be limited to the correction of structural distortions.[11]

Unfortunately, too often the reason behind the distortion-creating policies is the second one, that is, the convergence between the true objectives of governments and those that would warrant the adoption of irrational policies. The problem is compounded by the fact that governments usually do not like to admit to true objectives of this kind, preferring to pretend ignorance which no amount of educated argument can help overcome. In this situation to ask a government to adopt a social cost-benefit analysis of project evaluation is to ask it to give up its true objectives. If the government followed this suggestion comprehensively, including applying it to the private sector, the outcome would be identical with the situation in which it did nothing to pursue its true objectives. It would be utterly naive to hope that the government would undo by one hand what its other hand had been busy trying to achieve.

It could be argued that the government might be persuaded to use a social cost-benefit analysis which is limited to the public sector projects because it would still be free to pursue its true objectives with respect to the private sector. In the previous example the private traders, a dominant class with political power, would continue to amass wealth at the cost of the powerless peasants while public sector project selection, guided by shadow pricing, would be free of the distortions of the overvalued exchange rate. One might argue that this would be a more acceptable solution for the government than to give up the entire policy of overvaluing the rate exchange with all its redistributive consequences.

There are serious problems with this formulation. First, distortions will persist in the private sector and to that extent the adoption of the social cost-benefit analysis will do nothing to remove the adverse effects of policy-induced distortions in a part of the economy. More plausibly, the government would not accept such a dual solution because it would amount to the admission that its policies are distorted. It would be far more convenient to appear to be stubbornly ignorant than to admit, even implicitly, that it consciously distorted its policies to benefit powerful classes. Finally, there is little reason to expect that there would be a strong motivation to ensure social profitability in the public sector projects. It is much more likely that the social profitability of these projects, more than that of the private sector projects, would suffer as a consequence of the pursuit of wealth and power by the groups that control the state machinery.

When the enthusiastic professionals at the planning agency try to adopt a comprehensive method of social cost-benefit analysis while the agencies designing and implementing projects create an uproar about the difficulty and complexity of implementing the method, it would be natural for (the political and bureaucratic leadership of) the government to take the side of the latter. The method would be suspended or its implementation would be reduced to a halfhearted ritual. This must be a major explanation of the failure on the part of the professionals to translate their original enthusiasm for the method into actual operational systems of comprehensive project evaluation.

One would still want to know why the international development agencies, e.g. the World Bank, did not pursue the implementation of social cost-benefit analysis more vigorously. The Bank's neglect remains a puzzle. Is the Bank in alliance with the political élites of the borrowing countries? If so, why does it push price and other macroeconomic policy reforms intended to remove government-created distortions? Why is its enthusiasm for the removal of distortions so selective?

Even if it is true that the Bank *appears to try* to remove *all* distortions created by government action irrespective of which income classes they benefit, it is not necessarily true that its actual success in removing distortions is neutral with respect to their redistributive effect. No attempt has ever been made to see if the Bank succeeds as much in removing distortions that benefit the rich as it succeeds in removing the distortions whose benefits are more widely distributed. If indeed its success is heavily biased in favour of the latter, what reason is there to believe that the outcome is not due to the asymmetry of persistence in dealing with the two categories of distortions, e.g. paying lip service to the need to remove controls that redistribute incomes in favour of the rich while throwing all its weight into removing a subsidy that benefits wider groups of people? Systematic use of social cost-benefit analysis to screen out projects that have high rates of market profitability only because they are evaluated on the basis of the distorted prices that reflect government policy to redistribute income in favour of the rich is perhaps a declaration of total war on the government's income distribution objective, a much more serious business than demanding the removal of subsidies, with widely diffused effects, that the government was probably pushed into as a concessionary measure.

It is hard to accept the suggestion that the additional cost of implementing social cost-benefit analysis in evaluating projects would not be money well spent. With the vast financial and staff resources at its command, the World Bank should have found it possible to develop a comprehensive set of shadow prices for each significant borrowing country. A systematic application of the method would have substantially reduced the high proportion of projects that turned out to be unprofitable, provided too little benefits for the poor and produced adverse environmental effects.[12]

CONCLUDING REMARKS

As we have stated earlier, the reality behind the failure of the social cost-benefit analysis to be institutionalised is complex. It is not our intention to deny completely the validity of the usually cited reasons. Nor do we want to suggest that all the distortion-creating policies always end up redistributing benefits only in favour of the wealthy classes. The main point is that the neglect of the analysis of the political economy of the distortion-creating policies has often been the source of the naive hope that the invention of technically sophisticated methods of social cost-benefit analysis would cure the consequences of irrational policies on investment decisions.

Notes

1. Comments and help received from Keith Griffin are gratefully acknowledged.
2. Examples of the literature include Chenery (1953), Dobb (1960), Eckaus (1955), Galenson and Leibenstein (1955), Kahn (1951), Sen (1968) and Tinbergen (1958). Tinbergen (1958) advocated the use of accounting prices in the evaluation of investment projects, but his method was far less comprehensive than the major methods developed in the late 1960s and early 1970s.
3. See OECD (1968), UNIDO (1972) and Little and Mirrlees (1974).
4. The quotation is from Little (1982). He goes on to say: 'The first cookbook available was the Organisation for Economic Cooperation and Development *Manual*'. (p. 129).
5. *Ibid*.
6. See, for example, Squire and van der Tak (1975) and Anandarup Ray (1984).
7. Squire and van der Tak (1975), p. 3.
8. It should be noted that the latter are based on *actual costs* but *projected* benefits, and hence are nothing more than *projections* of the expected actual rates of return. Actual rates of return, i.e. the rates of return after the projects become fully operational, are rarely estimated and compared with the estimates at the time of appraisal.
9. Little, (1982), p. 397 (note 18).
10. In a system of overvalued exchange rate and accompanying protection and import quotas, the trading class is not the only one to benefit. Other recipients of import entitlement, e.g. capitalist farmers importing tractors, industrialists importing machinery, and the domestic producers of import substitutes, also receive income transfers in their favour.
11. Let it be made clear that we do not believe that a serious government can avoid creating distortions. 'Distortions' would be created by most forms of taxation, for example. Our concern here is with the removal of overt distortions that are not necessary for serious and effective governance.
12. The actual effect on the social profitability of overall investment in the recipient countries would still be limited by the consideration of fungibility; countries for which the borrowing from such agencies are rela-

tively small proportions of their total investments would still be able to implement all the projects they desire with low social profitability.

References

Chenery, Hollis B. (1953) 'Application of Investment Criteria', *Quarterly Journal Review (QJE)*, February 1953.

Dobb, Maurice (1960) *An Essay on Economic Growth and Planning*, London: Routledge & Kegan Paul.

Eckaus, R.S. (1955) 'Factor Proportions in Underdeveloped Countries', *American Economic Review*, September 1955.

Galenson, Walter and Harvey Leibenstein, (1955) 'Investment Criteria, Productivity and Economic Development', *QJE*, August 1955.

Kahn, A.E. (1951) 'Investment Criteria in Development Programs', *QJE*, February 1951.

Little, I.M.D., (1982) *Economic Development: Theory, Policy and International Relations*, New York: Basic Books.

Little, I.M.D. and J.A. Mirrlees, (1974) *Project Appraisal and Planning for the Developing Countries*, London: Heinemann.

OECD (1968) *Manual of Industrial Project Analysis for Developing Countries, vol. II, Social Cost-Benefit Analysis*, Paris.

Ray, Anandarup (1984) *Issues in Cost Benefit Analysis*, Washington DC: World Bank.

Sen, Amartya (1968) *Choice of Techniques*, Oxford: Basil Blackwell.

Squire, Lyn and Herman van der Tak (1975) *Economic Analysis of projects*, Washington DC: World Bank.

Tinbergen, Jan (1958) *Design of Development*, Baltimore: Johns Hopkins University Press.

UNIDO, (1972) *Guidelines for Project Evaluation*, New York.

III Rural Development

9 A View of Rural Development, 1980s Vintage (or why some of the Emperor's clothes – and his rice – should be made at home)

Gustav Ranis

INTRODUCTION

We are all aware of the fact that the field of development economics has been subject to extreme fads. In the fifties and sixties, industrial-isation was identified with successful development and the view firmly held by most of the profession, as well as policy-makers, that a rapid drive toward industrialisation could be counted on to drag the agricultural sector along with it. In the early 1970s, under the impact of the oil crisis, combined with a global food shortage, the same policy-makers and analysts finally became aware of the fundamental importance of the agricultural sector, but mainly as a source of food or as a way of substituting for the previous need to deploy scarce exchange for the importation of food in regions which often had been staple exporters before independence.

Since then, the realisation has grown further that it is indeed very difficult, if not impossible, to 'pull' a large agricultural sector into modernity without mobilising its own domestic surpluses and/or foreign exchange earnings, as the case may be, on behalf of the overall development effort. Included in that rediscovery of the im-portance of agriculture was the fact that the individual farmer was by no means an inert, plodding or necessarily non-optimising individual, but that he would respond well, given a reasonably secure price environment and access to information about new technologies and required inputs. Thus, food producing agriculture has been assigned an inreasingly important support role – along with cash crop export agriculture which was never really dethroned as part of the essential fuel for the national development effort. In other words, there now exists more of a recognition that agriculture should be asked to play an important historical role en route to the modern growth epoch.

While there is some recent evidence that the pendulum may be swinging back towards an industry-first strategy – now that the world has experienced a decade of relatively good harvests – this indeed is progress. But what is still missing is the recognition that what needs to be focused on in most LDCs is rural development rather than simply agricultural development, as part of a domestic balanced-growth strategy. In other words, while the traditional compartmentalisation between the rural and the urban sectors, well established during the colonial era, has been modified to some extent by the greater emphasis on domestic food crops, the realisation of the potential importance of rural non-agricultural activities for their own sake as well as for a way to maintain productivity change in agriculture proper is still extremely deficient.

This incomplete conversion to realising the full potential importance of the mobilisation of the rural economy has, of course, been exacerbated by current concerns with the LDC debt crisis, a crisis which fixes attention further on the open economy or enclave dimensions of development. Without deprecating for a moment the importance of exports, both of the traditional agricultural and the non-traditional industrial variety – the latter gaining increasing importance over time – the development literature in recent years has had a very strong bias in favour of examining post-colonial relations with the rest of the world, including trade, capital movements and technology transfers. Debate and analysis have focused attention on the industrial import substitution versus export promotion choice, including much concentration on the terms for the importation of foreign capital and technology, all in support of a shift from an inner- to an outer-orientated development strategy. But it is also fair to say that, in that context, the emphasis has been almost exclusively on how to redeploy agricultural surpluses, both those generated domestically and those generated via the retained proceeds from cash-crop exports, into export-orientated and away from import-substituting types of urban industrial activities. Very little attention has, at the same time, been paid to the locational dimensions of development, specifically to the importance of rural industrial and service activity as a complement to the sustained growth of agricultural productivity. It is this neglect of the sustainability of rural development through more analytical and policy-forming attention being paid to the locational dimension of the overall development strategy on which this paper is focused. And it is indeed most appropriate that such a paper be included in this particular volume, since Nurul Islam is one of the few who has persistently called attention to these matters.[1]

The basic problem that still needs to be fully appreciated is the importance of decentralised industrial and service activities in the rural areas, interacting on the one hand with agriculture and on the other with both urban industry and the rest of the world. Unfortunately, in most of the developing countries I am familiar with, there still exists a profound lack of faith in the capacity of both entrepreneurs and public officials in the rural areas. Even as peasants have finally been given their due under the pressure of the events of the 1970s this has not been accompanied by a similar recognition of the human potential for non-agricultural activity, private and public, existing in the hinterland. This potential can be realised in the context of a sustained development effort which recognises the important spatial dimensions of non-agricultural growth as part of a pattern of vigorous rural balanced growth. Indeed, such balanced growth in the rural areas has to be seen as occurring not at the expense of, but as a necessary support to, the more glamorous and well-recognised international dimensions of development focusing on the generation of labour-intensive industrial exports supported by capital and technology inflows.

Continued failure to recognise these spatial dimensions amounts to a serious handicap in the way of solving the problem of development, which I believe really lies below the surface of the current topical concern with the so-called debt crisis. It should indeed be emphasised here that even in the small East-Asian success stories, e.g. Taiwan, which is usually characterised as an example of a historically successful labour-intensive industrial exporter, what was really critical was the *prior* mobilisation of the rural economy, both agricultural and non-agricultural, as part of a domestic balanced-growth effort. While agricultural productivity increases, initially concentrated in rice and sugar, then in mushrooms and asparagus, provided the main initial engine of growth, it was rural industry and services, both for domestic and, increasingly over time, for the foreign market, which was asked to take the strain. Such rural industry was initially (in the sixties) largely based on agricultural raw materials, but gradually focused more on a subcontracting relationship with imported raw materials-based industries in the export-processing zones and else-where.

What is crucial here, and not yet fully understood, is the import-ance of agriculture and its relations to dispersed rural industry as a key to both successful domestic growth and the export-orientated performance which is so well known internationally. It is worth recalling, for example, that in 1951 only 34 per cent of all the industrial establishments in Taiwan were located in the five largest cities, quite low by LDC standards; but even more spectacular is the fact that this proportion was unchanged in 1971, after two decades of rapid growth which culminated in Taiwan's reaching the end of her labour surplus condition. The proportion of the total number of persons in manufacturing employed in the larger cities actually de-clined from 43 to 37 per cent of the total between 1956 and 1966, while the proportion for services also declined, from 41 to 34 per cent. Employment in rural manufacturing, on the other hand, in-creased from 47 to 52 per cent of the total and that in rural services from 49 to 56 per cent of the total during this decade; the rest were located in small towns.

It is, moreover, fair to say that in most contemporary developing countries, in contrast, colonial or post-colonial compartmentalisation of the economy has been only partially removed. Yet successful development clearly requires the mobilisation of the rural economy as an integral whole in a balanced, persistent and sustained fashion, simultaneously permitting the urban industrial sector to turn outward and begin to make its contribution to the financing of its own future growth through a labour-intensive export diversification drive of major proportions. This second line of approach of a two-pronged development strategy is being increasingly well understood by now; labour-intensive industrial exports, along with the contribution of foreign capital and, hopefully modified, imported technology are required not only to mop up additional unemployment but also so that the constraints imposed on the further growth of the urban industrial sector, – its needs for further capitalisation and/or debt reduction – can be lifted. But the complementary relationship with the first prong is usually ignored. Indeed, the analysis of the spatial characteristics of successful development has not been a prominent part of the development literature and/or policymakers' concern during recent decades: the potential historical role of this sub-sector en route to modern growth has not really been appreciated. It is indeed important not only that people in the rural areas be held in productive employment, both agricultural and non-agricultural, but also that a complementary relationship be established between agriculture and non-agriculture in the rural areas, on the one hand, and between rural and urban non-agriculture, including for export, on the other.

Analysis and policy focusing on this hitherto neglected first line of approach of an efficient development strategy therefore needs to be resurrected if the not uncommon problem of limping growth, along with secularly worsening poverty and income distribution outcomes, is to be addressed. In fact, this fundamental development strategy problem would have to be addressed even if the very topical contemporary debt problem were removed by fiat overnight.

AGRICULTURAL–NON-AGRICULTURAL LINKAGES, RURAL–RURAL AND RURAL–URBAN

The linkages most frequently cited in the literature are those which flow from agricultural to non-agricultural activities, the latter usually not differentiated by urban and rural. The assumption is customarily made that, somehow, agricultural productivity is rising exogenously, for example via increases in physical inputs, technology change and/or organisational change. Given such an exogenous change in agricultural productivity, three kinds of linkages can be identified:

1. Forward consumption linkages.
2. Backward production linkages.
3. Forward production linkages.

The first of these, forward consumption linkages, that is the demand for additional non-agricultural goods as a consequence of exogenous agricultural income change, has been found in all the previous empirical research on the subject to be quantitatively the most important. However, the size of this linkage effect depends crucially not only on by how much agricultural output or income has grown, but also on the distribution of that income, which, in turn, depends on both the initial asset distribution in agriculture, the crop mix in agriculture, and the choice of agricultural technology.

It is quite well understood that some crops are intrinsically more labour-intensive than others, for example asparagus and mushrooms are more labour-intensive than sugar and rice, and that for each and every crop there exists a large number of technology choices on the international shelf and/or resulting from domestic adaptations. The way in which primary incomes are generated in agriculture, due both to original asset distribution and to land tenure configurations, combined with process and product choices, clearly determines where the demand for additional non-agricultural output will make itself felt, such as for mass consumption goods or for luxury goods. Once that demand expresses itself, it either results in new rural linkages, or it is satisfied from production in the urban areas or even abroad, depending on the initial availability of locally-produced consumer goods. The response mechanisms leading to new rural activities are likely to be very positive as long as policy does not in a relative sense discriminate against such activities.

Unfortunately, the history of most non-agricultural activities in the rural areas of LDCs is a sad one. To the extent that such z-goods production existed historically, it was often destroyed by colonial imports – unless it was far enough away from the port cities to be protected by distance and transport costs. Later, during the post-independence import substitution era during which urban industry was definitively favoured it was discouraged even more, a trend which has continued to this day. Thus, while forward consumer linkages are likely to be potentially the strongest in a relative sense, the conditions for a vigorous response in terms of expanding rural non-agricultural activity are likely not to be met in many typically development settings.

The second kind of linkage referred to, the backward production linkage, focuses on inputs into agriculture, the demand for which will presumably rise given the same exogenous increase in agricultural productivity. This is an area in which technology choices with respect to the nature of agricultural implements and other inputs – thus the association between traditional and modern technologies and their respective output-generating as well as labour-absorbing character-istics – comes into play. One important consideration here is the quantity and quality of the R & D structure in existence which feeds in and diffuses the information on the range of potential technology options, i.e. the supply side of technology process and product choices. On the demand side we have the famous degree of distortion of relative factor prices, in addition to the overall macro-economic setting – exchange rates, protection rates, etc. – which affect, of course, not only the prices of alternative input combinations into agriculture but also the extent of workably competitive pressures on the agricultural decision-maker. The most obvious instance is the frequently-found subsidisation of tractors, which in some countries has exceeded the 50 per cent level, affecting the choice between power tillers and tractors for land preparation as well as the technology governing the extensive number of post-harvest operations. These backward production linkages, in other words, may be weak or strong, depending on the overall macro-policy environment as well as the particular institutional infrastructure with respect to R & D and the R & D diffusion and dissemination system. In the absence of decentralised information and an R & D diffusion system, and of realistic relative prices for final goods as well as inputs, the tendency is great for such backward linkages to have a relatively large effect on distant suppliers, including overseas suppliers – and a negligible effect on the growth of complementary non-agricultural input activities in the rural areas.

From the point of view of modernising agriculture through new 'green revolution' types of change in technology, inputs embodying new science and technology may well be an important contribution to additional changes in agricultural productivity. Such inputs can and are likely to be produced in medium-sized towns rather than in villages, but the more 'appropriate' mixes of seeds, fertiliser and so on are also more likely to emanate from within the region rather than from distant urban areas or based on relatively unadapted national or even international research findings.

Thirdly, there is the so-called 'forward production' linkage type, such as food processing, including the canning of cash crops and the processing of food crops. As in the backward production linkage case, what we encounter here is a very large range of alternative technologies. For example, in rice processing the choice often ranges from the deployment of 18–56 man-hours per ton, depending on the specific type of machinery being used. The precise processing choice is, of course, also affected by time or perishability, economies of scale and the quality of the product. But very often, once again, the range of alternative technologies, defined in terms of both process and product, is not widely known or diffused on the supply side, and is very dependent on the kind of macro-policy setting in which the rural economy finds itself on the demand side.

The three linkages referred to above, of which the first is quantitatively the most important at least in the static sense, all run from agriculture to non-agriculture and are fairly well established in the literature – even though they have not been given adequate emphasis in recent years. Also important, but relatively even more neglected, are the linkages which run from non-agriculture to agriculture. These were given some prominence by Ted Schultz, looking at the United States in earlier years, as well as by the so-called Vanderbilt School of Nicholls and Tang, who believed, as we do, that agricultural output is not only a function of physical inputs technology and organisation-cum-tenure arrangements, but also of the proximity in a spatial sense to non-agricultural activities.[2] In other words, the all important 'exogenous' agricultural productivity change which is required to keep the process going through the various kinds of linkages previously referred to, itself needs to be seen as a function, at least in significant part, of non-agricultural activity and its location. But this strand of thought and empirical analysis has virtually disappeared from the literature in recent decades.

Three sub-types of linkages running in that direction may be identified. One, somewhat reminiscent of the aforementioned backward production linkages, relates to the overheads, roads, marketing facilities, etc., which surely affect in a direct way the feasibility of contemplating a gradual but sustained further increase in agricultural productivity. A second sub-type, more subtle, and less frequently referred to in the literature, resides in the intrinsic importance of new consumer goods becoming available. Such a new window of opportunity in the form of non-agricultural incentive goods, either domestic or imported, could provide a powerful additional reason, *ceteris paribus*, for the individual farmer/operator to accept the usually higher risks of a new technology. A third sub-type, even less frequently referred to, even by the Vanderbilt School itself, is the issue of the importance of new investment opportunities becoming available, in a visible and relatively familiar setting, preferably close to home, that is in the rural areas – once again serving to enhance the willingness of farmers to take risks. This third sub-type of non-agriculture-to-agriculture linkage is, particularly in the early stages of development, important before a more sophisticated financial intermediation network is ready to convince farmers to take more 'distant' risks and channel their savings, through an ever more complicated financial intermediation system, to arms' length investors. As long as farmers are still willing to trust only their own family members, which is likely to be a feature of the scene for some time in most developing country contexts, the ability to discern new 'local' investment opportunities, including those via expenditure on education, remains an important source of productivity increase in agriculture at its source.

Thus, in a number of ways, farmers' attitudes towards risk and innovation are very likely to be substantially affected by contracts, via these various linkages, with the rest of the community, in particular various types of non-agricultural rural activity.

In summary, reviewing the bidding in terms of linkages moving from agriculture to non-agriculture and back to agriculture, the potential importance of such location-specific linkages for a virtuous circle of rural balanced growth needs to be more fully appreciated. Their importance may be overstated in the case of relatively small countries or city states, where it is, of course, geographically easier and more likely to have the stimulus come from the urban 'outside', including the rest of the world. But in any country with a significant agricultural hinterland these linkages, and especially their longer-term dynamic impact, must be viewed as a key issue. This has proved to be empirically verifiable, even in the context of the relatively small East Asian success cases of Korea and Taiwan, as their recent development experience has shown (see below).

Proceeding to a more detailed analysis of the make-up of these linkages, let us consider that in most LDCs we are initially faced with a dispersed agricultural population and a relatively concentrated non-agricultural population, including in the rural areas. In the absence of direct government intervention, the location of industry, urban or rural, will then depend on: (a) the size of that population and its dispersal; (b) the extent to which economies of scale play a role in relevant non-agricultural activities; and (c) the topography plus the stock of social overhead capital jointly determining transportation costs. Depending on the relative size of the rural and urban sectors at the outset, the size of the population and its dispersal, and the infrastructure in place, the relative importance of the rural balanced-growth approach as opposed to the export-orientated approach of an 'optimum' development strategy will, of course, differ. But they will both be important. Regardless of such initial typological differences among developing countries, the rural location of industry and its interaction with agricultural output, both food-producing and cash-crop, represents an important and underemphasised dimension of the development process. Neither the overall size of an LDC nor its organisational/political choice between a socialist or market-economy path affect this basic point, as the importance attached to balanced rural growth in both Taiwan and mainland China in recent years has fully demonstrated.

A key indicator of the relative success or failure of the rural

Table 9.1 Comparative indicators

	Non-agri. income share in rural families' total income (%)			Per capita real income growth rate %/year	Income distribution (Gini coefficient)		
	1960	1970	1980	1970–79	1960	1970	1980
Taiwan	32('64)	45	65	8.1	.44	.29	.29('78)
South Korea	–	15	25	7.5	–	.37	.38('76)
Colombia	14('50)	9	–	3.9	.53	.56	.52('82)
Philippines	–	17	16	3.3	.50('61)	.49('68)	.50('77)
Thailand	–	37	38	5.0	.41('62)	.43('68)	–

balanced-growth dimension of successful development is the percentage of non-agricultural income in total rural family income, absolutely and over time. This phenomenon reflects the importance of what has sometimes been termed a 'proto-industrialisation' process in the course of early Western European development (preceding the Industrial Revolution) and also goes under the name of off-farm employment opportunities in the contemporary language of development economics.[3]

Table 9.1 shows the marked difference in this critical statistics across countries and over time. Note, for example, the contrast between Taiwan, on the one hand, and the Latin American representative, Colombia, on the other, with South Korea lagging substantially behind Taiwan, and Thailand doing much better than the Philippines in the South-East Asian context.[4] Not only is the proportion of such non-agricultural activity as a share of total rural income initially absolutely much lower in Colombia and the Philippines, but it is also declining over time, while it is rising continuously in East Asia – even after the end of the labour-surplus condition was reached in the early seventies. We may, of course, expect the proportion of rural non-agricultural in total non-agricultural activity to decline in the modern growth era as economies of scale become much more pronounced, which, along with migration and Engel's Law, is more likely to lead to a higher relative concentration of industry in urban areas. But this modern economic growth phenomenon is representative of an era still not within reach of most of the countries we are considering here.

The comparative strength of the chain of rural linkages which yield such very different results across developing countries, both in terms of the size of non-agricultural rural activities and of aggregative bottom-line performance thus depends on: (a) the initial conditions, including the size of country, the importance of cash crops versus food crops, the size and dispersion of the population, the state of rural infrastructure, etc., already referred to; (b) the extent of equity of the primary distribution of income – a function, in part, of the initial distribution of land and the tenure arrangements in agriculture, and, in part, of the whole array of macro-economic policies of government affecting the realism of both relative input and output prices; (c) the state of the organisational institutional infrastructure with respect to R & D, information dissemination, credit availability, etc; and (d) the extent of workably competitive pressures affecting both sectors of the rural economy.

The relative importance of each of these links, in terms of the strength of the weakest member, of course differs depending on the stage of development. For example, in the early days or, perhaps of more relevance, in today's African or other low-income countries, a standard local market may still be nearly self-sufficient. But even there contact with a neighbouring self-sufficient area becomes increasingly crucial if agricultural and non-agricultural productivity increases are to feed on each other. In later stages the proximity effects of intermediate-sized cities and, ultimately, large cities and even the rest of the world, become more important with respect to the increased availability of new types of incentive consumer-goods but less important with respect to investment opportunities which can be entrusted increasingly to the financial intermediation network.

To measure the results of weak or strong linkages, one could, for each stage of development, for example, compute: (1) the ratio of population in the capital city to the total population, which, taking out the effects of such factors on economies of scale in non-agriculture, can be viewed as favourable if relatively low; (2) the size of small and medium cities' populations over the total population, which, for the same reason, can be viewed as favourable if relatively high; (3) the proportion of non-agricultural GDP generated in urban versus rural areas in comparison with the overall population distribution, with, once again, a higher proportion, *ceteris paribus*, viewed as favourable.

Turning to the important issue of causation, admittedly a tricky business when one deals with a chain of linkages, it seems clear, from work undertaken in the Philippines,[5] not only that forward consumption linkages, agriculture to non-agriculture, make the quantitatively largest contribution overall but also that the non-agriculture to agriculture linkage is of special importance in the poorer upland or rain-fed areas. This is clearly attributable to the more equal distribution of income in such regions as well as the relatively greater importance of linkages running from non-agriculture to agriculture at 'earlier' stages of development.

It is often contended that increasing the relative strength of rural linkages and the resulting balanced-growth process in rural areas may have to be purchased at the expense of a lower overall rate of growth. One need only appeal to the historical postwar experience of Taiwan and Thailand to put this criticism to rest. A high population density by itself is, of course, not necessarily helpful for the modernisation of agriculture or rural balanced growth generally. Static diminishing returns may be seen as likely to be in conflict with the dynamic linkage effects we have been discussing here. For example, Taiwan, an area with one of the highest population densities in the Third World, constitutes an unusually successful case of rural balanced growth. In contrast, Java (Indonesia) and Bangladesh, with an even higher population density, have achieved a much less satisfactory record of rural mobilisation. A high density of population can contribute to the successful transformation by converting a higher percentage of the rural population into non-agricultural producers, thus adding to the growth of standard market areas, as a larger volume of dualistic exchange on a per capita basis takes place. As the rural population becomes urbanised, in the sense of smaller towns growing up as counter-magnets, the area of the individual standard market ultimately begins to shrink because of the increasing relative importance of transport costs as compared to scale economies. In the case of Taiwan, for example, as agricultural labour productivity continued to zoom, this brought about a spatially dispersed industrial location which, in turn, ultimately generated increased linkages between the rural and urban populations, including via the export processing zones, because of the high volume of low-cost tradeables produced.

On the other hand, if agricultural productivity is relatively low, given an economy's initial conditions, it probably leads to a relatively large market area and a relatively low volume of dualistic exchange. This, in turn, is likely to reinforce agricultural stagnation because it is not conducive to rural–urban interaction. Economies of scale may at some point become sufficient to compensate for the higher transport costs of locating industry in the towns or ultimately even in the large cities.

In summary, the linkage between agricultural and non-agricultural activities thus has important spatial dimensions traceable to population size and dispersion, the scale economies of non-agricultural production, and transport costs. The gradual conversion of rural agriculturalists and non-agriculturalists into modern economic agents, aware of the potential of new agricultural and non-agricultural technologies, experiencing wider consumption horizons and aspiring to accumulate new kinds of assets, can be accomplished only through the strengthening of linkages with small towns and, ultimately, urban centres. A modern farmer or modern industrial entrepreneur is bound to become increasingly aware of the possibilities of carrying out all kinds of exchanges, not only with one another, but increasingly with far-away places, including even world markets. But a critical point is that he can start moving by dint of strengthened rural linkages and moving on from there rather than treading water within a compartmentalised set of relations, with resource flows riveted on import-substituting industrial production targets and/or foreign markets. In other words, our spatial perspective permits us to see that such compartmentalisation, usually inherited from colonialism, tends to restrict modernisation to the export-orientated enclave, which customarily touches only a small portion of the population, leaves much of potential agricultural and non-agricultural activity to one side and thus fails to make its human as well as fiscal contribution to the development process.

When a developing country is small, the task of transition into modern growth is relatively easier because the country can follow the option of attempting to achieve development mainly via the opportunities of foreign trade, foreign capital, and foreign technology – though this may not necessarily be optimal even in that situation. But as soon as there exists a substantial hinterland it is clearly sub-optimal to rely excessively on exchanges with far-away and foreign urban centres. While farmers can and should take full advantage of international trade, for example the asparagus, mushrooms and pineapples of Taiwan, which, incidentally, made these farmers just as entrepreneurial as the industrial exporters of Hong Kong, this can only be a part of a successful development story. The experience of both Taiwan and mainland China has shown that there indeed exist linkages through dualistic exchange between agricultural and non-agricultural activities which can be crucial to the chances of achieving sustained growth.

Let us finally turn to the kinds of policies, both macro and organisational-institutional, which are at the government's disposal in the event that it should seek to strengthen the various crucial links in the development chain as outlined here.

PUBLIC POLICY OPTIONS

In light of our earlier analysis, it should be clear that paying attention to balanced rural growth means that the seemingly inevitable primary import substitution sub-phase of development, with all its well-known interventions, should be kept relatively brief and relatively mild. This was certainly the case in East Asia and permitted a good deal of attention to be paid to the rural economy even during this relatively industry- and inward-orientated sub-phase of development. More importantly, once the inevitable export orientation sub-phase begins, a developing country will be much better off, to the extent that it does not unduly rely on continued import substitution of the secondary variety, coupled with export promotion, in contrast to the more market-orientated export substitution strategy, shifting from land-intensive to labour-intensive exports. The extent to which that second approach of the development process is utilised then makes the task for the complementary rural balanced-growth approach substantially easier, since the continued massive distortion of factor and commodity prices, protectionism, exchange rate overvaluation, etc., clearly hurt the domestic agricultural sector by taxing it 'under the table', discouraging competitiveness and maintaining the early colonial and post-colonial habits of compartmentalisation.

Macro-policy-related distortions, which weaken rural linkages, include the customary system of import licensing biased towards urban industry; credit markets similarly characterised by tight credit rationing in favour of urban industrial activities; tax incentives which usually are available only to firms with direct access to civil servants at the centre; exchange-rate overvaluation; direct interventions in the internal terms of trade; plus other direct allocations of rationed scarce resources that are familiar to the reader as part and parcel of the normal import substituting policy package. Less well-known but undoubtedly as important are the organisational/institutional features of the landscape, which usually serve to conspire against the building up of a sufficiently strong set of linkages in the rural areas, as well as, later, between urban industrial activities. These include the usually relatively meagre allocation of infrastructural and other public goods to the rural areas and are further reinforced by the precise composition and quality of the overheads placed there, that is, usually focused on assuring the supply of cash crops for export and luxury agricultural goods for the urban enclave, rather than on the mutual reinforcement of agricultural and non-agricultural activities in the food-producing hinterland. Most frequently, this requires a shift from the construction of main highways from ports to mining areas towards farm-to-market roads as a priority activity.

Similarly, the R & D institutional infrastructure and annual allocation systems are customarily focused very much on the same export-orientated cash crops rather than on the food crops; with respect to R & D for non-agriculture, whatever little public sector expenditure takes place here, it is likely to be focused on manufactured exports.

Finally, in addition to having a subsidised, heavily rationed credit system, not equally accessible to small-sized rural agriculturalists and industrialists, there is the frequent dearth of institutional or banking 'fingers' in the rural areas capable of reaching the dispersed population and thus preventing any deepening of financial markets. It almost goes without saying that the proximity to modern inputs, fertiliser, seeds, as well as access to new information embodied in either foreign or domestic technology, is likely to be very unequal, especially within the agricultural sector, along with the aforementioned access to credit. In most cases I am familiar with, to the extent that there is a meagre overall allocation of resources to the rural areas, priorities as to where public goods are to be allocated are most usually set by the central authorities. This is all part and parcel of the usual lack of confidence in rural actors, public and private, in sharp contrast to the rhetoric frequently invoked.

To sum up, when dealing with rural development as part of the overall effort at transition to modern growth, both analysts and policy makers must begin to think of agricultural productivity as a function not only of conventional inputs and technology but also of linkage variables as we have defined them here. In explaining differences in total factor productivity across villages in the Philippines, for example, we found labour inputs, a conventional input, to be significant, along with extension expenditures.[6] But equally significant were such variables as roads per hectare (directly related), the average distance to the nearest urban centre (inversely related) and the number of modern non-agricultural establishments within the same village (directly related). These results fit the notion that investment and consumption incentives in nearby non-agriculture help explain the famous 'residual' in agriculture.

Similarly, with respect to non-agriculture, in addition to conventional inputs and technology change, more attention must be given to explaining differential performance, especially in rural industry, in terms of both process and product choices related to linkage variables. Earlier work, for example contrasting the experience of Taiwan and the Philippines in pineapple processing and canning,[7] supported the notion that a concentrated industry choice (Philippines) had a much smaller impact on both cash-crop and food-crop production in the area, as compared to Taiwan where 23 dispersed national firms did a good deal of subcontracting. As a consequence, the capital/labour ratio for pineapple processing in the Philippines was from two to six times higher than that in Taiwan. Instead of reaching out only to the pineapple plantations in a vertically integrated set-up, as is typical of the post-colonial enclave, with minimum impact on the surrounding countryside, the Taiwan organisation affected large numbers of smallholders and led to a much more equal distribution of income, of substantial consequence in terms of the kinds of demand for industrial goods which were generated. The same sort of contrast can be found in the area of rice milling where we were able to compare and contrast the choice of technology in the concentrated large-scale public sector mills of the Philippines with the smaller-scale and much more labour intensive dispersed private mills of Taiwan.

Both the choice of suitable processes and appropriate goods in terms of the specifications for milled rice and for the non-agricultural goods purchased out of increased agricultural incomes can thus show marked differences across developing countries. Public policies which not only reduce the macro-economic distortions so frequently referred to but also concentrate on shifting public goods expenditures from the support of urban industry to strengthening the various links in the rural balanced growth chain can be expected to be highly effective. They will, in fact, make it possible not only for the rural balanced-growth approach of a successful development effort to go forward but also, by doing so, accelerate the much-needed complementary labour-intensive export orientation drive, en route to mopping up the system's labour surplus and entering the era of modern growth.

Notes

1. See for example, his 'Non-Farm Employment in Rural Asia: Issues and Evidence' in Shand (ed.), *Off-Farm Employment in the Development of Rural Asia*, National Center for Development Studies Conference, Australian National University, 1983 (published in 1986).
2. T.W. Schultz, *The Economic Organisation of Agriculture*, New York: McGraw-Hill, 1953; W. Nicholls, 'Agriculture in Regional Economic Growth' in C. Eichner and L. Witt (eds), *Agriculture in Economic Development*, New York: McGraw-Hill, 1964; A. Tang, *Economic Development in the Southern Piedmont*, Chapel Hill: University of North Carolina, 1958.
3. See Franklin Mendel's 'Proto-Industrialisation: The First Phase of the Industrialisation Process', *Journal of Economic History*, vol. 32, March 1982, and various working papers by Carl Liedholm et al, Department of Agricultural Economics, Michigan State University.
4. See also Harry Oshima's comparative work on monsoon agriculture in Asia, e.g. 'The Significance of Off-Farm Employment and Income in Post-War East Asia Growth', Asian Development Bank *Economics Papers* no. 21, 1984.
5. Gustav Ranis, Frances Stewart and Edna Angeles-Reyes, *Linkages in Development: A Philippine Case Study*, International Center for Economic Growth, (to be published).
6. Ranis et al., op. cit.
7. G. Ranis and F. Stewart, 'Rural Linkages in the Philippines and Taiwan', in Frances Stewart (ed.), *Micro-Policies for Appropriate Technology in Developing Countries*, Boulder, Colorado: Westview Press, 1987.

10 Poverty and Development: Prospects and Priorities for the 1990s

John W. Mellor[1]

INTRODUCTION

The decade of the 1980s marked an unfortunate set-back in the effort to eradicate poverty and hunger in developing countries. Rapid growth throughout the sixties and seventies gave way to stagnation in the eighties as massive structural imbalances were generated out of a combination of underlying economic forces and often misguided economic policies. The interaction of a series of oil shocks, rapid growth in the Third World's foreign debt, high real interest rates, depressed primary commodity prices, increasingly distorted prices in many developing countries, and grossly unbalanced public budgets combined to distort seriously the functioning of the world economy. The major restructuring of policies and economies that followed in both developed and developing countries further slowed growth, the cost of which was borne most heavily by the Third World's poor through lower incomes and consumption of food.

While adjustments to these problems are well under way, the prospects for the alleviation of poverty and hunger in the 1990s are currently overshadowed by pessimism growing out of the economic turmoil of the 1980s and from the view that Third World growth is largely dependent on capital goods imports financed by exports to the mature economies in developed countries. Slow growth and in-creased trade restrictions in the developed countries, and the massive foreign debt of a substantial number of developing countries limits the availability of foreign exchange to finance capital goods expansion, and opportunities for Third World countries to base their growth substantially on foreign markets.

A different and more optimistic view of the prospects for developing countries in the 1990s arises with the recognition that economic growth is basically a process of technological development that raises factor productivity. That provides the basis for rapid increases in national income which, in turn, stimulate other sectors which may have fewer opportunities to benefit directly from modern technology. Productivity-increasing technology, in turn, is the result of human capital formation and the development of institutions that can effectively mobilise that human capital for productive purposes. An important example of those processes is in the development of the research institutions responsible for generating modern agricultural technology.

Recent global imbalances have largely overshadowed these processes in developing countries. And yet, underlying the distortions of the past decade has been continued growth in developing countries' stock of human and physical capital, and improvements in institutional structures. These changes provide a framework for tremendous strides in the 1990s towards renewed economic growth and, more importantly, towards abolishing poverty and hunger throughout most of the Third World.

In low-income countries dominated by agriculture, growth in a large domestic market is only possible if incomes are rising in the agricultural sector. Therefore, technological change in agriculture, which boosts production, incomes and consequently demand in rural areas, is central to a strategy that produces high rates of economic expansion and broad participation in the development process. By spreading productive resources over the largest possible segments of the population, such a strategy creates large, direct increases in agricultural employment and incomes. More importantly for poverty reduction, the linkage and multiplier effects of agricultural growth, by generating increased demand for labour-intensive goods and services produced in the non-agricultural sectors, indirectly stimulates further employment and income growth throughout the economy.

The prospect of growth in the 1990s offers a significant opportunity to reduce hunger and poverty in developing countries. It requires cost-reducing technological change in agriculture. Also, if agricultural development is truly to make a widespread impact on poverty, the rural sector must be integrated into the larger economy through increased investment in infrastructure and services that promote farmers' adoption of that technology. Specifically, because of the commercial process involved in rural growth, those rural people not connected with effective infrastructure – particularly roads – cannot participate in and contribute to growth. Thus the whole rural area must be covered with adequate roads and other key infrastructure that require immense investment.

Efforts must also be undertaken to promote a climate of open trade among countries and to confront the problem of increasing instability in global agriculture. Finally, to make all this possible, the enlightened and coordinated participation of foreign donors is required. Foreign assistance, which is so susceptible to changing fads in development practice that can limit its potential impact, must be explicitly directed toward a strategy that uses agricultural development to foster and accelerate a broadly participatory process of growth. The remainder of this paper discusses each of these priorities in greater detail.

ELIMINATING HUNGER

Hunger as a proportion of the total population has been declining in developing countries in recent years; however, its absolute size has grown rapidly, by as much as 14 per cent over the 1970s (Tables 10.1 and 10.2). According to World Bank calculations, in the middle-income developing countries, the absolute number of the hungry dropped by nearly a half from 1970 to 1980, while in the low-income countries the numbers increased by more than half. In regional terms, absolute levels of hunger have grown most rapidly in Africa and South Asia. By 1990, an estimated 700 million people in developing countries will lack the food sufficient for a healthy, active life. Of those, about 350 million will be in South Asia, 140 million in Africa, and 75 million in China. The remaining 135 million will be about half in Latin America, with the rest in East Asia and the Pacific, and North Africa and the Middle East. The methodology used by the World Bank probably overstates the decline in poverty in the middle-income countries, particularly those with initially highly skewed income distribution. But the numbers do at least indicate very divergent potentials to reduce poverty through growth in the middle- and low-income countries.

Two conclusions follow immediately from these observations. First, intense hunger is increasingly a problem of the poorest countries, largely those in Africa and South Asia, suggesting that a

Table 10.1   Projected incidence of undernutrition, 1990 (millions)

	Total	Low-income countries	Middle-income countries
Africa	137	99	38
South Asia	350	350	–
East Asia/Pacific	31	–	31
Latin America	72	2	70
Near East	34	4	30
China	76	76	–
Total	700	531	169

Note: The estimated incidence of hunger in 1990 is calculated using the proportions undernourished in 1979–81 as reported by FAO (1985) and the projected population for 1990 as reported in World Bank (1988). The breakdown of the Far East into South Asia and East Asia/Pacific is on the basis of the distribution of poor in the two areas as given in World Bank (1986). Estimates on China are based on Riskin (1987). Division on the basis of low-income and middle-income is by the distribution of population in the two groups in each region. Incidence of poverty among low-income countries is assumed to be double that in the middle-income countries and this proportion is applied to each region specific number. Low-income countries are those with per capita income of $400 or less in 1983. Given the various assumptions in the calculations both in the original estimates and the projections, the numbers should be seen as broadly indicative, and not definitive.

general resource scarcity may be a major source of poverty. Second, given the experience of the middle-income countries, economic growth, albeit of a poverty alleviation orientation, is capable of producing major reductions in hunger.

However, large surpluses of food in the developed countries and in a few developing countries that were formerly deficient in food, have led some to the incorrect conclusion that poverty and hunger are problems not of production, but of distribution (Sen, 1981). But, because poor countries are generally short of resources themselves and the proportion of their population that is poor is very large, such redistribution would have to be substantially international. And it would have to grow enormously over time as the number of poor in the slow-growth countries continued to increase rapidly.

While reducing the number of poor purely through unending international redistribution is unlikely, reducing their number through economic growth can be highly effective, with considerable

Table 10.2 Changes in the prevalence of energy-deficient diets, 1970 to 1980

	Percentage change in share of population	Percentage change in number of people
Developing countries	−2	+14
Low-income	+3	+54
Middle-income	−9	−44
Sub-Saharan Africa	+4	+49
East Asia/Pacific	−14	−57
South Asia	+2	+47
Middle East and North Africa	−14	−68
Latin America, Caribbean	−4	−21

Note: The norm used is a calorie level which the World Bank defines as the benchmark below which there is 'not enough intake to prevent stunted growth and serious health risks'. The FAO in the Fifth World Food Survey shows somewhat different trends in that the proportions of hungry people declined in all regions, though for the least-developed countries as a group the proportions increased. It should be noted that not only is the FAO methodology different but their definitions of the regions are also not identical to those of the World Bank, e.g. the FAO does not separate out the poorer regions of South Asia from South-East Asia, aggregating them together as the Far East so that the disparate trends within the region are obscured. Nor do they separate out Sub-Saharan Africa from North Africa. Since we are interested in separating out the economically different regions, we use the World Bank trends. China is not included in the analysis.
Source: World Bank (1986).

scope for further progress. The reduction of poverty in the middle-income developing countries, such as in Latin America and East Asia, has been achieved largely in rural areas that are highly responsive to production-increasing agricultural technology, for which the employment multipliers are substantial both within agriculture and in the rural non-agricultural sector. While the number of poor in high-potential rural areas have been declining rapidly in the middle-income countries, that is not the case in the poorest countries. Some 250 million of the poor in low-income countries are still located in those high potential areas (Table 10.3). These data suggest that agricultural growth in those high-potential regions may be particularly effective in bringing about substantial future reductions in poverty and hunger in low-income countries.

Income growth from technological change in the high agricultural

Table 10.3 Rural–urban distribution of poverty and the estimated number of people living in areas of high potential, 1990 (millions)

	Total	Urban	Rural	Agricultural potential High	Low
Africa	137	14	123	61	62
South Asia	350	70	280	140	140
East Asia	31	5	26	6	20
Latin America	72	29	43	11	32
Near East	34	–	–		
China	76	–	76	26	50

Note: The distribution by rural and urban classification is based on a survey of country poverty studies. All poverty in China is grouped under rural poverty. There are indications that there is little malnutrition in urban areas but this should not be seen as a statement on the absence of poverty in urban China, rather a reflection on the paucity of definite data. All numbers are tentative and should be seen as merely indicative.

potential regions creates substantial employment multipliers within agriculture as well as in the rural non-agricultural sector. These effects are especially pronounced in the development of smallholder agriculture. Poor farmers spend as much as 40 per cent of their additional income on locally produced, labour-intensive non-agricultural goods and services and another 20 per cent on livestock and horticultural commodities that are also produced labour-intensively (Hazell and Roell, 1983). That increased spending provides for expanded employment in those regions and is responsible for a pronounced decline in the number of poor.

In addition, vigorous growth in the high agricultural potential regions can do much to alleviate poverty problems for the more than 25 per cent of the hungry located in urban areas, by alleviating the pressures of poverty through reduced migration. Good performance in the high potential areas and their urban enclaves also allows for increased migration from low potential rural areas, raising incomes in those regions by reducing stress on their resource base. In some cases, advances in technology might also be applied to low potential areas to transform them into high potential areas.

A critical component of a strategy to reduce poverty and hunger is the expansion of rural infrastructure. Rural roads, irrigation and drainage systems, communications networks and delivery systems are necessary to integrate farmers into outside markets for both modern inputs and their increased output. In parts of Africa, the scarcity of rural roads has produced marketing margins that are as much as four times higher than those in Asia, thereby increasing costs and limiting the potential for growth (Ahmed and Rustagi, 1987). Improved infrastructure also accelerates the growth of technology use and paves the way for linkages and multipliers to expand growth and eliminate poverty throughout the economy. In Bangladesh, for example, areas with good infrastructure use 92 per cent more fertiliser per hectare than areas with poor infrastructure. The linkage effects of that growth can produce a level of non-agricultural employment as much as 30 per cent higher than the poor infrastructure areas and wage rates as much as 30 per cent higher (Ahmed and Hossain, 1987).

Infrastructure investment also provides a vital link between the long-term, self-reliant removal of hunger, and short-term amelioration. Rural public works schemes to build infrastructure provide immediate increases in employment and are clearly the best proved means of targeting food and income to the poor. However, such efforts must not be driven so much by immediate employment objectives that they fail to provide the larger permanent employment multipliers of which they are capable. Roads must be of an all-weather type which, in Bangladesh for example, means they should be paved, if they are to fulfil long-term development objectives. The budgets of these projects should not be so dominated by the food component for labour that resources are not available for materials to build permanent establishments.

HUMAN CAPITAL AND INSTITUTIONAL DEVELOPMENT

Because the agricultural sector is subject to Ricardian diminishing returns, increased production can only be stimulated by increases in output per unit of input which, in turn, can only be obtained through technological change (Mellor, 1985). If attempts are made to stimulate production through higher prices, for example, the inelastic supply of land causes the productivity of other inputs gradually to decline. Unlike the response to price, the production response to the investments that embody technological change may be elastic or at least only moderately inelastic (Lele and Mellor, 1988).

Fully realising the benefits provided by agricultural research, however, requires lumpy investments of resources on a scale which small farmers cannot mobilise. A great deal of such investment must inevitably be undertaken by the public sector, at least at the initial stages of development. Whereas economies of scale do not necessarily obtain in agricultural production, they do hold in the provision of services such as research, input supply, and marketing. For example, Lele and Myers (1987) stress the importance of public sector investments in the processing of smallholder tea and coffee in Kenya and especially of Kenya's 'tea roads' in the production of those crops since the 1960s. However, because of their relative inability to mobilise capital and labour, obtain purchased inputs and gain access to knowledge, yields of smallholders were half those of large-scale producers in tea and 80 per cent lower in coffee production. In Cameroon, SODECOTON, a public sector organisation that provides access to technology and services for cotton producers, increased returns to labour use in that crop beyond the already high wages in the non-agricultural sector. The services provided by that organisation explain Cameroon's increased production in spite of an output price environment much less favourable than in countries that have done much less well in cotton production (Lele et al., 1988).

Of course, the basis of success in technological and institutional development rests largely on the rate of human capital formation. Agricultural research and service institutions and the management of rural public works programmes all require large numbers of people with highly developed technical and administrative skills. In addition, well-educated farmers benefit more from a good technical extension system than poorly-educated farmers. For example, complex management systems associated with raising cross-bred livestock, which are usually more productive and profitable than traditional breeds, require well-educated farmers for their adoption (Alderman, 1987; Mergos and Slade, 1987). Higher levels of education are thus necessary to the growth of a technically efficient livestock industry. While, in the short-term, technical assistance from the developed countries can be very influential in moving these processes forward, increased investment in education is vital to the long-term growth prospects of developing countries. And growing human capital must be mobilised into productive systems by effective institutional structures, which themselves require high-level human capital in the provision and use of foreign technical assets.

AGRICULTURAL TRADE

Development must largely be driven by growth in domestic demand generated out of the processes of technological and institutional development described above. With few exceptions, it cannot be led by export growth in the sense that the bulk of the demand for increased output from a developing country comes from abroad. Nevertheless, trade is extremely important to the development process. Because of the high elasticity of demand for food among the poorest in developing countries, once they accelerate their growth substantially, even their best efforts in the agricultural sector cannot keep up with the domestic growth in demand for food. Thus, trade is needed to facilitate the import of basic food staples, including cereals and vegetable oils, into developing countries. Equally important, if developing countries are to grow rapidly, they must spread their own capital resources across a high proportion of their labour force. This means they cannot concentrate on capital-intensive industries like steel, petrochemicals and fertiliser. They must import those capital-intensive goods and services as well.

Agriculture itself can play an important role in meeting the export needs to pay for those imports. The opportunities are particularly great in labour-intensive agricultural commodities like fruits, vegetables, and certain types of livestock commodities. In fact, developing countries have been increasing market share in horticultural trade and experiencing high growth rates of export – despite current trade policies in developed countries that limit incentives to developing country farmers – illustrating how large potentials in those commodities are (Islam, 1988).

Three further points on trade must be made clear. First, successful rural development efforts create broad-based internal markets that, in turn, can strengthen developing-country agricultural trade performance. Rising incomes create a dynamic structure of demand in developing countries, increasing domestic consumption of diverse foods including horticultural and livestock products which provides further stimulus to the export sector. Second, efforts to exploit the trade potential in developing countries require a strong research effort both to reduce costs in production of these crops and to develop new export markets. Third, and finally, eliminating trade restrictions in developed countries is essential in providing added incentives for small farmers to expand their production. Liberalisation of world markets can eventually contribute to increased trade on

Table 10.4 Changes in the coefficients of variations of world cereal
production, 1960/61–1970/71 to 1971/72–1982/83[a]

| Cereal | Coefficient of variation of production (per cent) | | |
	First period	Second period	Change
Wheat	5.46	4.83	−11.5
Maize	3.29	4.41	34.0
Rice	3.97	3.80	−4.3
Barley	4.81	7.50	55.9
Millets	7.78	7.66	−1.5
Sorghum	4.75	5.70	20.0
Oats	11.30	5.35	−52.6
Other cereals	4.57	9.22	104.2
Total cereals	2.76	3.40	21.7

[a] Does not include China.
Source: Hazell (1988).

the basis of comparative advantage that benefits both developed and
developing countries (Mellor, 1989).

AGRICULTURAL INSTABILITY

The world has experienced rapidly increasing instability in cereal
production in recent years. The coefficient of variation of total world
cereal production rose from 2.8 to 3.4 per cent between 1961/71 and
1972/83, an increase of 22 per cent (Table 10.4). Most of that increase
was accounted for by increasing variability in maize, barley, and
some other cereals. On the other hand, it appears that sizeable
increases in world wheat and rice production were not accompanied
by significant increases in instability.

Increasingly, production instability can be attributed to factors
associated with modern seed/fertiliser technologies. A country's production of a particular crop may be dominated by varieties from a
single parent, increasing the entire crop's susceptibility to particular
disease outbreaks. An extreme example was the devastation to the
United States' corn crop in 1970 caused by the southern corn leaf
blight (Figure 10.1). Susceptibility to that disease was limited to only
a few related hybrids which, unfortunately, were in wide use at the

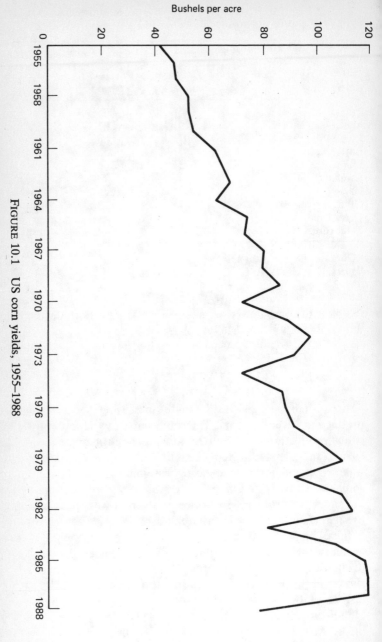

FIGURE 10.1   US corn yields, 1955–1988

Source: USDA (1988).

Note: The downward fluctuation in corn yield in 1978 was due primarily to widespread corn blight. Since then, most fluctuations can be attributed to severe weather conditions.

Table 10.5 Changes in coefficients of variation of world and national cereal prices,[a] 1961/71 to 1974/81, per cent

	Wheat		Rice		Maize	
	1961/71	*1974/81*	*1961/71*	*1974/81*	*1961/71*	*1974/81*
World	4.05	20.50	17.76	28.16	7.37	12.35
France	3.02	2.41			2.51	4.27
United States	15.03	20.20	2.56	20.29	7.98	16.77
Mexico	2.92	5.47			7.60	10.03
India	9.89	7.20	22.36	11.10		
Japan	3.37	8.39	13.50	4.24		
Canada	7.37	20.06				
Turkey	2.67	25.48				
F.R. Germany	2.92	3.00				
United Kingdom	2.68	4.78				
Italy	2.53	3.43				
Pakistan	7.84	8.11				
Argentina	24.58	50.17			23.15	33.05
Brazil			13.75	18.69	5.04	26.07
Yugoslavia					18.07	14.00
Kenya					10.91	10.00
Burma			2.54	0.66		
Philippines			12.57	4.17		
Colombia			14.05	9.32		

[a] Variation represented by fluctuations in prices around trend of the periods indicated.
Source: Hazell (1988).

time of the blight (Hargrove, Coffman and Cabanilla, 1979).

In addition to the widespread adoption of relatively few varieties, and in the developing countries especially, policies affecting the availability of fertiliser, electricity and water inputs can also affect production stability. Changes in those policies can have a large and unfavourable impact on production which becomes more and more dependent on the supply of those inputs with the increased adoption of new technologies.

As seen in Table 10.5, increasing price instability has accompanied greater production instability between 1961/71 and 1974/81. The coefficients of variation for world prices for the two periods increased 400 per cent for wheat, 59 per cent for rice and 67 per cent for maize. Many countries, however, have been able to insulate their domestic prices from fluctuations in world prices. Countries in the European Community have been particularly successful in that regard. Other

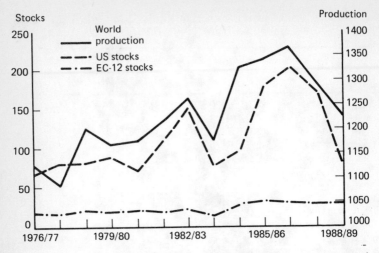

FIGURE 10.2   Responsiveness of US and EC-12 wheat and coarse grain stocks to world production, 1976/77 to 1988/89 (million metric tons)

Note: Data for 1988/89 based on USDA projections as of 11 August 1988.

Source: USDA (1988).

countries, like the United States, Canada and Argentina, on the other hand, have shown greater variability in their domestic prices.

Studies argue that the European Community's storage policies have actually exacerbated market instability (Koester and Valdes, 1984). The European Community relies mainly on trade to stabilise its domestic markets. On the other hand, in the face of increasing world production, the United States has historically increased its own stocks, limiting the potential decline in international prices (Figure 10.2). By extending price support loans to encourage farmers to store part of their output for extended periods of time, policies explicitly encourage food stockpiling during periods of low demand and/or high production, in order to make such stocks available when production declines or export demand increases. However, market-competitive actions authorised in the US 1985 Food Security Act have drastically reduced the level of carryover stocks of all major grains. The 1988 drought has accelerated the drawing down of US stockpiles, undermining the country's ability to be a stabilising influence on world markets. The US Department of Agriculture estimates a 56 per cent drop in US cereal stocks from the end of 1987 to the end of 1988 (USDA, 1988).

Instability in agriculture reduces and destabilises incomes and consumption in developing countries, a burden that is borne especially by the most poor. In India, for example, a 10 per cent reduction in supplies of food-grains results in reduced consumption of as much as 37 per cent for the poorest segments of the population, compared to only 8 per cent by the wealthiest (Mellor, 1978).

The impact of that instability makes it politically difficult for developing country governments to undertake a growth strategy based on increased production in agriculture. While most countries should be able to deal with instability by building stocks sufficient for a single poor year, the cost of providing for two successive bad years through a stocking policy is prohibitive. Therefore, a strategy of agriculture-led growth requires a broader scheme to deal with the threat of production instability.

Open international markets are the most effective way to deal with more severe shortages. But again, for developing countries to be able to import needed food supplies to provide stability, they must have access to markets for their own exports. Foreign assistance may also be necessary to finance the flow of agricultural goods to the neediest countries. Finally, international financial institutions, including the IMF's cereal facility, can be a major source of stability by providing concessionary financing for food imports by needy countries. However, in regard to the IMF facility, significant modifications are necessary to encourage developing countries to make full use of its resources (Ezekiel, 1985).

FOREIGN ASSISTANCE

Foreign assistance is an essential component of the development processes described above. In Africa, between 35 and 65 per cent of government expenditures and public investments since the early 1970s have come from foreign aid. However, aid has always been shown to have inefficiencies in the development context. If recipient country institutions and human capital are underdeveloped, for example, they use both foreign assistance and their own resources ineffectively. And, because there was relatively little growth or a slowing down of growth in much of the developing world foreign assistance has performed pretty badly in recent years.

In the context of the structural imbalances of the 1980s, the deficiencies of foreign assistance became spotlighted. First of all, both governments and donors grossly underestimated the importance of establishing human and institutional capital. In addition, the rapid growth in the number of foreign assistance donors over the last few decades has prevented meaningful coordination of their efforts. While in the 1950s, the United States dominated foreign assistance programmes, coordinating assistance efforts almost by default, it now provides only 29 per cent of the total official development assistance in the world (OECD, 1987). Since that is unusually heavily concentrated on just a few countries, the ability of the US to direct, coordinate and influence foreign assistance in the bulk of the developing world is very small indeed. Another, related shortcoming has been the tendency in recent years for development assistance to shift its emphasis quickly from one development fad to another, with each fad representing only a small portion of the developmental process, and all donors clustering around that particular fad. In moving from one fad to another – the infrastructure fad of the 1950s, the poverty orientation of the 1970s, and the market orientation of the 1980s – recipient countries have been overwhelmed with far too much assistance for certain aspects of their development, while other areas were sorely neglected. Without attention to complementary aspects of development, the objects of fads themselves failed to reach their potential.

Broad agreement among donors on an appropriate development strategy is the best solution to current problems in foreign assistance. For reasons outlined above, donors should focus initially on agriculture to raise factor productivity in that sector and thereby stimulate effective demand and even rapid growth in the non-agricultural sector. Such an agreement on an overall strategy would allow for natural coordination of assistance along the lines of something analogous to market processes. Donors would be free to use their resources to deal with different aspects of the agreed-upon strategy on the basis of comparative advantage and the support of their differing constituencies (Mellor and Masters, 1988).

CONCLUSION

The 1990s can put us firmly on the path of eliminating the bulk of poverty and hunger in the world. This is possible because of the vast investment in human capital and institutional structures that has been occurring for the past several decades. The returns are beginning to flow – first in the richer countries of Asia and Latin America, then in the poorer countries in these regions, and finally in Africa.

To realise those opportunities, developing countries must concentrate on a development strategy that emphasises growth in the labour-intensive agricultural sector. The prospects for that growth and for the alleviation of poverty and hunger in developing countries will depend largely on their ability to reduce costs and intensify agricultural production through technological innovation. That, in turn, will require increased investment in agricultural research to provide the basis for an accelerated increase in resource productivity in the high-production-potential areas, as well as in the more difficult environments. An expansion in rural infrastructure is also needed to integrate the poor fully in development processes by providing farmers with access to new technology and by providing the basis for employment multipliers to create new jobs in other sectors of the economy.

Foreign assistance must also be directed towards growth in small-holder agriculture and a broad agreement on that strategy must be obtained to allow donors to take full advantage for the comparative advantage of their resources and to maximise the impact of their efforts. Technical assistance from developed countries towards the further expansion of human capital and necessary development institutions – most importantly, those that undertake scientific research in agriculture – is crucial to progress in developing countries. In addition, recognising that rapidly rising incomes in developing countries generate a dynamic structure of demand and a consequent need to earn large amounts of foreign exchange through non-traditional agricultural exports, developed countries must open their markets to promote developing-country trade and take measures to ensure the stability of food supplies. Finally, food aid from the surplus-producing developed countries must be made available to support the expansion of rural infrastructure and meet the immediate needs of the hungry.

Cooperation by developing and developed countries can help both to eliminate hunger in the short-term and to encourage the long-term growth processes in developing countries. It is essential that they do so. Success in meeting the complex challenges and opportunities confronting us in the 1990s can ensure a shared and widespread prosperity well beyond the next decade.

Notes

1. The author greatly appreciates the assistance of Frank Z. Riely in preparing the text.

References

Ahmed, R. and M. Hossain (1987) *Infrastructure and Development of a Rural Economy*. Washington: International Food Policy Research Institute.

Ahmed, R. and N. Rustagi (1987). 'Marketing and Price Incentives in Asian and African Countries: A Comparison', in D. Elz, ed., *Agricultural Marketing Strategy and Price Policy*. Washington: World Bank, pp. 104–18.

Alderman, H. (1987) *Cooperative Dairy Development in Karnataka, India: An Assessment*. Research Report 64. Washington: International Food Policy Research Institute.

Ezekiel, H. (1985) *The IMF Cereal Import Financing Scheme*. Washington: Report of a study prepared for the Food and Agricultural Organisation and the International Food Policy Research Institute.

Food and Agriculture Organisation (1985) *Fifth World Food Survey*. Rome: FAO.

Hargrove, T.R., W.R. Coffman, and V.L. Cabanilla (1979) 'Genetic Interrelationships of Improved Rice Varieties in Asia', *IRRI Research Paper* Series 15, Manila: International Rice Research Institute.

Hazell, P.B.R. (1988) 'Changing Patterns of Variability in Cereal Prices and Production', in J.W. Mellor and R. Ahmed, eds, *Agricultural Price Policy for Developing Countries*. Baltimore: Johns Hopkins University Press, pp. 27–52.

Hazell, P.B.R. and A. Roell (1983) *Rural Growth Linkages: Household Expenditure Patterns in Malaysia and Nigeria*. Research Report no. 41. Washington: International Food Policy Research Institute.

Islam, N. (1988) *Horticultural Exports of Developing Countries: Past Performance, Future Prospects, and Policy Issues*. Washington: International Food Policy Research Institute.

Koester, U. and A. Valdes (1984) 'The EC's Potential Role in Food Security for LDCs: Adjustment in its STABEX and Stock Policies', *European Review of Agricultural Economics* 11: pp. 415–37.

Lele, U. (1988) 'Agricultural Growth, Domestic Policies, the External Environment and Assistance to Africa: Lessons of a Quarter Century', Paper presented at the World Bank's Eighth Symposium on Trade, Aid, and Policy Reform for Agriculture, Washington.

Lele, U. and J.W. Mellor (1988) 'Agricultural Growth, Its Determinants, and Their Relationship to World Development: An Overview', Paper presented at the XXth International Conference of Agricultural Economists, Buenos Aires.

Lele, U. and L.R. Myers (1987) *Growth and Structural Change in East*

Africa: Domestic Policies, Agricultural Performance and World Bank Assistance, 1963–1986. MADIA Research Report no. 1. Washington: World Bank.

Lele, U., A. Oyejide, V. Bindlish and B. Bumb (1988) 'Nigeria's Economic Development, Agriculture's Role and World Bank's Assistance, 1961 to 1986: Lessons for the Future', Washington: World Bank, mimeo.

Mellor, J.W. (1978) 'Food Price Policy and Income Distribution in Low-Income Countries', *Economic Development and Cultural Change*, 27 (1) pp. 1–26.

Mellor, J.W. (1985) 'Determinants of Rural Poverty: The Dynamics of Production, Technology and Price', in J.W. Mellor and G.M. Desai, eds, *Agricultural Change and Rural Poverty*. Baltimore: Johns Hopkins University Press, pp. 21–39.

Mellor, J.W. (1989) 'Food Demand in Developing Countries and the Transition of World Agriculture', *European Review of Agricultural Economics*, No. 15.

Mellor, J.W. and W.A. Masters (1988) 'The Changing Roles of Multilateral and Bilateral Foreign Assistance', in I. Nabi and U. Lele, eds, *Aid and Development: The Transition from Agriculture to Industrialisation and from Concessional Assistance to Commercial Capital Flows*. San Francisco: International Center for Economic Growth.

Mergos, G. and R. Slade (1987) *Dairy Development and Milk Cooperatives: The Effects of a Dairy Project in India*. Discussion Paper 15. Washington: World Bank.

Organisation for Economic Coordination and Development (1987) *Development Cooperation: 1987 Report*. Paris: OECD.

Riskin, C. (1987) *Feeding China: The Experience Since 1949*. WIDER Working Paper no. 27. Helsinki: World Institute for Development Economics Research.

Sen, A. (1981) *Poverty and Famines: An Essay On Entitlement and Deprivation*. Oxford: Clarendon Press.

United States Department of Agriculture (1988) World Grain Situation and Outlook. Circular Series FG 1–88. Washington: USDA, Foreign Agricultural Service.

World Bank (1986) *Poverty and Hunger*. Washington.

World Bank (1988) *World Development Report, 1988*. Washington.

11 Some Reflections on Bangladesh Development: Looking Backward to the Future

Mark W. Leiserson

My return to Dhaka in the summer of 1988 to contribute to a UNDP-financed review of the agricultural sector in Bangladesh was bound to stimulate reflections on the changes since my first visit to the then East Pakistan over twenty-five years ago. And since one of my responsibilities in that assignment was to provide some perspectives on the role of agriculture in Bangladesh's future development, I found myself seeking to recall what hopes, fears and expectations were prevalent then for East Pakistan's economic future and how they compare with Bangladesh's actual experience.[1]

For one naive traveller to East Pakistan in the early 1960s, the teeming population, the prevalence of time-honoured technologies (rickshaws, handcarts, country boats, bullocks, bamboo housing, etc.) and the 'ruralness' of the economy left indelible impressions. Feelings of dismay at the abject poverty were accompanied by admiration for the richness of the culture and the gentleness of the people which seemed to mirror the lushness of the landscapes and the warmth of the tranquil evenings.

While there was no gainsaying the vastness of the developmental tasks to be confronted, there were grounds for reasoned optimism. There were substantial near-term opportunities for accelerated agricultural development in the extension of modern small-scale irrigation by low-lift pumps and tubewells in combination with greater fertiliser use and the adoption of high-yielding varieties of rice. Early and vigorous advocacy of this strategy came out of the work at PIDE by Ghulam Mohammed prior to his untimely death.[2] In the longer term greater reliance would have to be placed on more extensive flood control and larger scale irrigation schemes.

Any optimism about the favourable prospects for agricultural

174

growth, however, was tempered by the inexorability of rapid population growth in the next two or three decades and the problem of providing remunerative employment for a burgeoning labour force. A prescient analysis by Swadesh Bose (also at PIDE) qualified the importance of accelerating demands for labour in non-agricultural sectors even under favourable assumptions about the effects of more employment-orientated agriculture policies.[3] The implications for greater efforts to mobilise domestic resources for development and, in particular, for the allocation of a greater proportion of industrial investment to East Pakistan were clearly seen.[4] At the same time the danger was recognised that higher investment expenditures might be accompanied by a reduction in the savings rate through 'consumption liberalisation'. This danger was felt to be particularly acute for East Pakistan where the higher rates of gross saving to gross product compared to West Pakistan (eight or nine per cent rather than three or four per cent) appeared to be connected with the export orientation of production.[5]

What could not be foreseen was that within the space of a very few years the tensions rooted, in part, to issues of development policy and resource allocation would lead to the emergence of Bangladesh as an independent nation. Despite the disruptions accompanying the struggle for independence and continuing political instability, impressive progress in agricultural development has been made. Acreage under modern high-yielding seed varieties has more than doubled while there has been a tripling in the area under modern irrigation and in fertiliser use per unit of cropped land. The trend rate of growth in cereal production increased from 2.6 per cent per year in the period 1950–71 to 3.4 per cent per year in the period 1971–85.[6] According to World Bank estimates, real agricultural product increased at an average annual rate of about 2.5 per cent between 1974 and 1985, while output of non-agricultural sectors grew at an average of about four per cent a year. During the same period per capita GNP growth averaged between 1.5 and two per cent per year.[7]

Despite this encouraging progress the fundamental long-run development problems of Bangladesh, already apparent in the sixties, remain and in certain respects have become more pressing. The most obvious factors conditioning Bangladesh development continue to be linked to the size and character of existing natural resource endowments in the face of high and growing population density. With cultivated acreage approaching its physical limits, inherent and environmental characteristics connected with climate, soil characteristics, rainfall and flooding are becoming more important cost-raising influences on Bangladesh agriculture. In the absence of another major and unforeseen wave of advances in agricultural technology, these fundamental natural resource limitations combined with the unavoidable prospect of a population of 200 million within the next 30 years will mean that higher relative returns to capital and labour will have to be sought in non-agricultural sectors if per capita incomes are to continue to increase.

An accelerating decline in the *relative* growth of agriculture appears to have begun already. One of the clearest indications is provided by recent trends in employment and wages. The absolute number of workers reporting their principal occupation in agricultural activities appears not to have increased between 1974 and 1984 even though the total civilian labour force increased by one-third. The proportion of the employed rural labour force in non-agricultural pursuits more than doubled – from less than 15 per cent to over 30 per cent – during the same period.[8] With agricultural output growing at an average rate of 2.5–3.0 per cent, the average real value added per employee in agriculture must have been increasing at about the same rate. (The rate of increase in average product per unit of labour services may have been less since yearly man-days per agricultural worker have probably increased as well.) The evidence on real wage levels indicates no strong upward trend during the past 12–15 years. Wage rates of male workers in agriculture have fluctuated around an essentially flat trend from the early 1970s, and only in the past two years have they reached average levels exceeding those prevailing in 1970/71.[9]

These trends imply rather high average rates of return to non-labour factors of production in agriculture – especially, one might suspect, in returns to fixed factors such as land. The distributional implications are disturbing. It seems more than likely that the benefits of increased agricultural output and productivity over the past 10–12 years have flowed disproportionately to those with control over access to land and water. Rural workers may have been able to maintain or possibly even increase the average level of real incomes by shifting wholly or in part to non-agricultural activities. This movement into urban or non-farm rural labour markets undoubtedly is largely responsible for the fairly flat trend observable in non-agricultural wages.

What is important to note in the present connection is that the future wellbeing of the rural population of Bangladesh (which still constitutes more than three-quarters of the total population) is as closely linked to the growth of non-agricultural activities as it is to agriculture. Consequently, agricultural development policies need to be designed and implemented keeping in mind the fundamental fact that rising incomes for the low income rural workers (and their children) will become ever more dependent on the growth in demand for non-agricultural labour and a greater and greater fraction of that will be in the demand for urban labour.

The explosive increases in the rate of urbanisation are apparent in the intercensal growth rates of urban population, rising from less than four per cent per year in the decade prior to 1961 to almost eleven per cent per year between 1974 and 1981. Over a third of the almost seven million recorded increase in urban population during those seven years took place in the four largest metropolitan areas. Dhaka – the quiet provincial capital (of about half-a-million persons) I first visited in 1962 – has grown to a bustling metropolitan centre with probably well over five million inhabitants, of which over a million have migrated in during the past seven years.

There are few if any of us who knew Dhaka twenty-five years ago who would have ventured to predict such a rapid population increase without a disastrous deterioration or complete collapse of municipal services. What is important to recognise, however, is that successful development in Bangladesh must involve a continuation of this rapid process of urbanisation, that the next twenty-five years will, one must hope, see the transformation of Bangladesh into an urban industrialised nation.

It is important to emphasise that neither rising *relative* costs of achieving incremental gains in agricultural output nor the relative decline in agricultural employment opportunities for a growing labour force implies there need be or should be absolute declines in the levels of agricultural investment or in the rates of growth of agricultural production and productivity. Indeed the higher rates of overall savings and investment which, as is argued below, are both possible and desirable should enable an increased flow of development resources into agriculture and rural development. A balanced development strategy must build upon the growth-promoting interactions between accelerating development in both agricultural and non-agricultural sectors. In particular, in Bangladesh circumstances where the population is predominantly rural, growing agricultural incomes are important to the increase in employment and earnings opportunities in urban and rural non-farm activities.

Moreover, there is ample evidence that productive investment opportunities in agriculture in general, and in food grains production in particular, are far from being exhausted in Bangladesh and can be expected to grow with advancing technology and improvements in rural infrastructure. It is well known that even currently available technologies are not being fully exploited. The shift to high yielding variety (HYV) cultivation is far from completed; even where this shift has taken place, yields at farmers' level remain well below the potentials revealed by experimental station yields, nationally and internationally . Estimates of the area suitable for HYV cultivation may be exaggerated, both because 'suitability' is too often defined in purely technical terms without regard to economic determinants, and because even the technical definition is too aggregated to capture micro-level variations. Similarly, experimental station yields achieved here or in other countries cannot be directly translated into targets that Bangladesh farmers might attain. But the gap between performance and potential with existing technology means that investments aimed at narrowing that gap are likely to be a relatively cost-effective way of achieving higher levels of agricultural production and limiting dependence on the import of foodgrains.

Emphasising the prospect of rising relative resource costs of agricultural growth, therefore, is not to argue against vigorous efforts to increase the flow of development resources into agriculture and rural development, especially for those projects and areas where high returns can be demonstrated in the near term. But it does argue for careful attention in the formulation of agricultural development strategy and policy to the alternative uses of investable resources in non-agricultural sectors. And it does imply, as stressed earlier, that Bangladesh development will be increasingly dependent upon other sources of growth, in particular higher levels of investment, faster technological progress and more rapid accumulation of human capital in non-agricultural sectors.

Overall, investment and saving rates have been discouragingly low since independence. Given the desperate poverty of a large fraction of the population, a comparatively low level of personal saving may not be surprising. However, the continuing low rate of savings and investment despite increases in per capita GDP is a cause for concern. Increased levels of foreign assistance and large inflows of workers' remittances from overseas have financed rates of consumption and investment somewhat higher than before independence, even though there was a sharp decline in the domestic saving rate. It has been estimated that without this decline, the rate of investment could have been substantially higher than 12–15 per cent.

To achieve higher and sustainable rates of economic development undoubtedly will require increased rates of saving and investment, the greater portion in non-agriculture. The higher degree of economic self-reliance associated with a more technologically advanced, more industrialised and more productive economy may well depend, somewhat paradoxically, on the gains from specialisation, technological access and expanding export industries that flow from greater exploitation of external market opportunities. With proper care in policy design and implementation the greater degree of interdependence entailed in more open goods and services and capital markets need not lead to greater foreign dependence; nor should it be inimical to the vigorous development of a more productive agriculture. Rather it should contribute to those increases in efficiency, higher rates of capital accumulation (both human and physical) and more rapid technological advances that will enable Bangladesh to compete in world markets as a self-reliant nation possessed of the managerial skills, institutions and economic resources sufficient to ensure the future economic security of its citizens.

An important implication of the above analysis is that, barring major technological breakthroughs in agriculture sufficient to offset the tendency towards comparatively lower returns in agriculture – and none of sufficient magnitude now appear imminent – the concentration of investment resources on the pursuit of self-sufficiency in foodgrains is likely to involve high costs in terms of forgone investment opportunities in other sectors of the economy. The result will be lower aggregate growth rates and adverse effects on poverty. Even if the goal of closing the 'food-gap' (somehow defined) were fully achieved, it almost certainly would prove to be a transitory accomplishment in the face of continuing population increases and (one would still hope) growing levels of per capita consumption.

Under the circumstances it is to be hoped that the issues surrounding food self-sufficiency will be examined as part of the process of framing the hard choices that have to be confronted in implementing a viable food policy as an integral part of overall development strategy and policy directions which strike an appropriate balance between sectors, both domestic and external, and which foster progress along a more efficient, more equitable and more self-reliant path of economic development.

Notes

1. That process brought back vivid memories of the professional and personal associations during my tenure as Joint Director of the Pakistan Institute of Development Economics from 1962 and, in the subsequent five years, as Director of the Yale University/Ford Foundation project in support of the Institute. As the last foreign director of the Institute, I take some pride in having had a role to play in arranging for the transfer to national leadership and in persuading Nurul Islam to accept appointment as Director.
2. See Ghulam Mohammed, 'Development of Irrigated Agriculture in East Pakistan; Some Basic Considerations.' *Pakistan Development Review*, Autumn 1966, pp. 315–75.
3. Swadesh R. Bose, 'Labour Force and Employment in Pakistan, 1961–86: A Preliminary Analysis'. *Pakistan Development Review*, Autumn 1963, pp. 371–98.
4. See, for example, John H. Power, 'Industrialisation in Pakistan: A Case of Frustrated Take-Off?' *Pakistan Development Review*, Summer 1963, pp. 204–7.
5. See Azizur Rahman Khan, 'Import Substitution, Export Expansion and Consumption Liberalization: A Preliminary Report'. *Pakistan Development Review*, Summer 1963, pp. 208–23; John H. Power, 'Development Strategy for Pakistan'. *Pakistan Development Review*, Autumn 1963, pp. 422f.
6. Mahabub Hossain, *Nature and Impact of the Green Revolution in Bangladesh*, Research Report 67. International Food Policy Research Institute, July 1988. Tables 6,7.
7. World Bank, *World Tables*, 1987, pp. 36–7.
8. Bangladesh Bureau of Statistics, *Statistical Yearbook of Bangladesh 1984–85*, Tables 3.1 and 3.2.
9. A.R. Khan and Mahabub Hossain, *The Strategy of Development in Bangladesh* (Draft manuscript dated 28 February 1988, Table 6, Chapter 7, p. 16).

12 Foodgrain Pricing Policy in Bangladesh: Procurement, Sales, Imports and Public Stocks

Abu A. Abdullah

INTRODUCTION

The determinants of agricultural performance – of the growth of output and the distribution of the resulting increases in income – are many. The availability of technology, the resource base, physical infrastructure, the agrarian structure, the formal and informal institutional matrix, the macro policy environment – all play a role. It would be highly convenient for the policy-maker if one could identify a particular factor as being the critical one, so that all efforts could be aimed at overcoming one clearly defined 'dominant constraint'. Adherents of such 'single factor' approaches are not in short supply. Unfortunately reality is more complex, and it is rarely possible to point to just one area of intervention where action will be sufficient to unblock the process of agricultural development.

One of these determinants of performance is obviously the price regime that confronts the farmer. Evidence from around the world shows that farmers do respond positively to price incentives, particularly once commercialisation had made some progress. Thus if the performance of the agricultural sector is considered unsatisfactory, one natural question to ask is whether this is at least partly because the existing price regime (i.e. the prices of outputs, inputs and consumer goods confronting farmers) is 'wrong', and if so, what actions can be taken to set it right.

When is a price regime 'right', and when is it 'wrong'? There is no simple or completely uncontroversial answer. This is because prices, especially the prices of basic foodgrains, have a multiplicity of effects

181

and serve a multiplicity of functions. There is not much point in using a high support price to elicit growth in output if at these prices the additional output finds no buyers – unless the government is willing and able to subsidise the consumption of the poor. Similarly, if prices needed to elicit domestic supply response exceed the price at which the food could be imported, a case could be made that, at least beyond a certain point, this would represent a waste of resources. (One may quite legitimately be willing to pay a price for self-sufficiency in food, but surely few countries would want, or could afford, to go to the lengths that Saudi Arabia has gone.)

A good logical starting point for assessing the 'rightness' of a price regime would therefore seem to be provided by world prices of the commodities in question. This approach, while fundamental, raises complex methodological and practical problems.[1] Here we leave aside considerations of the desirable degree of congruence between world and domestic prices and concentrate on a more limited range of issues. Specifically, in this paper we attempt to evaluate the Bangladesh government's policies with regard to domestic procurement, open market sales, and imports in terms of their efficacy as instruments to (a) support growers' prices, and (b) control seasonal price fluctuations. In the main we restrict our discussion to rice.

THE PRACTICE OF AGRICULTURAL PRICING POLICY

The main instruments the government utilises to influence food crop prices, both to growers and consumers, are procurement at administered prices and release of procurement and imports through various market and non-market channels.[2] The aim of the former is to assure a floor price to growers, and of the latter to ensure privileged access to selected groups (not necessarily, indeed in practice not primarily, the poor). Some basic data on the magnitude of these operations are assembled in Table 12.1. It may be noted that apart from the peak of 1980/81, procurement of both rice and wheat have stayed within a fairly narrow band.

Has price policy in Bangladesh, particularly as regards foodgrains, succeeded in its stated objectives of (a) ensuring growers an 'incentive price', and (b) moderating price fluctuations?

As regards (a), the notion of an 'incentive price' is problematic. It is usual to calculate this by adding a markup to the average cost of production. Clearly this price, even if effectively implemented, will offer no protection to farmers with above-average costs of produc-

Table 12.1 Availability of cereals (million metric tons)

Year	Production[a]			Imports			Domestic procurement			Offtake		
	Rice	Wheat	Total	Rice	Wheat	Total	Rice	Wheat	Total	Rice	Wheat	Total
1976/77	10.58	0.23	10.81	0.19	0.61	0.80	0.31	0.01	0.32	0.77	0.68	1.45
1977/78	11.67	0.31	11.98	0.30	1.34	1.64	0.55	0.01	0.56	0.60	1.40	2.00
1978/79	11.56	0.45	12.01	0.05	1.10	1.15	0.29	0.07	0.36	0.56	1.23	1.79
1979/80	11.46	0.74	12.20	0.71	2.07	2.78	0.23	0.13	0.36	0.69	1.71	2.40
1980/81	12.49	0.98	13.47	0.89	1.08	1.97	0.77	0.26	1.03	0.51	1.02	1.53
1981/82	12.27	0.87	13.14	0.14	1.11	1.25	0.27	0.03	0.30	0.76	1.28	2.04
1982/83	12.79	0.99	13.78	0.32	1.52	1.84	0.17	0.02	0.19	0.49	1.42	1.91
1983/84	13.06	1.91	14.97	0.18	1.88	2.06	0.14	0.13	0.27	0.50	1.51	2.01
1984/85	13.16	1.31	14.47	0.69	1.90	2.59	0.13	0.22	0.35	0.40	2.14	2.54
1985/86	13.53	0.94	14.47	0.04	1.16	1.20	0.22	0.13	0.35	0.37	1.15	1.52
1986/87	13.95	0.98	14.93	0.26	1.51	1.77	0.14	0.05	0.19	0.49	1.63	2.12
1987/88	13.81	0.94	14.75	0.59	2.33	2.92	0.29	0.05	0.34	0.47	2.03	2.50

[a] with 10% deduction for seed and wastage.
Source: Ministry of Food, *Food Situation Report*, May 1988, and unpublished files.

tion. There is no logical ground for choosing to support the average, rather than the highest (or the lowest) cost of production. In fact, world prices must play a key, though not exclusive, role in determining the appropriate procurement price. We therefore ignore the question of incentives, and ask ourselves instead (i) whether procurement policy has helped bolster growers' prices and (ii) whether procurement and offtake policies succeeded in narrowing seasonal price spreads.

On the first question, opinion is somewhat divided. Osmani and Quasem (1985) adjudge the programme to have been 'not successful on the ground that in years of good harvest growers' prices fell below procurement prices'.[3] From Table 12.2 we can see that our data also bear this out – indeed it would seem that, except for 1986, growers' prices have always been lower than procurement prices, though the margins were not usually very large.[4] Mahabub Hossain (1988) carries out a similar analysis with identical conclusions.

Chowdhury (1987, 1988) has however forcefully argued that the success or failure of the price support programme cannot be evaluated by looking at annual average prices, since what procurement is supposed to accomplish is to hold prices firm during the immediate post-harvest period. On the basis of a mensually disaggregated analysis, he concludes that '. . . procurement programme has raised the growers'-to-procurement price ratios quite conspicuously in harvest months . . . The performance of the procurement programme ex-

Table 12.2 Ratio of growers-to-procurement prices of rice, Bangladesh, 1976/77–1984/85

Months	1976/77–1978/79	1979/80–1981/82	1982/83–1984/85	1976/77–1984/85	Per cent increase (4) over (2)
1	2	3	4	5	6
July	78.26	96.32	107.43	94.00	37.27
August	80.88	91.92	105.68	92.83	30.66
September	92.82	99.60	115.43	102.62	24.36
October	97.04	101.27	127.90	108.74	31.80
November	82.47	93.52	105.67	93.89	28.13
December	89.85	94.91	109.69	98.15	22.08
January	92.53	103.67	117.54	104.58	27.03
February	97.39	117.37	119.64	111.47	22.85
March	109.39	126.21	123.27	119.62	12.69
April	101.45	97.71	103.37	100.84	1.89
May	96.12	80.97	98.87	91.99	1.07
June	106.49	81.57	100.56	96.21	– 5.57
Annual av.	93.7	98.8	111.2	101.2	18.68
Weighted av.	n.a.	100.9	108.1	n.a.	n.a.

Notes: Growers' price data were carefully compiled from BBS *Monthly Statistical Bulletin*, various issues. Growers prices were taken on the basis of harvest seasons for the three main rice crops. Aman harvest season was taken to range from November to March; boro from April to June; Aus, from July to August.
Source: Chowdhury (1987), Table VIII.

plains a good deal of the elevation of the bottom of the seasonal price movement'.[5] We reproduce in Table 12.2 opposite Chowdhury's Table VIII, with an added column showing the percentage change in the growers'-to-procurement price ratios between the first and the third trienniun. This last column shows quite clearly that the increase in the ratio in the four months November–February, which Chowd-hury pinpoints as critical, are by no means the largest registered; these occur in the July, August and October ratios.[6] Chowdhury notes this himself[7] and concedes that other factors must have been at work, but ends up arguing that raising the price in the post-harvest month will itself tend to raise the price throughout the year. This may well be so, but then this should show up in the annual average price figures, thus diminishing considerably the force of his critique of Osmani and Quasem.

To conclude, we may observe from Table 12.1 that except for the year 1980/81, domestic procurement has been a rather small percent-age of domestic net production, never exceeding 2.4 per cent in the last seven years. It is unlikely on the face of it that such a small operation would significantly affect prices.

While it must therefore remain an open question whether procure-ment has succeeded in supporting growers' prices, there appear to be some grounds for believing that the objective of containing seasonal price fluctuations through government offtakes in general and open market sales in particular may have been more successfully pursued. Table 12.3, reproduced from Chowdhury 1988, Appendix Table AV, shows that in general seasonal price-spreads have been clearly falling over the period. Indeed, while in the first quinquennium all the spreads were over 40 per cent, with two over 89 per cent, in the second quinquennium these were 31 per cent or less; while during the last six years only one was marginally above 30 per cent.

The question is, can we attribute this improvement, or at least a part of it, to government policy? Only a sophisticated modelling exercise, which to our knowledge remains to be performed, could give a definite answer.[8]

Chowdhury has aptly summarised some of the non-policy variables that may have contributed to this narrowing of the seasonal band:

Several economic-environmental changes are consistent with a secular fall in marketing margins: an improvement in the state of the grid of national highways, as also in intra-rural feeder roads, a possible increase in stock-turnover ratio, greater competition

Table 12.3 Difference between normalised high and low wholesale prices
of coarse rice, Bangladesh, 1972/73–1987/88

Year	Highest price	Lowest price	Difference	$\dfrac{HP-LP}{LP} \times 100$
1	2	3	4	5
1972/73	90.85	60.43	30.42	50.34
1973/74	133.19	81.19	52.00	64.05
1974/75	259.41	137.04	122.37	89.29
1975/76	195.75	100.70	95.06	94.40
1976/77	138.12	97.37	40.75	41.85
1977/78	149.19	124.57	24.62	19.76
1978/79	215.28	128.45	86.83	67.60
1979/80	231.07	176.38	54.69	31.16
1980/81	189.00	154.78	34.22	22.11
1981/82	189.67	171.49	118.18	68.91
1982/83	163.16	222.54	40.62	18.25
1983/84	285.00	231.38	53.62	23.17
1984/85	310.82	252.23	58.59	23.23
1985/86	313.80	257.20	56.60	22.01
1986/87	393.25	293.94	99.31	33.78
1987/88	377.36	321.75	55.61	17.28

Source: Chowdhury (1988), Table AV.

through entry into trade stemming from population growth not
matched by job opportunities in goods *production*, etc. Again, due
to a multiplicity of harvests, typical seasonal storage duration is
shorter.[9]

On the whole, therefore, it would seem that one has grounds to be
sceptical about the efficacy of pricing policy to date, either in supporting growers' prices or in moderating seasonal price spreads,[10] at
least pending further research on the subject.

IMPORTS, PUBLIC STOCKS AND PRICES

In Bangladesh foodgrain imports are the preserve of the government.[11]
Commercial import targets are set by setting the estimated 'food
gap', [(net production − consumption requirement at 16 oz per day
per head) + (current public stocks − target stock)] against aid
commitments.[12] As we can see from Table 12.4 and Figure 12.1, in

Table 12.4 Consumption requirements, food gaps and imports, 1974 to 1988 ('000 tons)

Year*	Net production[1]	Public food[2] grain stock	Consumption[3] requirement	Food gaps[4]		Imports[5]
				Target stock 700	Target stock 1200	
1974	10 818	302	12 649	2229	2729	n.a.
1975	10 264	217	12 997	3216	3716	2560
1976	11 683	761	13 265	1521	2021	1450
1977	10 811	863	13 543	2569	3069	790
1978	11 992	382	13 858	2184	2684	1610
1979	12 009	678	14 172	2185	2685	1156
1980	12 207	212	14 560	2841	3341	2783
1981	13 478	791	14 884	1351	1851	1076
1982	13 138	1249	15 265	1578	2078	1255
1983	13 780	615	15 629	1934	2434	1844
1984	14 147	611	16 054	1996	2496	2056
1985	14 478	800	16 407	1829	2329	2590
1986	14 471	1017	16 821	2033	2533	1200
1987	14 847	976	17 202	2079	2579	1767
1988p	14 879	727	17 664	2758	3258	2922

1. Total production – 10% deduction for seed and wastage.
2. As of end-June the previous year.
3. Estimated at 16 oz. per day per head.
4. Food gaps (1−3+2−700) and (1−3+2−1200).
p. Provisional.
Sources: (1), (2) and population figure for (3) from USAID (1988).
(5) from BBS (1986) and MOF (1988).
* 1974 = FY 1973/74, and so on.

most years (eleven out of fourteen) imports have been less even than the estimated lower food gap. Also notable is the fact that not only are the average annual stock levels higher in recent years, they also appear to be better managed in the sense that year-to-year fluctuations appear to be more moderate. However, by June 1988, stocks had doubled to 1.498 metric tons[13] which is arguably excessive.

Table 12.5 and Figure 12.1 provide information about the relative contributions of aid and commercial imports to total imports.[14] The graph makes it particularly clear that the grant element has been relatively stable, the match between the food gap and imports being achieved through fluctuations in commercial imports.

Have foodgrain imports in general, and food aid in particular, been systematically 'excessive' in the sense of dampening growers' incentives? Evidence is scarce, but what there is (Norton and Hazell, 1988;

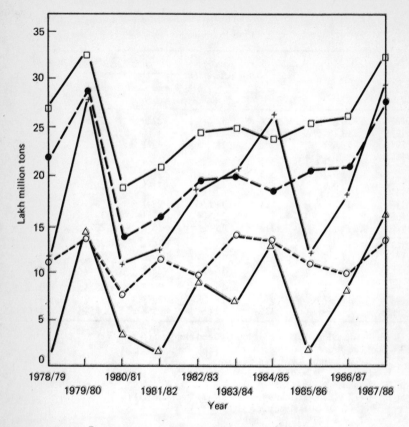

FIGURE 12.1   Food gaps, grant, loan/credit & cash and total imports

WFP, 1987; Hill 1988) suggests that the effect of imports on prices and hence on production was probably not very significant. Norton and Hazell find, for example, that in 1976/77, reducing food aid by 87.5 per cent, which would have cut imports by half, would have caused only a 1.2 per cent rise in the domestic foodgrain price level.

It is our contention, however, that quite apart from questions of producers' incentives, imports in recent years have been excessive in

Table 12.5 Production and import of rice and wheat ('000 tons)

| Year | Production | Import | | | | Total import as percentage of production | Grant as percentage of total import |
		Grant	Loan/ credit	Cash	Total		
1	2	3	4	5	6	7	8
1978/79	13 343	1108	20	28	1156	8.66	95.85
1979/80	13 560	1360	178	1245	2783	20.52	48.87
1980/81	14 974	751	65	260	1076	7.19	69.80
1981/82	14 597	1141	–	114	1255	8.60	90.92
1982/83	15 310	934	245	665	1844	12.04	50.65
1983/84	15 718	1397	91	568	2056	13.08	67.95
1984/85	16 084	1306	618	666	2590	16.10	50.42
1985/86	16 079	1087	103	10	1200	7.46	90.98
1986/87	16 587	980	445	342	1767	10.65	55.46
1987/88	16 397	1325	462	1135	2922	17.82	45.35

Source: MOF, *Food Situation Report*, June 1988, and BBS *Statistical Yearbook*, 1987.

the sense that scarce foreign exchange has been spent on commercial imports to build up unnecessarily high public stocks.

Since storage is a costly activity, it should be at a minimum level consistent with the need to stabilise supply over time. A good stock-management policy should allow stocks to come close to depletion at some points during the inventory cycle, without running the risk of offtake breakdown.

How close to depletion can one get without risking disaster? Looking back at Table 12.4, we see that since 1974 public stocks hit two all-time lows over this period, in 1975 (i.e. June 1974), and 1980 (June 1979). The low stock of 1974 contributed to the famine, but timely action in lining up aid and commercial imports averted a crisis in 1979/80.[15] Imports were high in both 1975 and 1980, but arrivals were timely only in the latter year, allowing both high offtake in the critical months and stock build-up. The lesson of this comparison is therefore that with competent import management (and, of course, reasonable aid climate and foreign exchange position), stocks can go down to about 200 000 tons without danger. With increasing population, this minimum requirement would of course rise. A determination to avoid 'crisis imports' would also justify higher stocks, but it is by no means clear that importing to build up stocks is the cheaper alternative. It would be the right policy only if one were confidently expecting world food-grain prices to be rising and/or the domestic currency to be depreciating at a rate that offsets storage costs.[16]

However, it is reasonable for every government to want some security reserves against emergencies. A stock of 200 000–250 000 could be depleted in one month during a time of crisis: in 1984, monthly offtakes over May–November averaged 250 000 tons[17], and as we can see from Table 12.6, in 1987/88 monthly offtakes came close to 300 000 tons in September and October (The total for the period July–December 1987 was 1.428 m metric tons, averaging 238 000 mt. per month). It is no doubt experiences like this that make the government designate 900 000 tons as the 'danger level' – the figure has possibly been arrived at as three months' potential high-offtake requirement.[18]

And yet it is noteworthy that both in 1984 and in 1987/88, current monthly imports were in general more than adequate to cover current monthly offtakes. This is clearly brought out in Table 12.7. We can see from the last column that in seven out of eleven months in that year 'inflows', mainly imports, exceeded outflows. In the other months the ratio never fell below forty-seven per cent. Indeed, for the thirty-five months for which data have been presented, the ratio fell below fifty per cent in only seven months, and exceeded unity in fourteen.

A comparison of Tables 12.6 and 12.7 shows that monthly opening stocks have usually exceeded monthly distribution by factors of two to fifteen. A frequency analysis shows that out of thirty-five months, only in four were the ratios between two and (less than) three, in ten between three and five, in fourteen between five and ten, in six over ten. These are excessive stocks by any reasonable standard. We would be inclined to suggest a target stock of about 800 000 tons, as representing two months' potential peak offtake (600 000 tons) plus 33 per cent for stocks in transit.

If the government has nevertheless gone on a veritable spree of stockpiling, this is clearly the result of an acute sense of insecurity based on distrust of the weather, of the world market, and of donors. Experience has shown the first fear to be exaggerated – flood damages are usually compensated by better-than average Boro crops. But undoubtedly a more robust production base, with extensive use of 'supplementary' irrigation[19] could help further reduce this source of insecurity. The distrust of the world market is understandable in view of the volatile nature of world foodgrain prices, but, as pointed out earlier, this does not really create a presumption in favour of buying

Table 12.6 Monthly imports, domestic procurement and distribution of food in 1985/86–1987/88 ('000 tons)

Month	1985/86			1986/87			1987/88		
	Imports	Domestic procurement	Distribution	Imports	Domestic procurement	Distribution	Imports	Domestic procurement	Distribution
Jul	102	39	84	70	6	92	462	34	167
Aug	31	19	93	89	1	109	106	3	216
Sep	8	8	125	323	–	151	199	–	295
Oct	104	9	165	123	–	240	400	–	291
Nov	22	1	133	194	–	196	509	2	242
Dec	73	36	115	–	10	120	702	–	217
Jan	40	55	148	–	9	194	151	–	204
Feb	21	38	155	76	3	220	288	4	233
Mar	95	17	159	153	1	246	87	11	248
Apr	197	83	161	256	20	244	161	40	187
May	210	23	53	219	44	171	122	110	121
Jun	136	30	65	379	97	136	n.a.	n.a.	n.a.
Total	1039	358	1456	1882	191	1633	3187	204	2421

Source: BBS, Monthly Statistical Bulletin, various issues.

Table 12.7 Monthly food grain stocks ('000 tons)

Month	1985/86			1986/87			1987/88		
	Rice	Wheat	Total	Rice	Wheat	Total	Rice	Wheat	Total
Jul	459	515	974	353	624	977	315	727	1042
Aug	482	589	1071	347	658	1005	283	659	942
Sep	468	515	983	313	632	945	208	598	806
Oct	474	502	976	270	844	1114	325	572	897
Nov	428	691	1119	192	746	938	367	627	994
Dec	374	572	946	194	740	934	451	732	1183
Jan	403	525	928	194	604	798	448	697	1145
Feb	448	411	859	193	428	621	426	822	1248
Mar	463	318	781	196	504	700	368	695	1063
Apr	447	283	730	184	365	549	372	719	1091
May	405	411	816	131	263	394	871	794	1665
Jun	358	534	892	146	273	419	n.a.	n.a.	n.a.

Source: BBS, *Monthly Statistical Bulletin*, various issues.

today and stockpiling rather than buying tomorrow when we need it. The distrust of donors seems harder to understand, since food grants have consistently been near the one million ton mark. But donors could help by agreeing to multi-year programming, at least at a base rate to be mutually agreed on (say of the order of 750 000 tons over the next ten years), with annual negotiations for any additional amounts.

What then of the 'cherished goal' of self-sufficiency? If the commitment to this goal is serious then clearly multi-year aid programming would reflect this by progressively reducing and finally eliminating food aid. This would need to be based on a realistic projection of the progress towards self-sufficiency.

PRINCIPLES OF PRICE FIXATION

We believe that a support programme for rice is warranted. How should the support price be determined? Current practice bases these prices on estimated average costs of production. We believe that this procedure is seriously flawed. We clearly need an independent standard to judge the desirability of protecting a particular level of costs.

World prices provide such a standard, but are notoriously volatile, with unpredictable year-to-year fluctuations and no reliably demonstrable trend. This is particularly true for rice, with its 'thin' international market. It would be manifestly absurd to change procurement prices in line with world prices from one year to the next. A smoothed series, perhaps a five-year moving average, could be used as a baseline.

What is a desirable markup over this international-market determined baseline? It is perfectly reasonable to put some premium on domestic production over imports. Domestic production is more easily and quickly available, and reduces a particularly dangerous form of aid dependency. Adhering strictly to the world pricing rule may also imply unacceptable levels of unemployment. We believe that the premium should be roughly equal to the protection offered to the industrial sector, which however should be reduced considerably. The Trade and Industrial Policy (TIP) study carried out by the Government of Bangladesh Planning Commission, has suggested nominal protection rates in the range 30–50 per cent for most industries. Some degree of preferential treatment for industry may be desirable, so perhaps a 20 per cent nominal protection rate would be appropriate for rice. Thus a first rule of thumb for determining the support price of rice (and any other tradable crop for which a price support programme is contemplated) might be

Support price = Five-year average world price in dollars × shadow exchange rate × 1.2

What implications does such a policy have for poor consumers? Past experience suggests that large, targeted, and subsidised public distribution systems are to be avoided; therefore, the market price must be kept within limits that ensure access to foodgrains for the poor. A high procurement price will translate into high prices to private traders and hence high retail prices. Since it is the poor who spend a larger proportion of their income on foodgrains, this will amount to a regressive tax, financing a subsidy to growers whose benefits are also distributed regressively. It must be remembered that the poor in Bangladesh are net purchasers of food: price increases directly threaten the food entitlements of such households.

There are two (not mutually exclusive) options to protect the poor: (1) the use of a 'Purchasing Power Parity' (PPP) rule in setting procurement prices, and/or (2) reliance on targeted food subsidies.

The first procedure aims to keep rice prices at a level which does not jeopardise the food entitlements of poor households. A potential procedure would derive the target price for rice by taking into account the income of the bottom quartile of the population, their consumption needs, and the share of rice in their consumption. However, such a procedure would not protect households with incomes below that average. Targeted interventions will still be needed, but on a smaller scale.

One way to resolve the dilemma that arises when the world price for rice exceeds the PPP price by a wide margin would be to switch the consumption pattern of the poor away from rice. Following the world price rule would go a long way towards encouraging such a switch, together with awareness programmes and some supporting services (e.g. milling facilities for maize). Taken to its logical conclusion, such a policy may see Bangladesh exporting high-value rice, with the domestic market being restricted to the affluent, and importing (and also to some extent growing) cheaper cereals like maize for mass consumption. If world prices of rice do indeed look like systematically exceeding PPP prices, this unpalatable solution may be the best one.

How can support prices be made effective? Currently not all growers can sell their produce at a certain minimum predetermined price because: (1) procurement volumes have been small compared to total production or sale; (2) the number of procurement centres (100–1200) is inadequate for comprehensive coverage; (3) cumbersome payment procedures raise transaction costs for small sellers; and (4) traders, in collusion with procurement centre officials, capture the margin between market and procurement prices. What can be done to circumvent these problems?

Solving the first two problems is relatively straightforward (in principle): more money should be spent to build more centres, recruit more officials, and increase purchases. The third problem is more intractable. It is frequently suggested that small farmers should be paid in cash, but this is unpractical. Cash payment increases the temptation as well as the opportunity to short-change the sellers. The risk of robbery also cannot be discounted. The only real solution would seem to lie in encouraging small sellers to sell and receive payment collectively, i.e. through cooperative marketing. This may also be the only way to handle the last problem of traders' intervention. The two-tier cooperative system of the Bangladesh Rural Development Board might be mobilised for this purpose.

Private trade in foodgrains will continue to be the dominant influence on price formation, with public food management playing the role of a regulator. This role is essential, but it does not preclude direct action to improve the performance of private trade. Such action should include (1) freer availability of credit to private traders, specially in good harvest years, and (2) removal of outmoded restrictions on stock holdings and stock movements. Increasing private sector participation in imports and exports should also be encouraged, with tariffs and exports taxes being used to ensure consistency with procurement and issue prices set by government.

CONCLUSION

In this paper we have dealt only with a few selected aspects of price policy. Broadly, our conclusions are that the procurement programme should be expanded, the procurement price should be fixed with due regard both to international trading opportunities and the purchasing power of the poor, and that public stock targets should be lower, with correspondingly lower volumes of commercial imports.

In the context of Bangladesh agriculture, how much can we expect from price policy? In this author's opinion, something, but not a great deal. The tendency for cereal prices to lag behind other prices, both agricultural and non-agricultural, which has characterised the eighties, is symptomatic of a deeper malaise – the poverty of the masses and the resulting stagnating demand for cereals. Price policy can at best be a holding operation, while more basic policy changes are undertaken to provide productive employment in non-crop and non-agricultural activities. It is beyond the ambit of this paper to spell out the elements of such policy changes.

Notes

1. These are ably discussed in Ahmed (1988) and Valdes and Siamwalla (1988).
2. Macro-economic policies, in particular exchange rate policies, exert a powerful and possibly dominant role in agricultural price formation.
3. See Osmani and Quasem (1985) pp. 249–51.
4. For the years of overlap, there are differences between Table 5.7 of Osmani and Quasem and our Table 12.4. We suspect this is because they use the procurement price of rice, and convert growers' paddy prices to

rice-equivalent. Since procurement is over-whelmingly of paddy, we have preferred to directly compare procurement and growers' prices of paddy.

5. See Chowdhury (1987), p. 126.

6. The data from his Table IX, which gives ratios between trend growers' and procurement prices, show broadly similar results. However, October shows the third highest percentage increase, and the period April–June registers 10–11 per cent increase instead of the very low (for June negative) change in the actual price ratios.

7. See Chowdhury (1987), p. 124.

8. Chowdhury (1988, p. 31) cites a study by Montgomery which in his opinion shows convincingly that in 1982/83, 'OMS offtake was significantly effective in moderating price increases in the lean season of that year', but also reports his own failure to replicate these positive results for 1983/84 or 1984/85. As he says, 1984/85 was a year of 'there to fore record OMS deliveries and quite large trend-normalised seasonal variation'. He also notes that in 1986/87, 'OMS deliveries were at an all-time high. Seasonal spreads were quite tolerable'. In fact, as can be seen from Table 12.3, the 1986/87 price-spread, at 34 per cent, was far and away the highest in six years.

9. *Ibid*. 1988, pp. 38–9.

10. This is not to deny that the government has demonstrated a greater capacity to cope with crises, as compared to, say, 1974. However, as stressed by Osmani (1987, pp. 42–4), this has more to do with an improved foreign exchange and aid position than with any significant change in policy or implementation procedure.

11. Last year private importers were given licences to import 20 000 mt of foodgrains, but these remained largely unutilised (personal communication from Assistant Director General, Ministry of Food).

12. Target stocks are fixed annually by the MOF. Ahmed and Bernard (1988, pp. 7.7–8) use 700 000 mt. But according to MOF officials, since at least 1980 a figure of 1.2 million mt is being used. Both estimates are shown here.

13. MOF, 1988, p. 31.

14. The category 'loans/credits' seems to be a combination of concessional and commercial credit. In the graph it has been added to 'cash' imports.

15. See Osmani (1987), pp. 36–45, for an excellent comparative analysis of 1974, 1979, and 1984.

16. 'It is not advisable for a developing country to take speculative positions in the world grain market, which is what importing grain for storage against the prospect of a rising price implies, unless its information on the market is as reliable as that of the multinational grain companies and other speculators against whom it will be competing.' (Valdes and Siamwalla, 1988, p. 84) 17.

17. See Osmani (1987), p. 41 footnote.

18. Personal communication from Food Ministry official.

19. Droughts on the whole cause more damage. See for example Ahmed and Bernard (1988), pp. 5, 8–5, 11.

References

Abdullah, Abu (1988) 'Fertilizer Pricing and Distribution Policy', Background Paper for the Agriculture Sector Review; Dhaka, March.

Ahmed, Raisuddin (1988) 'Pricing Principles and Public Intervention in Domestic Markets' in Mellor and Ahmed (eds) *Agriculture Price Policy for Developing Countries*, Baltimore and London: Johns Hopkins University Press.

Ahmed, Raisuddin, and Andrew Bernard (1988) *Seasonality of Rice Prices. Effect of New Technology, and an Approach to Rice Price Stabilisation in Bangladesh*, International Food Policy Research Institute (IFPRI).

Alauddin, Mohammad, and Clem Tisdell (1987) 'Trends and Projects for Bangladeshi Food Production: An Alternative Viewpoint', *Food Policy*, vol. 12 no. 4.

Asaduzzaman, M. (1988) 'Feeding Our Future Towns: An Overview of Urbanisation and Associated Food Policy Issues', Paper presented at the GOB/EEC seminar on 'Food Strategies in Bangladesh', Dhaka, October.

Bangladesh Bureau of Statistics, *Statistical Yearbooks*, 1986 and 1987.

Boyce, James K. (1985) 'Agricultural Growth in Bangladesh, 1949–50 to 1980–81: A Review of the Evidence' *Economic and Political Weekly*, vol. 20, no. 13.

Chowdhury, Nuimuddin (1987) 'Seasonality of Foodgrain Price and Procurement Programme in Bangladesh since Liberation: An Exploratory Study', *The Bangladesh Development Studies*, vol. XV, no. 1, March.

Chowdhury, Nuimuddin (1988) 'The Changing Food System: Storage, Transport, Marketing and Distribution Issues in Bangladesh', paper presented at the GOB/EEC seminar on Food Strategies in Bangladesh, Dhaka, October.

Government of Bangladesh (1973) *The Third Five Year Plan*, Dhaka.

Hossain, Mahabub (1988) 'Green Revolution in Bangladesh: Its Nature and Impact on Income Distribution', BIDS Working Paper no. 4, Dhaka.

Hill, Marianne T. (1988) 'Modelling the Macroeconomic Impact of Aid', *Bangladesh Development Studies* vol. XVI, no. 1, March.

Kahlon, A.S. (1985) 'Integrated Structure of Wheat Production, Marketing and Price Policy', Report to the Department of Agricultural Marketing, October.

Mellor, John W. and Raisuddin Ahmed (eds) (1988) *Agriculture Price Policy for Developing Countries*, Baltimore and London: Johns Hopkins University Press.

Food Planning and Monitoring Unit, Ministry of Food, *Food Situation Report*, June 1988.

Norton, Roger D. and Peter B.R. Hazell (1988) 'A Model for Evaluating the Economic Impact of Food Aid', IFPRI.

Osmani, S.R. (1987) *The Food Problem of Bangladesh*, Helsinki: World Institute for Development Economics Research.

Osmani, S.R. and M.A. Quasem (1985) 'Pricing and Subsidy Policies for Bangladesh Agriculture', Dhaka: BIDS, August. (mimeo).

Rahman, Sultan H. (1986) 'Supply Response in Bangladesh Agriculture', *Bangladesh Development Studies* vol. XIV, no. 4, December.

Siamwalla, Ammar (1988) 'Public Stock Management', in Mellor and Ahmed (1988).

Timmer, Peter, Walter Falcon and Scott Pearson, (1983) *Food Policy Analysis*; World Bank/Johns Hopkins University Press.

Management Unit Trade and Industrial Policy Reform Programme, *An Overview of Assistance Policies For Agro-Based Industries*, Dhaka, 1988.

Navin, Robert, and Ibrahim Khalil, (1988) *The Agricultural Sector in Bangladesh – A Database*, Dhaka: USAID, June.

Valdes, Alberto, and Ammar Siamwalla, (1988) 'Foreign Trade Regime, Exchange Rate Policy and the Structure of Incentives' in Mellor and Ahmed (1988).

Wennergren, E. Boyd, and Morris D. Whitaker (1986) 'Foodgrain Sufficiency in Bangladesh: A Reappraisal and Policy Implications', *Journal of Developing Areas*, 21, October.

World Food Programme, 'Interim Evaluation of Project' Bangladesh 2197 (Exp. 5), Report of WFP Mission, 1–29 March 1987; WFP, Dhaka.

13 Returns from Education in Rural Bangladesh

Mahabub Hossain

INTRODUCTION

The most dismal performance of the Bangladesh economy since independence is perhaps in the field of basic education. The literacy rate is very low and has remained stagnant for a long time: 23.8 per cent in 1981 compared to 24.3 per cent in 1974 and 22 per cent in 1961.[1] About 40 per cent of the primary school age population never attend school, and among those who enrol in school about 31 per cent drop out by Grade 2, and 70 per cent by Grade 5.[2] According to the 1981 census, in the prime school age group of 10–14, 33 per cent of the population attended school in 1981 (31 per cent in rural areas, compared to 45 per cent in urban areas); and 38 per cent among male population, compared to 28 per cent among females. For the male population there was in fact a decline in the school attendance rate during the 1974–81 period.

Achieving universal primary education has been the avowed policy of the government for a long time. The government allocates about 8 per cent of public expenditure (revenue plus development) on education which amounts to about 1.5 per cent of the GDP. In the 1988/89 budget 41 per cent of public expenditure was allocated for primary schools and 29 per cent for secondary schools.[3] Since 1976 allocation to the education sector increased at a rate of 17 per cent per year compared to the rate of inflation of about 10–11 per cent. The government has undertaken large projects for primary schools for development of curriculum, supply of text books and development of school facilities. Apparently these efforts from the supply side to improve the literacy situation had limited success.

This leads one to look at the issue from the demand side. Being able to read and write may give a person psychological satisfaction. But that may not be enough incentive for a poverty-stricken household to send the children to school. They might prefer to have some material gains since there is some opportunity cost in sending children to school. Even when education and textbooks are provided free, the household would have the additional cost of better clothing for school attendance, and purchase of teaching materials. More important, after a certain age which may be quite early depending on the economic status of the household, the children may be used for various household activities, such as rearing of cattle and poultry, production of fruits and vegetables in kitchen gardens and supervision of hired workers, which would earn income for the household or save expenditure. Extremely poor households may even hire out the services of their children to upper-income groups as attached workers for domestic service or various agricultural activities, and thereby save at least the cost of food and clothing on account of the child and in some cases may even earn some income. The return from education must be high enough to compensate the cost on account of these opportunities forgone. The removal of the supply-side constraints may be a necessary but not a sufficient condition to attract children to schools.

This paper makes a modest attempt to assess the returns from education in rural Bangladesh. The information is drawn from various secondary sources as well as from a survey of rural households conducted by the Bangladesh Institute of Development Studies (BIDS) in 1982. The survey was conducted in 16 purposively selected villages scattered through the four administrative divisions of the country and represent the principal ecological zones.[4] A census of all households in the selected villages was carried out to serve as the sample frame for the study. The households were classified into eight groups based on the size of landholding (four groups) and the occupation of the head of the household. A proportionate random sample was then drawn from each stratum so as to have 40 households in each village. The total sample size consists of 640 households with 4006 members. In addition, information is drawn from an on-going BIDS study for which a sample survey has been conducted in 60 villages in 1988.

The paper is organised as follows: As a background to the study, the next section reviews the level and changes in educational status of adult population in rural Bangladesh from the available national statistics and household surveys. The third section assesses the impact of different levels of education on input use and productivity in rice cultivation and on the adoption of modern technology. The fourth section studies the impact of education on occupational mobility and employment in agriculture and non-agricultural activities by using a multivariate regression technique. The fifth section as-

Table 13.1 Level and changes of educational status of adult population in rural areas, 1974 and 1981 (figures in per cent of total population in the age group)

Age group of population	No formal schooling		Attended primary school		Attended secondary school		Attended College or University	
	1974	1981	1974	1981	1974	1981	1974	1981
15–19	68.3	63.0	12.9	18.9	18.0	14.5	0.7	3.6
20–24	74.3	65.4	11.1	18.3	11.0	10.6	3.5	5.7
25–34	81.3	69.7	10.5	17.2	6.1	7.4	2.1	5.7
35–44	84.3	74.4	9.8	16.6	5.2	5.7	0.7	3.4
45 and above	87.0	77.4	8.7	15.5	4.0	5.6	0.3	1.5
Total	80.5	70.8	10.3	17.1	7.9	8.3	1.3	3.8

Source: Bangladesh Bureau of Statistics, Reports of 1974 and 1981 population censuses, Dhaka, 1978 and 1984.

sesses the return from education in general and for different landholding groups. The final section recapitulates the major findings and draws some policy implications.

EDUCATIONAL STATUS OF RURAL POPULATION

Information obtained from the population census of 1974 and 1981 regarding educational attainment of adult rural population (who actively participate in economic activities) is presented in Table 13.1. The following features emerge from the table.

Adult illiteracy is widespread. Nearly 71 per cent of the adult population recorded in 1981 never attended school and another 17 per cent had only up to primary level education, many of whom would not have the skill of reading and writing with comprehension. Only 8.3 per cent of the population attended secondary school and 3.8 per cent had higher education.

Temporal and across age-group comparisons reveal some progress in educational attainment, contrary to the popular notion that there has been no progress at all in the field of literacy. The proportion of adult population with no formal schooling was reduced from 81 per cent in 1974 to 71 per cent in 1981. The higher-age population cohort spent their school-age period earlier than the lower-age population cohort. So across age-group comparison regarding educational attainment for a particular year (from static, cross-section data) provides dynamic information regarding changes in educational attainment. In 1981 about 37 per cent of the population in the 15–19 age group attended school compared to about 25 per cent for the population who were at least 20 years older. In 1974 thirty-two per cent of the 15–19 age group attended school compared to only sixteen per cent for the population aged 35 years or more. One should note however that the progress in educational attainment is too slow in relation to the need, particularly if the government wants to achieve universal primary education within a short period of time. Also, the comparison of the figures for the two younger age groups (the 15–19 and 20–24 age cohorts) show that the progress has become slower in recent years.

Advancement in the attainment of secondary education appears to be much slower in comparison to both primary and higher education. Among the 15–19 age group, for example, the proportion of population who attended only primary schools increased from 12.9 to 18.9 per cent during the 1974–81 period, and those who attended college or university increased from 0.7 to 3.6 per cent, while those who attended secondary school dropped from 18.0 to 14.5 per cent. Thus, a larger proportion of those who enrol in schools drops out after primary level, but a larger proportion of those who cross the secondary level continue to higher education.

The population census reports do not provide information on educational attainment for different socio-economic groups. A 1988 BIDS field survey of 60 randomly selected villages however noted vast differentiation among various landownership groups in this respect. Educational attainment of the head of the household was found to be highly positively correlated with the amount of land owned by the household (Table 13.2). About 54 per cent of the sample-household heads in 1988 reported that they never attended school; the figure was 68 per cent for the functionally landless households (those with less than half an acre of land), compared to only 28 per cent for the households with more than five acres of land. The differentiation was even wider among household heads who attended at least secondary school. There were 44 per cent among large landowners compared to only 10.4 per cent for the landless and 24.1 per cent for small owners.

The figures in Table 13.2 also suggest a strong negative correlation of school drop-out rates with the amount of land owned by the household. For the landless 32.5 per cent sample heads of household

Table 13.2 Distribution of heads of household by landownership status and level of education, 1988 (per cent of total members)

Level of education (completed years of schooling)	Less than 0.5 acres (N=4882)	0.5–2.5 acres (N=3122)	2.5–5.0 acres (N=1088)	5.0 and over (N=782)	All households (N=9874)
Nil	67.5	45.3	35.3	28.3	53.8
Up to two years	7.1	8.2	6.5	5.6	7.3
3–5 years	15.0	22.4	20.5	22.0	18.5
6–10 years	6.8	12.7	18.9	21.0	11.1
11 and over	3.6	11.4	18.4	23.1	9.3
Total	100.0	100.0	100.0	100.0	100.0
Per cent of samples in the group	49.5	31.6	11.0	7.9	100.0

Source: Census of 60 randomly selected villages conducted by BIDS for the study on 'Differential Impact of Modern Rice Technology in Bangladesh' (work in progress).

reported having some formal education, but about 68 per cent of them dropped out before reaching secondary schools. For the large landowner group 71.7 per cent of the household heads had some formal education; among them only 38 per cent dropped out before reaching secondary schools. The corresponding figures for the small and medium landowners are 56 per cent and 42 per cent, respectively.

The status of land ownership of the household is also found to be an important determinant of the attendance of the children in school. The BIDS sample survey of households in 60 villages in 1988 found the school attendance rate in the primary school age group (6–10) was 60 per cent: it varied from 47 per cent for the landless households to 83 per cent for the large landowner group (Table 13.3). But the attendance rate was also found to be highly positively related with the level of education of the head of the household; from 46 per cent for those having no formal education to 82 per cent for those who completed secondary school. Similar findings are noted for attendance of children in secondary school (Table 13.3). The effect of education on attendance rate is however found to be very pronounced

Table 13.3　Extent of attendance of children in school by level of education of household head and landownership status of household, 1988 (per cent of school age population)

Completed years of schooling of head of household	Land owned by household (acres)				
	Less than 0.5 acres (landless)	0.5 to less than 2.5 acres (small farm)	2.5 to less than 5.0 acres (medium farm)	5.0 acres and more (large farm)	Total
Primary school age group (6–10):					
nil	35.7	47.0	66.6	80.4	45.8
1–5	56.6	65.9	66.0	77.2	63.7
6–10	65.4	82.6	76.9	90.0	77.3
11+	86.6	78.1	77.5	86.3	81.5
Total	47.3	62.3	70.5	82.6	59.8
Secondary school age group (11–16):					
nil	20.6	40.2	60.4	57.8	35.3
1–5	42.2	62.5	76.9	56.5	57.3
6–10	62.1	77.5	66.6	61.5	69.0
11+	82.3	67.4	79.4	66.0	71.7
Total	34.2	57.3	70.5	60.8	52.5

Source: Unpublished information from a sample survey of 60 villages for the study on 'Differential Impact of Modern Rice Technology in Bangladesh', conducted by BIDS (work in progress).

for the landless households and not highly significant for the large landowners. Also, households whose heads had attended secondary school seem to send most of their children to school, irrespective of the size of landownership (Table 13.3). Even in landless households the attendance rate in both primary and secondary schools is more than 80 per cent for the heads of household who had completed secondary school. The findings point to the dynamic role of education in extending literacy in rural Bangladesh.

EDUCATION, AGRICULTURAL MODERNISATION AND FARM PRODUCTIVITY

Agriculture is the main economic activity of the rural households and nearly two-thirds of the total income are derived from it. In Bangladesh, agricultural production centres around crop husbandry. So the first step in assessing the return from education in rural areas should be to look at its impact on the management of crop production.

It is argued in the literature[5] that education would have very little role to play in improving farm management in a static, traditional environment, where the optimum crop husbandry practices were developed long ago and hence the knowledge has already been disseminated widely, and the skills have become family tradition. Better education could provide a higher pay-off to farmers only in a changing and modernising environment, which would need exposure to new information and extension services. Access to information about sources of new inputs, the knowledge of how they can be optimally used, and the channels and timing of marketing of additional output could be important factors in determining the rate of adoption of a new agricultural technology and the extent of economic gains from it. A better-educated farmer could acquire the new knowledge quickly and could have more contact with the extension agents who supply this information. In Bangladesh, the growth of agricultural production now depends on the diffusion of the modern 'seed-fertiliser-water' technology. So farmers' education should assume a critical role in promoting agricultural growth.

Table 13.4 reports the findings of the BIDS household survey on the relationship of some key variables regarding input use and farm productivity with the level of education of the adult members (age 16 and over) of the household. No systematic relationship is observed from the data. As expected, the better educated had larger land holding and they also had more fixed non-land assets per acre of land. The access to irrigation and the amount of labour used per unit of land was found almost random across the scale of educational attainment. In fact, the less-educated adopted the modern crop varieties relatively more than the better-educated, a finding contrary to the *a priori* hypothesis. The households with less-educated adults also used more fertiliser per unit of land than the better-educated, which is the result of higher rates of adoption of modern varieties, as they are highly fertiliser-intensive. The per-acre yield of paddy for both local and modern varieties was found invariant across the education scale up to the secondary education level. Only those households whose adults had more than secondary level education achieved higher crop yields. But the number of observations in this cell is so small (13 out of 484 farm households) that it would be unwise to draw firm conclusions from this information.

Agricultural performance may depend on many factors besides the farmer's education. The effect of those factors needs to be isolated for the estimation of the true effect of education. Since education may affect agricultural production by facilitating the adoption of

Table 13.4 Relationship of some variables with average level of education of adults, 1982

Variables	No formal schooling	Up to two years' schooling	3–5 years	6–10 years	Over 10 years
Average size of land owned (acres)	1.33	2.44	3.00	3.37	4.46
Capital per acre of land (Tk)	2992	2746	3322	4979	4276
Percentage of land irrigated	21.80	34.40	26.00	38.90	32.50
Percentage of area under modern variety of cereals	49.70	48.20	44.80	33.40	33.50
Fertiliser use per acre (lb)	145	129	145	119	102
Labour use per acre (days)	57	52	51	45	53
Paddy yield (maunds/acre)	26.30	25.90	25.50	24.30	27.90
Paddy yield for modern varieties (maunds/acre)	36.60	36.50	36.60	36.30	46.10

Source: Unpublished data from BIDS Field Survey.

modern agricultural practices, a multi-variate regression model was fitted to explain the adoption of modern varieties of rice, in which education was included as one of the explanatory variables. The following results were obtained from the farm survey data:

$$MVP = 0.17^* - 0.429 \ OWNL + 0.283^{**} \ TNC + 1.084^{**} \ IRGP$$
$$\quad (2.34) \quad (-0.74) \quad \quad (4.64) \quad \quad \quad (12.56)$$

$$-0.550 \ LBR + 0.337 \ FSZ - 0.416 \ EDN + 0.742^{**} \ CRDTI$$
$$(-0.25) \quad \quad (0.38) \quad (-0.66) \quad \quad (2.74)$$

$$+0.695^{**} \ CRDTN - 0.290^* \ NAGRI \quad \bar{R}^2 = 0.48$$
$$(3.82) \quad \quad (-1.99)$$

where *MVP* is the proportion of land cultivated with modern varieties of rice, *OWNL* is the area of land owned by the household (acres), *TNC* is the proportion of land under tenancy, *IRGP* is the proportion of land irrigated, *LBR* is the amount of land cultivated per worker (acre), *FSZ* is the number of members in the family, which is a measure of the consumption-pressure in the household, *CRDTI* is the amount of loans received from institutional sources (Tk 100 per acre), *CRDTN* is the amount of loans received from non-institutional sources (Tk 100 per acre), *NAGRI* is the income from non-agricultural sources (Tk 100) and *EDN* is the level of education of the head of the household measured by completed years of formal schooling.

Since the observed values of the dependent variable have a limited range (zero to one), which is the case of a limited dependent variable model, a Tobit (two limit probit) model was applied to estimate the parameters of the equation. The figures within parentheses are asymptotic 't' values of the regression coefficient. The value of the adjusted coefficient of determination, $\bar{R}^2$, is for the ordinary least square estimate of the equation. The sign** denotes that the coefficient is statistically significant at 1 per cent probability level, and* at 5 per cent level.

The results show that the factors which significantly affect the adoption of modern crop varieties are availability of irrigation facilities, credit received from both institutional and non-institutional sources and the area under tenancy.

The statistically significant positive coefficient of the tenancy variable indicates that the extent of adoption of modern varieties is higher on rented land than on owned land. This is contrary to the *a priori* hypothesis that the terms of tenancy (sharecropping, which is the most common arrangement) discourages adoption of modern varieties.[6] Since the modern varieties are more labour intensive than the traditional ones, and the tenant rents in land for minimising the underutilisation of family workers and farm establishment, large landowners may gain more by getting modern varieties cultivated by sharecroppers than by self-cultivating with wage labourers. Since there is excess demand for land, the tenancy market may be governed more by the interest of the landowners than by that of the tenants, who would be discouraged from cultivating modern varieties on rented land under a crop-sharing arrangement.

Another surprising result is the negative coefficient of the non-agricultural income variable, which is also statistically significant.

Farmers who earn some income from non-agricultural sources may have less liquidity constraint than those who depend mostly on agriculture. So access to non-agricultural income should ease the capital constraint to adoption of modern varieties. The negative value of the coefficient however indicates that farmers who have more access to non-agricultural income have adopted less, which is contrary to the above hypothesis. This suggests that the association between the two variables may be the other way round. Farmers who cannot adopt modern varieties due to technical constraints (non-availability of irrigation, deep flooding of land, etc.) try to augment household incomes by engaging in various non-agricultural activities.

The value of the coefficient of education variable is negative, which supports the earlier finding that the less-educated adopt modern varieties more intensively. The value of the coefficient is not however statistically significant. N.I. Hossain tried to explain the determinants of the adoption of modern varieties with district level cross-section data and also found similar results on the effect of education.[7] He however found positive relationship between education and the use of chemical fertilisers.

Thus, in Bangladesh education does not seem to contribute to agricultural production even under modernising circumstances. It may be explained by the fact that the type of education provided in schools is not work-orientated. Schooling is basically regarded as a means to escape from the hard manual labour which farming requires. Those who have some formal education seek non-agricultural jobs which are less arduous and often better paying than agriculture. This type of education may promote occupational mobility and not increase efficiency of labour in a particular occupation. The role of education in the choice of occupation and employment is examined in the next section.

EDUCATION, OCCUPATION AND EMPLOYMENT

Does education affect the choice of occupation in rural Bangladesh? Table 13.5 presents information on the educational status of the heads of household according to the major sources of income of the household obtained from a census of 60 villages, conducted by BIDS in 1988. The following features can be noted from the table.

The illiterate are concentrated mostly in manual occupations like

Table 13.5 Education attainment of household head by major source of income for the household, 1988

Major source of income	No. of sample house-holds	Level of education of the household head				
		No formal schooling	Classes 1–2	Classes 3–5	Classes 6–10	Classes 11 and higher
		(in per cent of row total)				
Cultivation of own farm	4323	46.5	7.9	21.5	14.1	10.0
Agricultural wage labour	2605	79.5	0.4	10.6	2.9	0.6
Cottage industry	291	51.2	7.6	22.3	14.1	4.8
Trading and shopkeeping	871	38.2	10.3	26.2	14.5	10.8
Transport operation	319	67.1	9.1	16.3	6.9	0.6
Construction work	104	71.1	9.6	11.5	4.8	2.9
Services	931	14.0	3.9	25.2	21.1	35.9
Others	430	77.2	5.3	6.5	5.1	5.8
Total	9874	53.8	7.3	18.5	11.1	9.3

Source: Census of 40 randomly selected villages conducted by BIDS for the study on 'Differential Impact of Modern Rice Technology in Bangladesh' (work in progress).

agricultural wage labour, transport operation and construction work. About 54 per cent of the household heads reported having no formal schooling, the proportion was 80 per cent for the households engaged in agricultural wage labour and 71 per cent for construction workers and 67 per cent for transport operators (cart and boat operators and rickshaw pullers). Persons with secondary-level education were only 3.5 per cent, 7.5 per cent and 7.7 per cent in these three occupations respectively.

The higher-educated on the other hand were concentrated in two occupations, services, and trade and shopkeeping, which are the major sources of income for about 18 per cent of rural households. Only 16 per cent of the heads of household reporting services as the major source of income had no formal schooling while 36 per cent had at least secondary school certificates, and another 21 per cent attended secondary schools. About 25 per cent of the persons reporting trading as the major source of income had at least secondary-level education, while 36 per cent in this occupation were illiterate. Quite a large proportion of people who cultivate their own land are also better educated (about 24 per cent attended at least secondary school). Some of them may pursue trading and services as a supplementary source of income.

For a rigorous analysis of the effect of education on farm and non-farm employment, we estimated a labour supply function on the 1982 household survey data, in which education was included as one of the explanatory variables. The survey collected information for the adult members of the household on their participation in productive work for each day of the week preceding the day of interview, for eight weeks scattered throughout the year 1982. The periods were selected on the basis of *a priori* knowledge of the cropping pattern of the area so as to represent the normal, busy and slack periods of employment. The supply of labour of the household was built up from these eight weeks' data.

Following Yotopoulos and Lau, and Bardhan[8] the following labour supply function was fitted on the data:

$$SLBR = f(WAGE, FSZ, WRKR, FEM, OWNL,$$
$$TECH, CPTL, EDN, LVNG)$$

where *SLBR* is the average weekly hours of labour put in by all adult members of the household; *WAGE* is the wage rate (Tk/day) prevailing at the village level; *FSZ* is the number of members in the household; *WRKR* is the total number of workers and *FEM* is the number of female members participating in income-earning activities; *OWNL*, the amount of land owned by the household (acres); *TECH*, the amount of land cropped with modern varieties (acres); *CPTL*, the amount of non-land fixed assets owned by the household (Tk 100); *EDN* is the number of completed years of schooling for the head of the household; and *LVNG*, is the standard of living in the village as measured by per capita consumption expenditure (Tk 100).

In the utility function of an individual, leisure is considered as one of the consumer goods. Its cost is the wage income which has to be sacrificed if leisure is consumed. So the choice between leisure and consumer goods is determined by their relative prices, i.e. the wage rate and the prices of consumer goods. An increase in income from non-wage sources shifts the consumption possibility upwards and hence the individual can have more leisure and consumer goods at the same level of relative prices. Thus labour, which is the residual of the time available for work, is determined mainly by the wage rate, the prices of the consumer goods and the income from non-wage sources. The main determinants of the non-wage income are physical and human capital. The variables *OWNL*, *TECH*, *CPTL* and *EDN* have been incorporated to capture the effect of this factor. Education, by increasing the quality of human resource, provides scope for increasing labour productivity or mobility to higher-paid employment in the service sector, and hence for earning higher income from the same amount of labour.

The decision regarding the consumption of goods and services and the supply of labour is determined at the household level. So the composition of the household and the working members may also affect the supply of labour. The higher the number of consumers (*FSZ*) relative to workers (*WRKR*) the lower would be the per capita income from labour in the household and the higher would be the supply of labour. The larger the proportion of female workers, the lower would be the supply of labour, since women have to supply domestic labour which reduces the time available for income-earning work. So, other things remaining constant, labour supply would be positively associated with family size and negatively associated with the number of female workers.

The results of the exercise are presented in Table 13.6. For the present purpose we are interested in the coefficient of the education variable. After controlling for the effects of the other variables, the coefficient of education is found negative in the equation for agricultural labour, which suggests that the higher-educated supply less labour to agriculture. The value of the regression coefficient indicates that with each additional year of schooling the supply of labour to agriculture is reduced by 1.44 hours per week, that is about 9.4 standard eight-hour days a year. The coefficient of education in the equation for non-agricultural labour is however positive, which shows that the higher-educated supply more labour to non-agricultural activities. The value of the coefficient indicates that with each additional year of schooling the supply of labour to non-agricultural activities is increased by 0.78 hours per week or about five days per year. Thus, on balance, education seems to reduce the supply of labour. The value of the estimated coefficients would mean, other things remaining constant, that a worker with secondary school

Table 13.6 Effect of education on labour supply to agriculture and non-agricultural activities – a regression estimate

Explanatory variables	Agriculture	Non-agriculture	Total
	(Average number of hours per week)		
WRKR	13.34**	12.72**	31.06**
	(15.23)	(9.47)	(9.47)
FSZ	1.55**	−0.27	1.28**
	(3.78)	(−0.61)	(3.34)
FEM	−11.33**	−0.14	−11.27**
	(−4.38)	(−0.05)	(−4.76)
WAGE	0.07	1.03**	1.10**
	(0.29)	(3.73)	(4.71)
OWNL	0.77	−1.86**	− 1.09**
	(1.83)	(−4.04)	(−2.80)
TECH	1.86**	−4.04**	−2.18**
	(2.34)	(−4.65)	(−2.95)
CPTL	0.61	0.18	0.34**
	(1.74)	(1.72)	(3.89)
EDN	−1.44**	0.78**	−0.66**
	(−4.97)	(2.43)	(−2.42)
LVNG	−0.97**	−0.50	−1.47**
	(−4.00)	(−1.88)	(6.51)
Constant	28.34**	4.26	32.60**
	(3.54)	(0.88)	(4.38)
$\bar{R}^2$	0.47	0.21	0.67

Note: The sample size consists of 624 households with valid observations for all variables. Figures within parentheses are estimated '*t*' values. The sign * denotes that this coefficient is significant at five per cent probability level, and ** at one per cent level.

certificate would work about 44 days less in agriculture and 50 days more in non-agricultural activities. Since the labour productivity of the educated person may be higher than the illiterate, the income of the former need not necessarily be lower because of the reduced work effort.

RETURNS FROM EDUCATION

It is estimated from the BIDS field survey that the sample households earned on average Tk 20 984 during 1982 at the prevailing prices.[9] The per capita income was estimated at Tk 3300, which compares with the per capita income of Tk 3015 estimated by the Bureau of

Statistics for the country as a whole for 1982/83. About 64 per cent of the income was earned from agricultural activities and 36 per cent from non-agricultural activities.

The following regression model was fitted to study the determinants of household income:

$$INCM = f(OWNL, OWNL^2, TNC, TECH, WRKR, DPND, EDN)$$

where *INCM* is the annual income of the household, and *DPND* the dependency ratio in the family as measured by the number of consumers per worker. Other variables are as defined earlier. The dependency ratio was included to test the Chayanovian hypothesis that in a peasant economy, the motive force behind the economic activity is the consumer-worker balance in the family. The square of owned land was added to allow the marginal return from land to vary with the size of landownership. In Bangladesh, land productivity varies inversely with farm size,[10] and we have already noted that larger landowners prefer more leisure, which indicates that marginal returns from land would decline with the increase in the size of landownership.

The estimates of the parameters are reported in Table 13.7. The main determinants of agricultural income are land, technology and family workers, while the main determinants of non-agricultural incomes are the number of workers in the family, accumulation of non-agricultural assets, the level of education of the worker, and the consumption pressure in the family.

The results show that education increases household income mainly through involvement of the worker in the non-agricultural sector which support the findings of the previous two sections. The estimated value of the regression coefficient suggests that an additional year of schooling increases non-agricultural income on the margin by Tk 250 per annum, but it is achieved partly at the expense of agricultural income, so the effect of education on total household income is less. An additional year of schooling reduces agricultural income by Tk 77, and raises total income by Tk 172 per annum.

We may now make an attempt at estimating the rate of return on education, for which we also need information about the cost of education. The government spent about Tk 164 per student per year at the primary level in 1983. There is no accurate estimate of the private cost on account of books, teaching aids and improved clothing. An unpublished BIDS survey in 11 villages conducted during

Table 13.7 Determinants of rural household incomes: regression
estimate, 1982

Variables	Agricultural income	Non-agricultural income	Total income
Constant	1978	256	2045
	(1.56)	(0.24)	(1.20)
OWNL	3287**	200	3459**
	(14.87)	(1.08)	(11.26)
OWNL^2	−43**	−2.5	−43**
	(−5.28)	(−0.36)	(3.93)
TNC	627	−183	351
	(1.90)	(−0.66)	(0.78)
CPTL	−0.005	0.205**	0.101
	(−0.13)	(6.04)	(2.66)
WRKR	975**	2095**	3125
	(2.65)	(6.68)	(6.22)
TECH	1729**	357	1973**
	(7.22)	(1.89)	(6.13)
DPND	799	827*	1649**
	(1.75)	(2.13)	(2.65)
EDN	−77	249**	172
	(−1.37)	(3.50)	(1.52)
$\bar{R}^2$	0.55	0.19	0.52

Note: The sample size consists of 629 households with valid observations for
all variables in the equation. Capital is measured as value of non-land
agricultural fixed assets in the equation for agricultural income, and non-
agricultural fixed assets in the equation for non-agricultural income. Figures
within parentheses are estimated t-values.

1981 estimates this cost to be approximately Tk 250 per annum per
student. Thus the total cost per annum per student for primary
education comes to about Tk 414. If a student incurs this cost for a
period of five years and then from year 6 gets an additional return of
Tk 860 (172 × 5) per annum for a period of 45 years,[11] the internal
rate of return from this investment is calculated at about 25 per cent.
If the cost paid by the government is excluded, the internal rate of
return from private investment comes to 35 per cent. At this rate of
return there should be enough incentive to continue schooling to the
primary level.

The above calculations assume that there is no opportunity cost in
sending children to primary school. But this may be an unrealistic

assumption for the secondary school-going age. Many students at this age would have participated in various expenditure-saving household activities if they had not attended school. The 1981 BIDS survey estimated the alternative earnings forgone at about Tk 1200 per annum (at 1982 prices) and the cost of books, materials and additional cost on improved clothing at Tk 800 per annum. If a student incurs these costs for a period of another three years in lower secondary schools, and from year 9 (since beginning school) earns Tk 1376 per annum (172×8) as additional income from that investment for a period of 42 years, the rate of return from the private investment works out at 14.5 per cent. It is estimated that the government spent Tk 210 per student in secondary school in 1982. If this cost is included the rate of return on investment becomes 12.2 per cent. At these rates of return there would be a limited incentive to continue schooling even up to the lower secondary level.

Of course, the rate of return on education may not be the same for different socio-economic groups, and the return per year of schooling may vary at different levels of education. The estimates of annual income for households classified by the educational attainment of adult members will be seen from Table 13.8. The estimates are provided separately for different landownership groups since land is

Table 13.8 Average household incomes by size of landownership and level of education of adult members

Level of education (years of schooling)	Less than 0.5 acres	0.5–2.0 acres	2.0–5.0 acres	5.0 acres and above
Nil	12 165	13 413	22 418	36 324
Up to two years	11 449 (−358)	18 910 (2785)	28 564 (3073)	41 922 (2819)
3–5 years	12 252 (22)	19 919 (1627)	24 404 (497)	47 315 (2748)
6–10 years	11 655 (−75)	21 648 (1029)	31 115 (1087)	55 000 (2335)
Over 10 years	–	25 196 (1178)	48 182 (1707)	80 113 (4379)
Total	12 039	17 136	26 269	45 693

Note: The figures within parentheses are additional income per·year of schooling. Sample sizes for the four landholding size groups are respectively 195, 217, 165 and 62.
Source: Unpublished data from BIDS field survey.

the major determinant of rural income, and hence its effect needs to be isolated. The table also gives an estimate of the incremental income per year of schooling for different levels of education. The estimates should however be taken with a grain of salt because, as we have already noted, income may be determined by a host of other factors besides land and education. With this qualification in mind the following points may be noted from Table 13.8.

The functionally landless households who are the bottom 30 per cent of the sample in the landownership scale do not seem to get any return from education at all. Even for households whose adult members attended secondary school, the income was almost the same as the households whose members never attended school. Although this result is surprising, it is consistent with the observation that the landless households are not interested in sending their children to school. Members of this group of households generally work as agricultural labourers for others. In this occupation education is of little use, since the employer would not provide higher wages to a better-educated than to a less-educated worker. An educated member in this group of households could be self-employed in more productive non-agricultural activities such as trading, in which he could utilise the skill acquired through education. This would however, require some fixed and working capital, which very few landless households can afford to accumulate. Also, these people do not generally have access to credit from financial institutions. Only if a person could get at least a secondary school certificate, could he find a job in the service sector, but the opportunity cost of keeping children in school for so long may be very high for this category of household who, for the obvious reason of intense poverty, are more concerned about immediate needs than about investment in children's education.

For other categories of household the return from education appears to be positive and quite substantial. But for small and medium landowning households the incremental income from an additional year of schooling does not increase beyond the primary level. Since the opportunity cost of sending the children to school increases with age, particularly when the child crosses the primary level, the constant marginal return from additional schooling would discourage parents from keeping their children in school beyond primary level.

The return from additional schooling is highest for the large landowning group, and the return appears to increase with the level of schooling. In this category, households with illiterate adult members earned only Tk 36 328 (at 1982 prices), while those whose members attempted secondary school earned Tk 55 000 and with members having higher secondary education the income increases to over Tk 80 000. The incremental income per year of education was about Tk 2800 for primary education, and Tk 4400 for higher secondary education. This level of earning would give a very high rate of return on education.

The findings suggests that formal education is a necessary but not a sufficient condition for increasing incomes. For raising labour productivity and incomes by the application of skills acquired through education, one needs to have access to other productive resources such as land and capital. Because of the type of education provided in schools, which discourages manual labour, education may not increase labour productivity and income through better management of land. But ownership of land provides access to capital, credit and public services, which could be combined with education to move from agriculture to higher-paid non-agricultural occupations. By facilitating this occupational mobility, education raises income for the households with larger land-ownership.

CONCLUSIONS

In Bangladesh illiteracy is widespread and in spite of the government's emphasis on universal primary education, very little progress has been achieved in this field since independence. This paper relates economic performance of rural households with educational attainment of members in order to see whether the demand side factors pose constraints to progress in this field.

It is found from the study that the efficiency of management of agriculture has no relation to the educational attainment of the head of the household. This is surprising because the growth of agricultural production now depends on the adoption of the new 'seed-fertiliser-water' technology and education should have facilitated better understanding of the technology and its proper use. But the rate of adoption of the new technology is found invariant with the level of education. A multivariate regression analysis of the household level data shows that the higher the level of education the lower are the supply of labour and the earnings from agriculture.

Education however provides some return through facilitating occupational mobility to higher-paid non-agricultural jobs. The higher-educated in rural areas are concentrated in trading and services while the illiterates pursue agricultural labour, transport operations and construction work, which require manual labour. The supply of labour to non-agricultural activities and non-agricultural incomes is found to be significantly related to the level of education of the household head.

An additional year of schooling is found to increase income by Tk 172 per annum at 1982 prices. This gives a rate of return of 25 per cent on investment on schooling at the primary level, but it is reduced to about 12 per cent for the lower secondary level, as the children reach the age when they can earn something for the household, which is part of the cost of sending them to school. It is found that the landless do not gain at all from education since they do not have the capital necessary to take up the opportunities of employment in the non-agricultural sector. For the large landowning group however the return from education is high and it increases for successively higher levels.

In order to make schooling more attractive, there is a need to change the curriculum so that education becomes more work-orientated and increases efficiency of labour in the workplace. Knowledge about new agricultural practices and their practical applications should be taught in schools so that students find education useful in increasing income from farming. The landless could be induced to send their children to school if the educated landless were given access to institutional credit without collateral security (as provided by Grameen Bank), so that they could use the skills acquired through education for generating self-employment in more productive non-agricultural activities.

Notes

1. The concept of literacy used in various censuses has not been uniform. The 1981 census treated a person as literate if he or she could write a letter in any language, while the 1974 census defined literacy as the ability to read and write, and the 1961 census, as the ability to read and write with understanding. Because of changes in definition, one may raise questions about the observed stagnation in the literacy ratio. It will be shown that there has been some improvement in the educational status of adults.
2. See *Survey of Primary Schools and Evaluation of Primary School Agriculture Programme in Bangladesh*, Part I, Institute of Education and Research, University of Dhaka, July 1977, p. 51.

3. Government of Bangladesh, *Demand For Grants and Appropriations, (Non-Development)*, 1988–89, Ministry of Finance, Finance Division 1988.
4. The survey design and methodology is described in detail in, *Development Impact of the Food-for-Work Programme in Bangladesh*, Bangladesh Institute of Development Studies and the International Food Policy Research Institute, Washington DC, 1985. pp. 1.3–1.11.
5. See, among others, Dean T. Jamison and L.J. Lau, *Farmer Education and Farm Efficiency*. Baltimore and London: Johns Hopkins University Press, 1982; M.E. Lockheed, D.T. Jamison and L.J. Lau, 'Farmer Education and Farm Efficiency – A Survey', *Economic Development and Cultural Change*, vol. 29, 1980, pp. 37–76; Baldev Singh, 'Impact of Education on Farm Production', *Economic and Political Weekly*, 1974, pp. 92–6; Craig C. Wu, 'Education in Farm Production: The Case of Taiwan', *American Journal of Agricultural Economics*, vol. 59, no. 4, November 1977, pp. 699–709.
6. The effects of tenancy on the adoption of modern agricultural technology are discussed in Amit Bhaduri, 'A Study in Agricultural Backwardness Under Semi-Feudalism', *Economic Journal*, vol. 83, March 1973, pp. 120–37; David Newberry, 'Tenurial Obstacles to Innovation', *Journal of Development Studies*, vol. 11, no. 4, July 1975, pp. 263–77; Pranab K. Bardhan and T.N. Srinivasan, 'Crop Sharing Tenancy in Agriculture: A Theoretical and Empirical Analysis', *American Economic Review*, vol. 61, no. 1, 1971, pp. 48–64.
7. M. Iqbal Hossain, *Regional Agricultural Poverty Differences in Bangladesh*, Unpublished PhD dissertation, University of Dhaka, 1988.
8. Yotopoulos and Lau derive a labour supply function of the household from an indirect utility function, while Bardhan employs a pragmatic approach to explain the labour market participation behaviour of peasant households. See, P.A. Yotopoulos and L.J. Lau, 'On Modeling the Agricultural Sector in Developing Economies', *Journal of Development Economics*, vol. 1, no. 2, September 1974, pp. 105–27; Pranab K. Bardhan, 'Labour Supply Functions in a Poor Agrarian Economy', *American Economic Review*, vol. 69, March 1979, pp. 73–83.
9. See, Mahabub Hossain, *Nature and Impact of the Green Revolution in Bangladesh*, Research Report no. 67, International Food Policy Research Institute, Washington DC, July 1988, pp. 119–21.
10. A large number of studies confirmed this relationship. See among others, Mahabub Hossain, 'Farm Size, Tenancy and Land Productivity: An Analysis of Farm Level Data in Bangladesh Agriculture', *Bangladesh Development Studies*, vol. 5, no. 3, 1977, pp. 285–348; *Nature and Impact of Green Revolution in Bangladesh*, IFPRI Research Report no. 67, July 1988; and M.A. Sattar Mondal, 'Farm Size, Tenure and Productivity in an Area of Bangladesh', *Bangladesh Journal of Agricultural Economics*, vol. 3, no. 2 December 1980, pp. 21–42.
11. It is assumed that a student will complete his primary education at age 12 and his working life will continue up to age 57.

IV In Lieu of a Conclusion: A Personal Reminiscence

14 Economics Comes of Age in a Developing Country: the Case of Bangladesh

Austin Robinson

My own first acquaintance with the part of the world which included what is now Bangladesh came soon after the separation of India and Pakistan. It happened that the central economic administration of India was comparatively little affected by the separation: on the other hand rather few senior economic officials opted for Pakistan. Mohammed Ali, the first Secretary General of the Government of Pakistan and later Minister of Finance and Prime Minister, found himself faced with the task of setting up a financial administration for a new country with insufficient experienced officials to do the job satisfactorily. He asked the British Treasury to lend him someone for a few weeks to help set up an economic planning department. Since I had been occupied in that sort of work and was now back in Cambridge, they asked me to go out on a Cambridge vacation.

My memory of my first day is vivid. I asked whether they had the rudiments of a plan. I was given the in-tray off the table of the head of the department. It contained a large number of letters suggesting projects, in hardly any cases with any estimate of cost. The advocate, of course, gave his project a very high priority. I had nothing except my own inadequate knowledge of the country, or rather two countries, to guide me.

One obviously needed some criterion as to how large a plan might be in total. I asked whether there existed any attempt to estimate the order of magnitude of the national income. Not unexpectedly, I was told that they knew of no attempt. This was nobody's fault. The first attempts to estimate the national income of India by V.K.R.V. Rao and others had been made only a few years before. Rather it was a perhaps inevitable consequence of trying to superimpose the techniques of a very modern country on what was, temporarily at least, a very primitive country. A few days later they told me that they had found someone who had tried to produce a national income. They brought to see me a lad who looked as if he was about nineteen years old, very shy and very diffident. His attempt was enormously praiseworthy and heroic. I played with it myself for the rest of my time in Pakistan. As it was it had, as so often, both considerable gaps and considerable doubled-counting as well as much guesswork. I do not think I ever turned it into anything that I would have dared to use.

All this I have mentioned because I want to emphasise the extreme ignorance that existed at that time regarding many of the essentials of the Pakistani economy, apart from the few things, such as guesses of crop yields, which the Government of India had long collected. Some of the gaps in knowledge obviously needed an improvement of the Government's own statistical service. This has been done, to the immense advantage both of national administration and economic investigation. But not all problems are best handled by regular annual returns. There are many problems that are best examined once for all in considerable depth. One can use the study in depth to interpret annual statistics. Such studies in depth are in many cases better conducted by an academic non-governmental body.

Inevitably while I was in Pakistan on this first occasion I got to know the local representatives of the Ford Foundation and discussed with them the teaching of economics. A year or two later I was asked by them to go out again. They were interested in particular in various suggestions that an economic institute should be set up, and were themselves considering whether they should play a major part in doing this. Since they knew that I had acquired a certain knowledge of Pakistan in addition to an earlier knowledge of India they asked me whether I would go round the various universities of the two wings, talk to as many as I could of those concerned, and advise the Foundation. This I was able to do not very long after my first visit.

I did in fact travel round both wings and visit five of the six universities of the two wings a year or two later. What I found was very interesting. The economics was being taught very thoroughly and very conscientiously. But it was a very academic subject. It was about the way that people behaved in England or North America. It assumed the institutions and repercussions of England or North America. It was not about Pakistan. It did not assume the institutions of Pakistan. It all seemed to me infinitely remote from their own everyday life.

Equally it seemed to me that a pupil was learning more English economic history, more about the development of economic technologies and institutions in England than in his own country. When I argued that this was very wrong, that having secured their independence they ought to teach their own history, I was told that there were no adequate books because not enough was known and this or that had never been measured. I naturally argued that those teaching economics ought to get out, do research and write books. It was quickly made clear to me that there was neither money nor facilities then available for research and precious little leisure to do it in a country that was large and in which distances were long and made fieldwork expensive.

Despite all the difficulties I was very greatly impressed by the capacity of some of those that I met, and by the quality of teaching in some of the institutions despite unusual difficulties. I have irrelevant memories of the immense size of the class to which I was asked to speak impromptu at Government College, Lahore, and of the strange experience in Peshawar of being faced, as I talked to an audience of students, by the end of a blanket which separated the male students from the female while allowing both to see me and neither to see the other. But I was also impressed by the smallness at that time of the number of absolutely first-rate well-trained potential members of the staff with adequate research experience for an institute if one were created and the damage that their withdrawal might inflict on their universities.

Nonetheless the conclusion was obvious: the good government of what were then the two wings of Pakistan required that more should be known about the detailed working of the national economy; the good teaching of economics required that more should be known both qualitatively and quantitatively about the national economy. Even at some short-term cost to teaching it made good sense to set up the proposed institute.

It was substantially more difficult to know how to staff it. Ideally both the Ford Foundation representatives and I would have liked to start and continue with a Pakistani Director. But it was equally important that the first Director, who would have to establish the rules, procedures and traditions of the institute, should be someone with recent experience of working in a really good institute and senior enough to exercise a certain amount of effortless authority over younger colleagues. It was decided, very rightly in my view, that the first Director should be an experienced American and that we should seek to increase as rapidly and effectively as we could the number of Pakistani post-graduate economists doing research in the good research schools in Europe and North America and hope to bring them back to staff the Institute.

The Ford Foundation was very fortunate in recruiting Gustav Ranis to be the first Director. He was followed successively by Irving Brecher, Henry Bruton and Mark Leiserson. They brought to the new Institute just the combination of experience, scholarship and enthusiasm that was wanted. Opening in Karachi in 1958 their tenures carried the Institute through to 1964. We had been equally fortunate in recruiting Nurul Islam, educated at Harvard University and then teaching at Dhaka University, who had the experience and seniority to take over as the first Director born and bred in the country.

Meanwhile a number of remarkably able younger economists had been emerging. Of these A.R. Khan and Swadesh Bose with Cambridge PhDs, and several others, came back from foreign graduate schools to work in the Institute.

There was, however, one major difficulty. The Institute was very rightly located in the Western wing, alongside the national government and most national institutions. The major problems of poverty, underemployment, deprivation were in the Eastern wing. Thus the Institute was many hundred miles from much of its most urgent fieldwork. Nurul Islam discussed this with Gustav Ranis, myself and some others at an International Economic Association conference at Bled during the summer of 1970. We agreed with him that it made sense to move a part of the Institute to Dhaka. A number of the new recruits to the research staff were themselves Bengalis and would be glad to move nearer to home.

The consequence of the move was that, with other Bengalis, the staff of the Institute was exposed to all the dangers of the War of Independence. Many were smuggled out and collected as research groups in Oxford, the United States and Calcutta. But with the end of the war they were quickly back in Dhaka, acting as the planning organisation of Sheikh Mujibur Rahman's first post-independence administration, with Nurul Islam as Deputy Chairman of the Planning Commission.

For a short time it was difficult for those who were not formally absorbed into the Planning Commission to know whether they were informal assistants to those who had been or an independent institute. But quickly they became once more an independent institute, with Swadesh Bose as Director.

This happy situation did not last long. With the assassination of Sheikh Mujibur Rahman his administration was superseded and a number of those previously in the Institute who had been closest to him found employment with international bodies who valued their expertise, to the advantage of the wider developing world, but the grave loss of Bangladesh.

It must not be suggested that, important as it was, the Institute was the only thing that was happening to improve the teaching of economics during these years. A number of outstanding economists came back from post-graduate work abroad to teach and have subsequently become professors in their universities.

Perhaps more important, the International Economic Association had held in 1958, at the instigation of Nurul Islam, what we called a Refresher Course. The first of these had been held most successfully in India in 1955, planned by Professor Vakil. He had argued that during the war years the Asian countries, including his own, had been out of touch with current thought in the advanced countries in which important changes in economic thinking had been going on in the later 1930s. The Indians wanted four or five participants in those arguments to come to India for four or five weeks and bring a hand-picked group of younger Indian economists up to date. Joan Robinson, Nicholas Kaldor, Lorie Tarshis and Jack Downie had done this. It had been a great success. There was obviously a strong case for doing the same for Pakistan if it were wanted.

It clearly was wanted. Held in 1958 before Independence it took place in the summer of that year in Murree and lasted four weeks. The visitors were Arthur Brown, Harry Johnson, Peter Bauer, Ken Berrill, G.M. Meier and Brian Reddaway. The International Economic Association records show that between thirty and forty Pakistani economists attended; they do not show how many came from each wing. The intention was that the numbers should be equal.

I have heard less at first hand from actual participants about this refresher course than I have about the Indian course, but it was a lively team of visitors and I suspect that, as certainly happened in India, those who attended completed the course fully abreast of the then current state of European and North American economics.

The refresher course played its part in bringing some of the teaching staff of the country into touch with post-1939 developments in Keynesian and other economic thinking in Western Europe and North America. Closer touch with developments of socialist thinking was achieved in a very different way. Initially Nurul Islam and I had planned to hold in 1972 a conference of the IEA based on the work of the Bengali group abroad and dealing with the problems of the development of the area now known as Bangladesh. When the war ended with unexpected speed and they returned quickly to Dhaka that proved impossible. But when Nurul Islam and the group took over the responsibilities of writing the first plan for the new country a new possibility emerged. The group as a whole and individuals within it were much more competent and experienced as economic theorists than as administrators. They were collectively aware that they needed the criticisms of some experienced socialist administrators. Nurul Islam and I (I was ex-President at the time and he was Treasurer) accordingly revived the idea of a conference, now to be held in Dhaka, in which those Bangladeshis responsible for each programme would prepare the papers, in which there would be as many experts from socialist countries as from non-socialist, in which we would be primarily concerned with practical policies.

We deliberately called the conference 'The Economic Development of Bangladesh within a Socialist Framework'. We were anxious that it should not degenerate into one endless argument about the rival merits of capitalist and socialist systems. That issue had already been decided at the highest level. The socialist economists included, apart from any Bangladeshis, Andreas Brody (Hungary), Joseph Pajestka, Jan Lipinski (Poland), Vladimir Kondratiev, Ilya Redko (USSR), Branko Horvat, Alexander Bajt (Yugoslavia), Konstantin Gabrouski and Konstantin Kolev (Bulgaria).

The proceedings during our formal meetings are recorded in the volume edited by Keith Griffin and myself, but my memories are of endless private arguments between individual Bangladeshi economists and individual socialist economists, many of them seeing for the first time a backward Asian country and in some cases, in my view, over-optimistic about the practical possibilities of very rapid development to the standards of an Eastern European country. I think that out of that conference and the short period during which the Institute and the planning organisation of the country were very closely integrated came an atmosphere of reality which had not been there in equal degree before. At a slightly later stage I remember well the difficulties of sorting out the functions of the Institute and of giving it again an independent existence and research programme, independent of service to those of its staff who preferred to remain permanently in government service.

In this record of my memories I have dealt perhaps excessively with the Institute because for many years my links with it were close.

When I come to undergraduate teaching I feel less confident of my facts. My impression in the earlier years after independence was that the undergraduate facilities and standards had fallen in the same way that they had in similar conditions in my own country. The library facilities suffered particularly and I have memories of the efforts of our British undergraduates to give books to help teaching to come back to normal after the damage to libraries during the war. We collected enough textbooks to fill two transport aircraft. It happened that I was in Dhaka and I have memories of sorting the books and trying to ensure that each university had enough copies of the same text to make it possible to teach a class. For some years shortages of all sorts made the working of the universities difficult. Apart from that it proved as difficult to reconcile postwar undergraduates with the circumstances of a university as it had with my own generation of ex-service undergraduates in my own country.

In all this reconstruction I have vivid memories of the determination of the local officers of the Ford Foundation, which financed the conference and (if I remember right) the transportation of the books, to get Bangladesh on to its feet. I naturally have memories also of the energies of the British Council officers and the many other friends of Bangladesh.

By the mid-1970s there was in Dhaka a group of economists fully abreast of modern academic economics and of the thinking of those who were currently administering the most advanced capitalist and socialist countries. The limits on progress were those imposed by climate, by war damage, and as in all countries by political factors.

If I may look back over the longer period since I first set foot on the Indian continent in the late 1920s, the change is astonishing. At that time almost all the teaching of economics in the universities of the continent was in the hands of British professors. They were conscientious, well-informed, but slightly second-rate – not quite good enough to get posts in their own country. A few Indians, including a very few Muslims, came to British universities to study economics. They were so few as to make little impact when they returned home and very little impact on the wider international world of economists. Today things are wholly different. Oxford, Cambridge, London, Harvard and many other universities in Europe and North America have professors drawn from the Indian continent, a number of them from the Muslim countries. The various United Nations organisations draw a considerable proportion of their ablest officers from the dian continent. The **International Economic** Association and other international economic bodies depend upon Asian officers equally with officers from North America and Europe. The economic skills and reputations of Bangladeshi economists have very much come of age.

Index

231

TRADE, PLANNING AND RURAL DEVELOPMENT

Also by Azizur Rahman Khan

THE STRATEGY OF ECONOMIC DEVELOPMENT IN BANGLADESH
  (*with Mahabub Hossain*)
COLLECTIVE AGRICULTURE AND RURAL DEVELOPMENT IN SOVIET
  CENTRAL ASIA (*with Dharam Ghai*)
AGRARIAN SYSTEMS AND RURAL DEVELOPMENT (*editor with
  Dharam Ghai, Eddy Lee and Samir Radwan*)
THE ECONOMY OF BANGLADESH
GROWTH AND INEQUALITY IN PAKISTAN (*editor with Keith Griffin*)